Differentiating

in Number & Operations

and the Other Math Content Standards

preK–grade 2

Differentiating

in Number & Operations

and the Other Math Content Standards

A **Guide** for

- Ongoing Assessment
- Grouping Students
- Targeting Instruction
- Adjusting Levels of Cognitive Demand

Jennifer Taylor-Cox

HEINEMANN
Portsmouth, NH

Heinemann
361 Hanover Street
Portsmouth, NH 03801–3912
www.heinemann.com

Offices and agents throughout the world

Library of Congress Cataloging-in-Publication Data
Taylor-Cox, Jennifer.
Differentiating in number & operations and the other math content standards, preK–grade 2 : a guide for ongoing assessment, grouping students, targeting instruction, and adjusting levels of cognitive demand / Jennifer Taylor-Cox.
p. cm. — (Differentiating in number & operations and the other math content standards, preK–grade 2)
Includes bibliographical references and index.
ISBN-13: 978-0-325-02183-6
ISBN-10: 0-325-02183-X
1. Number concept—Study and teaching (Early childhood)—Activity programs—United States. 2. Number concept—Study and teaching (Elementary)—Activity programs—United States. 3. Arithmetic—Study and teaching (Early childhood) —Activity programs—United States. 4. Arithmetic—Study and teaching (Elementary)—Activity programs—United States. 5. Individualized instruction—United States. 6. Differentiation (Cognition)—United States. 7. Mathematical readiness. 8. Classroom management. I. Title. II. Title: Differentiating in number and operations and the other math content standards, preK–grade two.
QA141.15.T39 2008
372.7—dc22 2008017184

Editor: Emily Michie Birch
Production: Lynne Costa
Cover design: Jenny Jensen Greenleaf
Typesetter: Publishers' Design and Production Services, Inc.
Manufacturing: Louise Richardson

Printed in the United States of America on acid-free paper

12 11 10 09 08 VP 1 2 3 4 5

When your heart is in your work, it doesn't seem like work. That doesn't mean it is effortless. It just means you enjoy it.

This book is dedicated to all the students, teachers, administrators, and parents that I have worked with over the years. It is for you and because of you that this book was written.

CONTENTS

INTRODUCTION

Why Do We "Aim for the Middle" When We Teach Math?

Aim for the middle and pray for ricochet!

Let's face it. Most math lessons are directed toward the middle of the group. We ignore the reality that some students already know the information and some students are not ready to learn the information. We aim for the middle and pray for ricochet. We hope the knowledge we impart to the center will bounce around until everyone gets it. I used to teach this way. Many educators teach this way. Why?

Perhaps we aim for the middle in our instruction because we are inundated with standards-based ideals. Politically charged and socially propelled standards drive educators to teach *the curriculum*. The merits of standards-based instruction and increased expectations are sound, but assuming that all students at the same grade level need to learn the same thing at the same time is a problem.

Our national focus on assessment in mathematics may also encourage a tendency to teach to the middle. However, it is important to remember that educators need to incorporate mathematics assessment in ways that are beneficial to both students and teachers, and that not all *assessment* involves students taking state and national tests. Ongoing assessment tells us where students are in their math knowledge before, during, and after instruction. It is the heart of differentiated instruction in math. Educators can use formal, informal, and personal types of assessment. Such tools provide opportunities to question learners in ways that reveal their thinking and provide insight to the teacher. As we implement productive assessments, we gain rich information and come to understand and value assessment as a critical tool for differentiated instruction. Perhaps another reason we aim for the middle is that we simply do not have command of the content. Teachers need to pay attention not only to concepts themselves but also to what comes before and what comes after those concepts. Let's say my goal is to teach addition using single-digit numbers to a class of first graders. Some of my students may already be comfortable working with two-digit addends, while others may not yet understand what addition is. Often, teachers are left with no clear guidance as to what to do for these students, and the *aim for the middle* approach isn't going to help them.

Perhaps it is an issue of pedagogical expertise. Think about how many times you have heard a teacher say, "I taught it, but they didn't learn it!" What the teacher may actually be saying is, "I told them or I showed them, but they didn't get it." Traditional mathematics instruction often includes a lecture followed by examples shown to the whole class. Unfortunately, this type of instruction is not suited for all students. Still, in many classrooms, the instruction centers around the teacher demonstrating problems and concepts on the board or overhead projector. The teacher, then, often is the only person actively engaging in mathematics.

Recent professional development opportunities for math teachers have started to address some of the pedagogical and contextual hurdles. With an increased focus on active learning, many math classrooms—especially grades Pre-K–2 classrooms—have come alive with hands-on mathematics. Teachers are beginning to express more comfort with mathematics. However, the one-size-fits-all whole group approach remains pervasive. Consequently, we still have students frustrated because the level of instruction is beyond them; we still have students bored because they already know the information. All students are entitled to instruction that meets their needs, not just those fortunate enough to be in the middle.

The answer is clear—targeted, differentiated instruction; yet it is hard to find truly differentiated math classrooms. Teachers tell me, "Of course, I want to meet the needs of all my students in mathematics, but I don't have time." "Yes, I believe in the power of differentiated instruction, but not in math. We have too much to cover." "Differentiated instruction is great for literacy and social studies, but how to use it in math is a real mystery." These statements and others launched me into a quest for making differentiated instruction in mathematics a reality. My journey started in my classroom and has expanded through professional development models to classrooms across the country. While there are numerous ways to differentiate instruction, this book focuses on a targeted approach to differentiation of math content. This focus is in no way intended to minimize the positive impact associated with other types of differentiation. In fact, we'll explore the importance of incorporating students' learning frameworks, which include styles, preferences, needs, and interests, because these are powerful ways to increase student achievement.

The problem is that there are so many avenues and so many possibilities when differentiating instruction that implementing it can become an unobtainable ideal instead of a reality for many educators. To remedy this problem, I encourage teachers to begin by focusing on one aspect of differentiated instruction—not at the expense of other ways to differentiate, but as a way to start. Given today's focus on standards-based instruction, I prefer to begin with the math content. My goals are to use quick and effective ways that are research-based and have been tested in hundreds of classrooms to assess student understanding; employ purposeful, flexible grouping; utilize levels of cognitive demand; and target instruction for all students. In order to differentiate instruction in math using a standards-based curriculum, without extra hours of planning, I target math instruction for students. You can easily implement these strategies in your own classrooms.

Why Is the Focus of This Book on Number and Operations?

Why is number so important?

The number and operations content strand provides a foundation for all other areas of mathematics. All students need to establish solid groundwork in number and operations to help them be successful in mathematics. The goals are to help students foster their number sense by working with numbers in accurate, efficient, and flexible ways. To do so students need their teachers to provide targeted, differentiated instruction in number and operations.

For young students, number and operations involve much more than counting or writing numbers. Math educators need to understand all of the components that comprise number and operations so that they can easily target the instruction for students.

Using This Book with the *Content Companions*

Why are there Content Companions?

The purpose of the *Content Companions* is to provide prekindergarten through second grade mathematics educators with the tools needed to target instruction through differentiation in all math content areas. The number and operations book offers ideas, techniques, and strategies to use when targeting instruction in number and operations. The *Content Companions* allow educators to understand how to use these same ideas, techniques, and strategies when teaching algebra, geometry, measurement, and data analysis and probability. The *Content Companions* offer specific content examination, student work samples, and lesson ideas. The rationale behind the *Content Companions* is that while number and operations is a critically important math standard, it is not the only standard that prekindergarten through second grade math educators teach. Algebra, geometry, measurement, and data analysis and probability are also very important content standards.

Throughout this book you will notice small boxes in the margin that indicate where other mathematics content explanations and examples are offered in the *Content Companions*. Each time you see this cross-reference box in the number and operations book, you can turn to the corresponding page in a *Content Companion* to find specific information pertaining to algebra, geometry, measurement, or data analysis and probability. There are far too many books out there that attempt to explain to readers that similar strategies can be applied in all areas of mathematics; but these resources often fail to provide specific examples. Likewise, some resources attempt to cram all content into one resource; but these resources are often limited and incomplete. To address these problems, the *Content Companions* provide a comprehensive set of resources that prekindergarten through second grade educators can use to target instruction through differentiation in mathematics.

The fabulous news is that we don't have to teach to the middle and pray for ricochet anymore! We have the knowledge and tools to help us meet the needs of young math students. I invite you to read these books to learn how to implement a targeted approach to differentiated instruction in mathematics. Please accept my invitation. . . .

CHAPTER 1

Targeted, Differentiated Instruction

What Is a Targeted Approach to Differentiated Instruction in Math?

Targeted instruction in action

Classroom teachers are busy with no time to reinvent the wheel again and again. We need quick and effective ways to target math instruction. The beauty of this book is in the real classroom examples and explanations. Without lengthy lesson plans or hours of preparation, teachers can easily implement targeted, differentiated mathematics instruction on a daily basis. By knowing where students are in their learning journeys and connecting this knowledge to curricular goals and standards, differentiation in mathematics can become as second nature as "hands-on learning."

Command of the Content

Targeting math instruction on the fly requires us to encompass a new way of thinking about teaching. *What* to teach and *how* to teach are important, but they are not enough. Simply put, even the best-scripted lessons will never accomplish what targeted, differentiated instruction can accomplish. We need to understand mathematics in a way that allows us to identify the previous concepts (back-mapping) and subsequent concepts (forward-mapping). The great news is that many districts across this country have already organized this information for us! Math researchers and math supervisors have created various models of the goals and objectives for each grade level. However, when teaching first grade number and operations, the teacher needs to know the number and operations concepts that are taught in kindergarten and in second grade. The teacher may even need to know the prekindergarten and third grade objectives. This knowledge enables the teacher to have command of the content—allowing the teacher easily to build bridges, repair gaps, and provide challenges for all students.

I know what you are thinking . . . teachers have enough with their own grade-level benchmarks. However, if we focus only on one grade level, we may not reach many students, because students are at various levels of understanding. "When a teacher tries to teach something to the entire class at the same time, chances are, one-third of the kids already know it; one-third will get it; and the remaining third won't" (Lilian Katz, in Tomlinson 1996). Essentially, two-thirds of the students are not learning anything. To meet the needs of all students, try looking at one topic at a time. Find out the benchmarks for the previous grade level and find out the benchmarks for the next grade level. You'll then have valuable tools for targeting math instruction, because you will have a greater understanding of the sequence of skills within any given concept, allowing you to use back-mapping and forward-mapping. Having command of the content enables the teacher to target instruction on the fly.

Traditionally teachers thought—and were often told—that they could not tread on another teacher's turf. If you teach something that the student is supposed to learn next year, what will the teacher teach next year? I remember being told by a supervisor many years ago, "Don't even look at next year's math objectives because you don't want to accidentally teach something that is supposed to be learned in the next grade." How disconcerting, perhaps even scary, this advice is. Let's move past this type of thinking. Every student deserves to have learning opportunities targeted to specific academic needs. If next year's teacher is good, she will continue to differentiate instruction and will have plenty to do! Even if she does not differentiate instruction, you will have provided optimal academic growth, ultimately better preparing the students for their next classroom. You may have even inspired many of the students to seek out self-directed opportunities to continue learning at their levels.

Time Is Precious

Time is so valuable. We always need more of it. There's simply not enough time. Not enough time to teach. Not enough time to plan. Not enough time to assess knowledge. Not enough time to reflect upon our practice, let alone change the way we are teaching. Perceived lack of time often keeps teachers from trying new strategies or implementing new programs. The brilliant thing about targeted, differentiated instruction, however, is that it can actually give you more time in the classroom. *The more you differentiate instruction, the more time you actually have to focus on essential instruction.* The teacher is not teaching the curriculum; instead, the teacher is teaching children. It doesn't happen overnight. Targeted, differentiated instruction is just like most everything else—the more you learn about it and practice it, the better you become at it.

Think about the first lesson plan you ever wrote. If you are like most novice educators, you devoted more time to thinking about and writing the lesson than you actually did teaching the lesson. Now, as a seasoned educator, you don't write lesson plans in the same manner. Sure, you may write an extensive lesson for an observation or for course work, but you no longer write lengthy, detailed lesson plans on a daily basis. You went through the process of learning how to teach and now you know what to do. The process for learning how to target differentiated mathematics instruction is similar.

To target instruction in mathematics without adding extra planning hours to my day, I think in threes—concept, next concept, and preceding concept. I define the math concept and think about how to *bump it up* to a higher level and how to *scaffold it down* to a lower level. Thinking in threes prepares me for the potential levels of my students. My goal is to have ideas to challenge those who already know the concept and to build bridges for those who are not yet ready to learn the concept. The challenging and the scaffolding are manifested through the adjustment of the levels of cognitive demand and targeted instruction, both of which we will examine in detail in this book.

Successful teachers are time grubbers. Because there is rarely extra time, teachers need to look for small chunks of potentially available time during the course of the school day. Analyze your day. Look for idle time. Can I meet with a small group during the morning routine? Can I assess learning during centers or seatwork? Is it possible to have a five-minute reteach group while students pack up supplies at the end of the day? Can I teach students how to lead a portion of circle time (time where the class sits as a whole group to discuss various daily routines such as calendar, weather, announcements, daily schedule, etc.) so I can explain the math challenge to a group of students? Find the hidden time and use it to target and differentiate instruction. Every minute counts!

Leading and Managing the Class

Contrary to popular belief, a differentiated classroom necessitates more leadership than a nondifferentiated classroom. As Tomlinson (1995) clarifies, teachers who differentiate instruction "exert more control in their classroom, not less" (5). We need to identify our definitions of leadership and *control.* They do not mean dictatorship. The leader is not the constant *sage on the stage.* Controlling the classroom does not mean students must remain silent during math time. Instead, the teacher provides vision, support, and challenge to facilitate student learning.

In addition to being a strong leader, the teacher must also be a skilled manager. Establishing ground rules that make sense and are consistently utilized is a critical factor in making the differentiated math classroom successful. One of the most important ground rules that needs to be established is uninterrupted small group instructional time. When the teacher is working with a small group, other students need to find out the answers to their questions through means other than asking the teacher. If the classroom rules include *no talking* or *no getting out of your seat,* we've created contradictions in the expectations. To avoid classroom contradictions, teachers need to encourage students to engage in productive conversations, which include clarification of directions and math discourse. Additionally, students need to know how to get the manipulatives they need to solve math problems. Teachers don't have time to be waiters and waitresses, bringing things to students. Students need to do these things themselves, so teachers can focus on teaching.

Managing and leading the classroom involve setting realistic expectations and focusing on progress. One year I had a class of first graders who needed constant encouragement and support. It seemed the only way the students could accomplish a task was when I was right beside them. To make differentiated instruction a reality, I had to step back and reflect upon what was happening. I wanted the students to be independently productive, so I could work with small groups; yet I had become a crutch for nearly all of my students. I enabled them to be completely dependent upon me. I fixed this problem one step at a time. First, I provided a simple task for everyone and explained to them that I would be working with a small group without interruption for two minutes. Other students were to work without my help for the two minute period. We accomplished this small step and celebrated our success! Students shared how they solved their own problems. Jonathan asked Maria if he could borrow a pencil. Sharon asked Darrell if he wanted some base-ten blocks to use. Tony asked Marc to re-read the directions to him. The students were empowered by their two minutes of success, and I used this experience as a springboard.

Next, we successfully implemented three minutes of small group time during math. Within a week, we were up to seven minutes. Within a month, I was able to work with three small groups for at least ten minutes each, allowing me to target the instruction for all students. Now don't get me wrong, I couldn't just ignore the rest of the class for thirty minutes straight. Between groups I checked on the progress of students and provided hurdle help as needed. Many times I helped my small group get started on a task and then left them working so I could make a quick walk around the classroom to monitor progress and provide support and academic challenges to those who needed it. As I began to differentiate the independent work for students, I met with my small groups for less time until we could build the structure back up to where we had previously been. It was the modified management and leadership that opened the doors to multiple opportunities for targeted, differentiated math instruction.

Types of Ongoing Assessment

To know what to address, we need to assess!

To know what to teach as we target instruction in mathematics, we need to utilize assessment. In a recent workshop, I referred to assessment as education's *A-word*. Some people disregard the A-word. Others are afraid of it. Still others use it without really understanding what it means. Honestly, assessment is not a bad word—just misunderstood, no wonder. We have formative and summative assessments, direct and indirect assessments, qualitative and quantitative assessments, embedded assessments, developmental assessments, and authentic assessments (just to name a few). As educators think about assessment, other connected thoughts emerge—evidence, feedback, records, grading, reporting, rigor, reliability, validity, objectivity, subjectivity, standards, blueprints, dipsticks, portfolios, quality, and fairness. So many thoughts and emotions are wrapped up in the word *assessment*.

While all of these types and thoughts of assessment have value and are applicable to the classroom, it is their very existence that makes things so overwhelming for teachers. Which type of assessment is best? When will I have time to teach if I spend so much time assessing? Can't it just wait until I'm finished teaching? To achieve the National Council of Teachers of Mathematics (NCTM) (2000) recommendation that "assessments should support the learning of important mathematics and furnish useful information for both teachers and students" (372), mathematics educators need to focus on using assessment in purposeful, productive ways. In the classroom, we need to use assessment to reveal the information we currently need to teach all of the students. Essentially, the assessments drive the instruction and can be categorized in three basic forms—formal, informal, and personal.

Formal Assessment

Formal assessments include tests, quizzes, exams, diagnostic tools, and other traditional forms of assessment. Many formal assessments are designed to evaluate the overall effectiveness of the instructional program. While these types of assessments can be beneficial in ways that may help educators evaluate student competency and may pinpoint instructional areas that need improvement, they are not particularly useful to teachers on a daily basis. Often these tests are designed poorly because feedback on performance is not timely or inclusive and the tasks often have little value to students (Wiggins 2003). Give the test, post the scores, and the school year is over. Or give the test, record the grade, and move on to the next chapter—these cycles do not give the teacher a chance to use the assessment data to target instruction.

Fortunately, not all formal assessments have to be used in a summative manner. Teachers can actually use the information to revise teaching and learning! These are the formal assessments that directly impact classroom instruction. The chapter test can be used as a preassessment. A quiz or a diagnostic tool can be given in the middle of the lesson or in the middle of the unit. We can make some reteach plans after the postassessment. In these examples, formal assessments are used in formative ways.

Formative assessment gives feedback to teachers and students in ways that influence instruction. Even when a test is given at the end of the unit, the teacher can still use the information to create reteach groups and challenge groups that can meet during subsequent chapters of study. The reteach group focuses on concepts that preceded the current concept of study. The challenge group focuses on concepts above the current concept of study. The point is using the information from the assessments, not merely recording results in a grade book or on a report card.

Informal Assessment

Most of the ongoing assessments that I use to target instruction in mathematics are informal. The goal is to find out what students know before, during, and after instruction. As recommended by the National Association for the Education of Young Children (NAEYC) and NCTM (2002), "Early childhood mathematics assessment is most useful when it aims to help young children by identifying strengths and needs so as to inform teacher planning" (12). The focus is on improving student learning through the use of purposeful data. Informal assessments such as index questions, observations, interviews, and journal reviews give teachers information they can use to guide instruction.

Index Questions

An index question is a very simple way to gain knowledge of where students are in their understandings of a particular concept. A teacher poses questions or gives tasks that are directly related to what is being taught (or will be taught next). The questions or tasks give an "index" of where each student is in terms of their level of understanding. Typically the questions or tasks require more than a one-word or one-number response. Students have an opportunity to show what they know about the given topic. Each student writes or draws a response on a note card or piece of paper. The teacher collects them, sorting them by levels of understanding. Index questions may be administered to students as preassessments, assessments during instruction, or assessments after the instruction.

These formative assessments are not intended to be time consuming. Typically, the students have five minutes or less to write or draw responses and then the teacher uses a few minutes to sort the indexes. Sorting the indexes into levels of understanding becomes faster and easier for teachers as they gain more experience. Some teachers prefer to sort the indexes when the students are not in the classroom (during planning time or after/before school). Other teachers sort the indexes while the students are doing a practice problem or other independent activity.

I always encourage teachers to think about the indexes as *at-a-glance* knowledge indicators. What do you think the student knows about the topic? What evidence do you see? Does the index show that the student has a strong understanding, a mediocre understanding, or a weak understanding? Often the student responses fall into three groups—students who already know; students who know something about the concept, but don't have a complete grasp of the concept; and students who are struggling with the concept. Sometimes there are only two groups, sometimes there are four groups—it varies with each class and each math topic. The teacher decides how many groups are needed and, most importantly, how many groups are manageable. Having too many groups can be a disaster for the teacher. Let's say the indexes show eight levels. Just the thought of eight different levels of instruction is overwhelming. Not to mention the fact that the more groups, the less time the teacher can spend with each group. If there are too many levels, combine some. Try to make a quick decision about which group to put the child in based on the evidence the student provides on the index and based on what the teacher knows about the student. If it is later determined that a student should be in a different group, simply move the student—that's the beauty of purposeful, flexible grouping of students.

Basing the quick sort of indexes on evidence is key. The last thing we want to do is assume a student should be in a specific group. We are trying to move away from the stereotypically stagnant achievement grouping. The groups need to be formed based predominately on the evidence presented on the index. Using index questions allows the teacher to cater the instruction to the current needs of each student. Index questions are such cornerstones for targeted instruction that an entire chapter of this book is devoted to their use with number and operations in prekindergarten through second grade.

Observation

Observation is another important type of informal assessment. By observing students engaged in mathematics situations, educators can assess the strengths and needs of students. It is essential that we uncover what students know before, during, and after instruction. In this way, informal assessment is dynamic and ongoing, not merely something done at the end of a unit. For example, as kindergartners count objects, the teacher can take notice of each student's mathematics knowledge. These observations may be recorded in many forms—anecdotal records (which include verbal responses and behaviors), note cards, and checklists. Through observation the teacher is looking for these skills and others:

Student has one-to-one correspondence.
Student knows the rote counting sequence.
Student can keep track of what has already been counted.
Student can name the number of elements in the set.
Student knows the quantity even if the objects are rearranged.

The goal in this situation is to find out where students are in their understanding of numbers and counting. With this information, educators can then target instruction for their students. In turn, assessment through observation can be incorporated to focus on the progress of learning. Strengths and potential gaps in the students' knowledge are revealed and addressed. As Copley (2000) specifies, "Teachers must observe children's actions, behaviors, and interactions and listen carefully as they talk" (24). Undoubtedly, observation is a helpful way to gather information to target differentiated instruction.

Interviews

Interviews are another way to informally assess students. Asking them how they solved problems and why they used specific strategies reveals a great deal about their mathematical abilities. Manipulatives often enhance students' abilities to express their mathematics understanding. Hence it is important to provide an assortment of manipulatives for students to use to show, explain, and prove their thinking. For example, by inviting first grade students to show the number 28 in a variety of ways, the teacher can pose questions to determine the students' understanding of how numbers are composed and decomposed. Insight into student understanding may be revealed through interviews that address these and other questions:

Can the student show and explain 28 as 2 tens and 8 ones?
Does the student understand that 28 can also be represented as 1 ten and 18 ones?
Is the student comfortable composing (building) and decomposing (breaking apart) numbers?
How developed is the student's sense of how this number is related to other numbers?

As students explain and justify solutions to math problems, educators learn which concepts students know and which concepts students need to learn. Assessments that inform practice enable mathematics educators to meet students where they are as they target the math instruction.

Reviewing Journals

Even very young students can and should keep math journals. Math journals provide students with opportunities to use pictures and words to characterize and describe mathematics situations. Math journals serve as a powerful way for students to communicate and represent their thinking. Reviewing journals provides teachers with additional means of informal assessment. This practice enables teachers to examine evidence of students' growth in mathematics understanding over time. While reviewing math journals, the teacher is looking for answers to these and other questions:

Can the student accurately apply mathematical concepts?
Does the student use math vocabulary?
Which strategies are evident?
Is the math thinking accurately represented?

As with index questions, observations, and interviews, journals can be used to assess math knowledge of students before, during, and after instruction. Clearly, the best assessments are those that align with productive instructional strategies. Allowing students to "show" what they know in the same ways they "learn" new knowledge is a powerful way for the teacher to target instruction.

Personal Assessment

Personal assessment is unlike other forms of assessment in one very distinct way. The teacher is not the evaluator. Students appraise their own levels of math knowledge. At first, the thought of students deciding what and how much they know may seem a little daunting! As teachers, we feel so accountable and spend a great deal of time evaluating. So it is sometimes difficult for us to break away from being the judge of a student's knowledge or comfort level; however, it is empowering to students when we put them in charge of assessing these things.

Okay, I know the questions that follow. And yes, I have worked with many students who think they know more than they actually do. Likewise, I have worked with many students who are not as confident as they could be about their knowledge. And, yes, some students initially choose to mimic their friends just to get to work with them. Still other students are embarrassed if they do not know something. These are some of the reasons teachers may shy away from personal assessments. They worry students' assessments of their knowledge are not accurate. They worry students will say they know when they really don't or that students will think there is a smart group and a stupid group. As teachers, our job is to teach the students how to accurately assess their levels of understanding within a safe classroom community. Students need to know that no one (including the teacher) will make them feel inadequate because they do not know something. It is all about knowing what you know and learning what you need to learn next. It takes time. With some students, it takes more time. But the time is worth it because if students can accurately judge where their understanding lies, they are empowered to move on in their learning journeys, which will ultimately save your time.

One of the ways to help students gain accuracy in assessing their level of knowledge is to combine personal assessments with index questions. Some of the indexes can include a scale. Students are asked to rate their levels of understanding when they respond to the index question. Combining indexes and personal assessments helps the teacher know how well the students judge their knowledge of any given math topic.

Options for different types of personal assessments are numerous. The more you use them, the more various formats come to mind. I started with the common *thumbs-up* signal. Thumbs-up if you understand the concept. Thumbs-sideways if you understand some of the concept. Thumbs-down if you are confused about the concept. Like many teachers, I have used these signals to gather a general sense of where my class is functioning at any given time. In the past, I asked for the thumb signals and then continued with whatever

I was doing. Now I use these signals as a way for students to personally assess where they are in their current learning journey. I respond to the thumb signals. Perhaps I need to meet with my thumbs-up group to give them a challenge. Or perhaps I need to meet with my thumbs-down group to provide some support. The point is the teacher needs to use the information to make adjustments in the level of cognitive demand required for the task and to target instruction for specific groups of students.

Students can evaluate their levels of understanding on different types of scales. Using vertical and horizontal number lines, students rate personal degrees of understanding. Students can use individual number lines as scales to mark levels of understanding, as shown in Figure 1–1.

The scales can have any given range. With primary students, I usually begin with simple whole-number scales such as zero to ten. Later, I increase the complexity of the scale by adjusting the range. Hearing a student announce, "I understand this idea at a level of about three-fourths," is music to the math teacher's ear! Students are self-evaluating *and* using mathematics language.

Using class line plots can also be beneficial. Students place a name sticker in a location on a line that indicates knowledge level of or comfort level with a specific concept (see Figure 1–2).

The line plot is then used to group students purposefully and to target instruction using the personal assessment information.

Graphs and comparison circles are additional ways to gather personal assessment information. Students place name cards in specific columns, rows, or locations to indicate their level of understanding. As shown in Figure 1–3, the bar graph labels offer ways to indicate degrees of understanding of or comfort with the math topic.

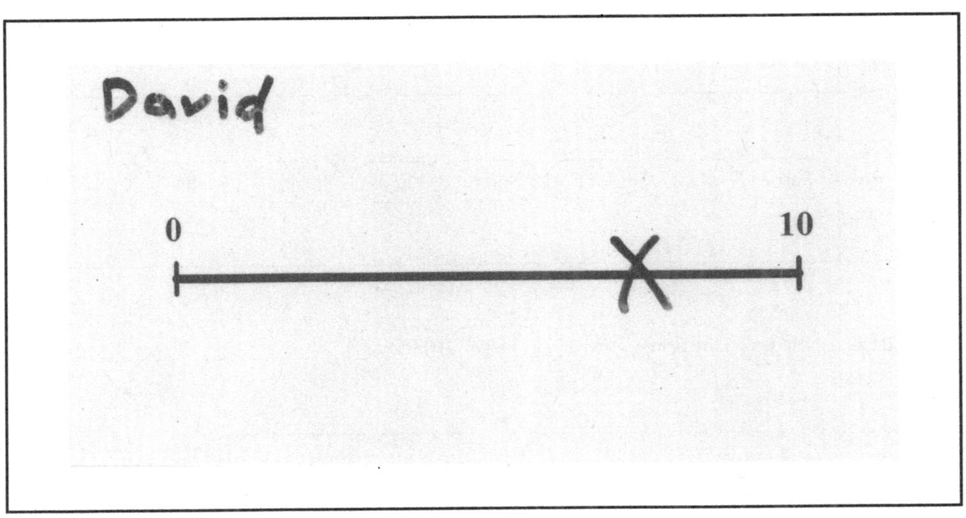

Figure 1–1
Student Scale

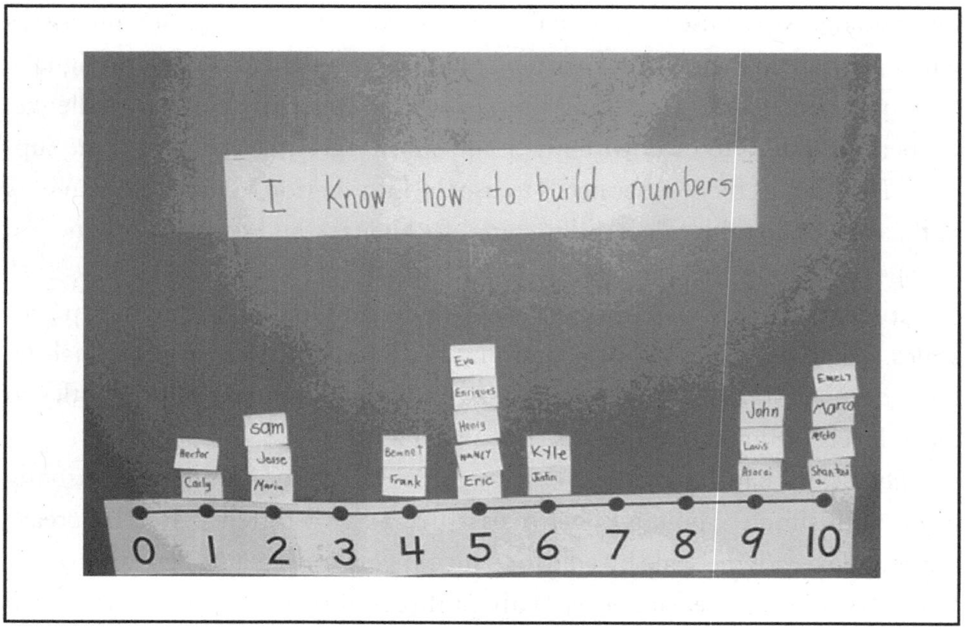

Figure 1–2 *An Example of a Class Line Plot*

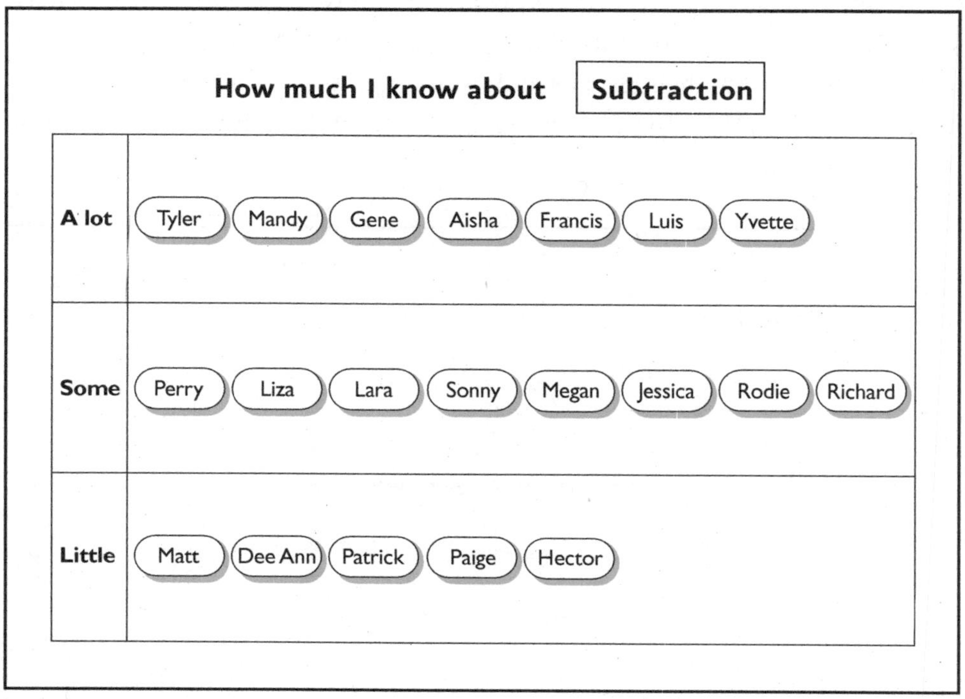

Figure 1–3 *An Example of a Class Bar Graph*

If the class is learning about composing and decomposing numbers, the comparison circle labels could be "I know how to make twelve with groups of two" and "I know how to make twelve with groups of four." At a glance the teacher can see which students need more support and which students need more challenge (see Figure 1–4).

Personal assessments can also be used before, during, and after instruction. Most of the time students gain knowledge from the instruction. Because we use stickers or magnetic name tags, students can easily relocate names or use *before* and *after* name tags to show the potential increase in knowledge or comfort level. Student comments such as, "I'm going to move my name up on the line because I get it now!" prove the power of personal assessment tools. By encouraging students to accurately determine where they are in their learning, the teacher is afforded a quick and easy way to form learning groups. The benefits multiply because the graphic organizers used to determine learning levels actually open the door to more math thinking and more math discourse! Using graphic organizers to gain personal assessment data is such a new and exciting idea that an entire chapter of this book (Chapter 7) is devoted to

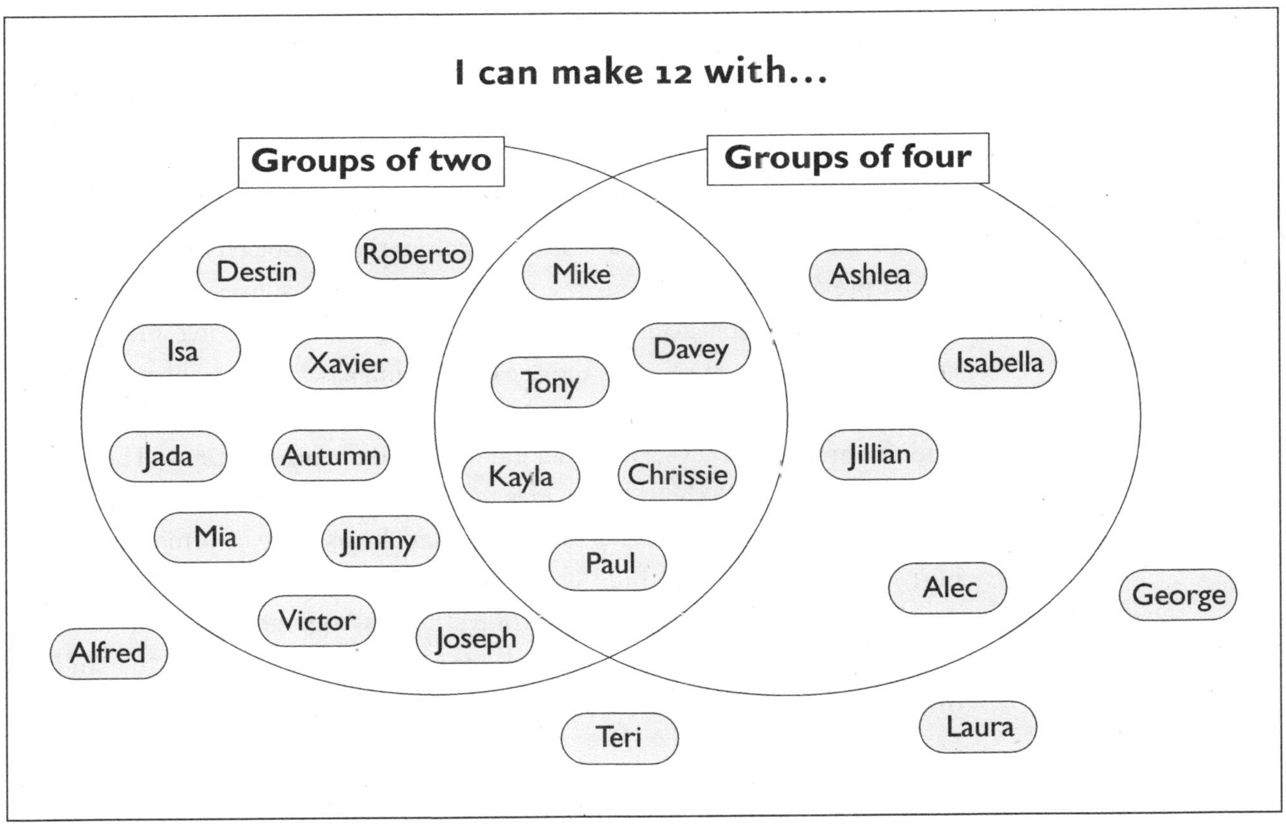

Figure 1–4 *An Example of Comparison Circle Labels*

providing examples and explanations—specifically for prekindergarten, kindergarten, first grade, and second grade.

The Differentiated Instruction in Mathematics Cycle

The phases of differentiated math instruction in action!

There is a cycle of actions that illustrates a powerful way to implement differentiated math instruction.

The steps include (see Figure 1–5):

1. Define Concepts: Include previous and subsequent concepts
2. Use Ongoing Assessment: Include formal, informal, and personal assessment
3. Form Groups: Make groups purposeful, flexible, and fluid
4. Target Instruction: Focus on specific academic needs
5. Adjust Levels of Cognitive Demand: Find the right LCD
6. Reflect and Analyze: Evaluate learning progress and make adjustments.

The process begins with defining the concepts that need to be taught. The teacher identifies the on-grade-level benchmarks or objectives *and* the connected previous and subsequent concepts. This process gives the teacher content knowledge for accurately and efficiently differentiating mathematics instruction. The next phase is the use of ongoing assessment. The teacher uses formal, informal, and personal assessment methods to gather data about where students are in their levels of understanding of the math concepts. The teacher has many choices. Perhaps he decides to give the students an index question to assess knowledge. When the data are collected, he uses the information to form purposeful, flexible, and fluid groups. The groups are not arbitrarily or randomly assigned. The teacher may group students homogeneously or heterogeneously depending on the goals of the teacher and the needs of the students (more about purposeful, flexible, and fluid group structures will be addressed in Chapter 3).

After forming the groups, the teacher targets instruction and adjusts the levels of cognitive demand for students. Some tasks may need to be simplified. Other tasks may need more complexity. This adjustment in the level of cog-

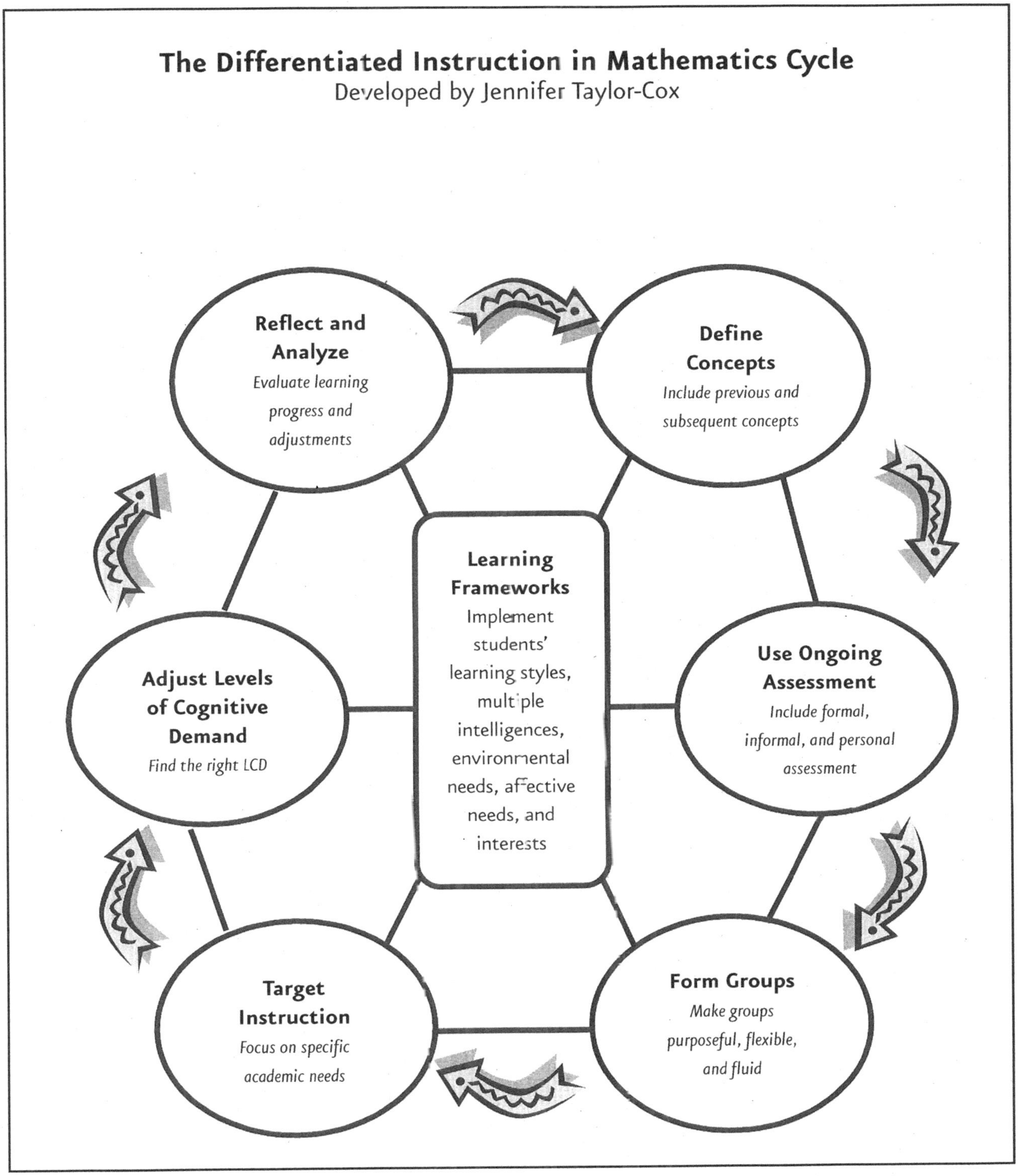
The Differentiated Instruction in Mathematics Cycle
Developed by Jennifer Taylor-Cox
Reflect and Analyze
Evaluate learning progress and adjustments
Define Concepts
Include previous and subsequent concepts
Use Ongoing Assessment
Include formal, informal, and personal assessment
Form Groups
Make groups purposeful, flexible, and fluid
Target Instruction
Focus on specific academic needs
Adjust Levels of Cognitive Demand
Find the right LCD
Learning Frameworks
Implement students' learning styles, multiple intelligences, environmental needs, affective needs, and interests

Figure 1–5

nitive demand may be present in the assignments students work on, the questions that are posed to them, and the follow-up tasks they are given. Sometimes the targeted instruction occurs simultaneously with the adjustment of the levels of cognitive demand; other times the targeted instruction follows or precedes it. In any case, the teacher focuses on the explicit academic needs of the students. If some students have a gap in understanding a specific concept, the teacher may have a small group mini-lesson on the topic, which can serve as the targeted instruction. If other students already understand the on-grade-level concept, the teacher may meet with this group of students to provide challenge by targeting instruction to the next grade-level concept. The options are many, but the goal is singular—focus on the needs of the students.

The differentiated instruction cycle encourages the teacher and students to analyze and reflect. How is the learning progressing? What changes need to be made to set students up for success? Certainly, reflection and analysis can and should occur at all times during the cycle; we don't have to wait until the end of the lesson or school day. However, we need to make sure we include reflection and analysis in our educational practices.

Incorporating students' learning frameworks serves as the backdrop of the differentiated instruction in mathematics cycle. Learning styles, multiple intelligences, environmental preferences, affective needs, and interests are ways to connect students with positive learning experiences. Students' motivation and commitment are increased as teachers incorporate learning frameworks. Each of the phases in the differentiated instruction in mathematics cycle can occur at anytime, and they do not have to happen in a specific order. The differentiated instruction in mathematics cycle is intended to provide a foundation for teachers who want a map of a way to successfully implement differentiated mathematics instruction. The cycle also gives us insight into the most important ideas to consider when differentiating mathematics instruction.

CHAPTER 2

Number and Operations in Prekindergarten Through Second Grade

The Importance of Number Sense

What is number sense?

In many ways number sense is the core of all mathematics. Having a strong sense of number involves having a high level of comfort with numbers and number relationships. Number sense is a blend of comprehension of numbers and operations *and* fluency with numbers and operations. It involves using a broad understanding of number and operations in flexible ways to make judgments and develop practical and effective strategies (McIntosh, Reys, and Reys 1993).

In mathematics we are after accuracy and efficiency. We want to teach children to get it right and do it quickly—not at the expense of understanding but because of understanding. To build number sense, the fluency with numbers and operations needs to be based on comprehension—not rules and procedures. Number sense is having a good intuition about numbers that is established bit by bit through exploring, visualizing, and relating numbers in ways that go beyond traditional algorithms (Howden 1989). Prekindergarten through second grade mathematics instruction involves helping children establish genuine number sense through their experiences with number and operations.

The three *big ideas* in number and operations are understanding numbers and relationships of numbers, understanding operations and relationships of operations, and computing fluently and estimating (National Council of Teachers of Mathematics 2000). These major ideas incorporate and enhance number sense.

Understanding Numbers and Number Relationships

Nifty numbers

Mathematics is based on understanding numbers and number relationships. Prekindergarten through second grade mathematics teachers devote a great deal of time to teaching children about numbers and number relationships. We ask children to count and show numbers and quantities. We encourage them to use numbers to name sets and amounts. We focus on teaching children the whats, hows, wheres, and whys of our number system in order to build their understandings of numbers and number relationships.

Understanding numbers and number relationships involves counting, representing numbers, composing and decomposing numbers, understanding relative position and magnitude of numbers, place value, and fractions. Each facet plays a major role in the development of children's understanding of number and operations.

Counting

Counting is one of those math concepts that begins very early and continues throughout our lives. Babies count. Toddlers count. Children count. Teenagers count. Young adults count. Not-so-young adults count. While the quantities and strategies may be different, everyone counts! From the infant who mimics *one* to the grandparent who counts cross-stitches, counting serves as a way for everyone to engage in mathematics.

While it may seem like counting is a simple part of understanding number and number relationships, there is actually much involved in counting.

One-to-One Correspondence

Interestingly, the initial use of the term *one-to-one correspondence* dates back to 1873 (*Oxford English Dictionary* 2007). Even though the concept has been around for a long time, it is important to clarify its application to early childhood understanding of number and number relationships. One-to-one correspondence is an understanding that one group has the same number of things as another group. It involves matching one member of a set with a member of another equal set. One spoon goes with one bowl. One mitten goes on each hand. One cookie goes on every napkin. One thing matches with another thing. We can see that children have one-to-one correspondence when they can match things one for one.

At any given time, children can have one-to-one correspondence up to a specific number. A young child may currently have one-to-one correspondence through three, which means the child can match each item in a set of up to three with another item in an equal set of up to three. Suppose a three-year-old is given three pretzels and three plates. If the child has one-to-one correspondence, the child can place one pretzel on each plate. Perhaps when given four pretzels and four plates, the child inaccurately performs the task. This helps the teacher identify the scope of one-to-one correspondence a child currently has. Obviously, the scope of the one-to-one correspondence changes as the child learns and develops.

Sometimes children show inconsistencies. One day the child shows that he can match one for one with up to six items. Yet the next day, the same child may only be able to match one for one with up to five items. These inconsistencies can be a normal part of the child's development. To capture a child's one-to-one correspondence scope, it is best to provide multiple experiences using a variety of objects. Uncovering inconsistencies and looking for trends can help the teacher identify instructional needs. The focus is not on what children can't do; instead the focus is on what the child can learn to do next.

Teaching one-to-one correspondence involves providing multiple and varied opportunities to children. Setting the table is a great chance to experience authentic one-to-one correspondence. One plate for each person. One napkin beside each plate. One fork on each napkin. When we serve meals or snacks in the classroom, we need to allow the children to prepare the table. Of course it takes more time when children set the table—but by giving children opportunities to set the table, we are providing valuable, authentic experiences that will help them increase their scope of one-to-one correspondence.

Another way to gain more experiences with one-to-one correspondence is through distribution of materials and supplies. Many classrooms have student jobs including the weekly *teacher's helper* whose job it is to pass out papers, materials, and supplies. When each child needs a work mat and bag of counters, the teacher can give opportunities for children to engage in one-to-one correspondence by having the children distribute the supplies to their classmates. These tasks give students further experiences with one-to-one correspondence.

Rote Counting

Rote counting is an important part of counting. Counting by rote means counting in a memorized sequence. Because the term *rote* signifies *without meaning*, rote counting is understood as counting by memory without understanding the values or how to use the numbers. While we always want mathematics to be meaningful for children, *meaningless* rote counting is an important step toward *creating meaning*. When children memorize the alphabet or a nursery rhyme, they learn how to exercise their memory. They also learn about sequencing and patterning. The same is true with rote counting. While rote counting is considered meaningless counting, it is actually a quite meaningful exercise for children. Using your memory to understand the sequence and interrelated patterns is not meaningless! Perhaps it would be better to call it memorized counting or recall counting rather than rote counting because there is meaning in the task. Yet children rote count without understanding what the numbers mean, so I suppose we're stuck with the term. Considering it meaningless, however, short shrifts its value.

Children learn to rote count by listening to others count, watching others count, and by attempting to join or repeat the rote counting. Teachers give children experiences with rote counting through songs, games, rhymes, poems, and chants. As determined by the child's level, rote counting should include forward counting, backward counting, counting by ones, skip counting, and counting starting with numbers other than zero or one. Rote counting experiences can happen anytime and anywhere—just start counting.

Rational Counting

Rational counting is when the one-to-one correspondence and the rote counting are synchronized. Rational counting involves matching each number name (in order) to each object in a group. It gives purpose to rote counting. Rational counting is alive and well when a prekindergartner successfully counts five shovels in the sandbox and is also present when a second grader accurately applies skip counting (by tens and fives) to finding the value of a group of dimes and nickels. As children count objects in a set they use rote counting and one-to-one correspondence to give meaning to the mathematics situation.

When rational counting, many children touch or point to the objects as they count. Sometimes children *slide* objects one by one as they count. Other times they place the objects somewhere (e.g., in a cup) one at a time as they count. Each of these experiences enables the child to pull together the one-to-one correspondence and rote counting to create meaningful, rational counting.

When young children are learning rational counting, sometimes they mistakenly omit numbers. This means they may need more rote counting experiences. Other times they do not touch each object, which means they may need more experiences with one-to-one correspondence. Knowing that rote counting and one-to-one correspondence serve as the ingredients for rational counting allows the teacher to analyze the child's counting and then address the child's specific needs. Saying that a child can't count is much like saying a child can't read. It is not helpful because we need to identify the child's exact strengths and weaknesses in order to provide appropriate instruction. Additionally, we can increase or decrease the quantities a child counts to allow us to identify the range of rational counting abilities the child has. In this way we can find the child's independent rational counting level (the greatest quantity a child can consistently and successfully count) and the instructional rational counting level (slightly greater than the greatest quantity a child can consistently and successfully count). The independent and instructional levels can be found in counting by ones or in skip counting.

Keeping Track

Keeping track is another important part of successful rational counting. Keeping track means knowing what has already been counted and knowing what is left to count at all points in the rational counting process. Sometimes when counting, children count and recount the same objects. Say there are six toy cars, but the child touches several cars twice and reaches the count of ten. The rote counting is accurate. The one-to-one correspondence is correct, in that a number name is given to each object touched. Yet the rational counting is impaired because the child does not keep track of what has already been counted. This is a common part of the process of learning how to count. Teachers can use the information for instructional purposes.

There are several ways to help children keep track as they count. One way is to teach the students to *line up* the objects prior to counting. Lining up the objects gives structure to the counting situation because the child is more likely to know where to start and where to stop. Moving objects (sliding or placing objects somewhere) as they are counted can help students keep track of what has already been counted. We use these strategies to help children establish accuracy in counting.

After children learn how to keep track we can help them progress to more efficient strategies. For example, a kindergartener who keeps track by placing each object in a cup as it is counted has learned a way to accurately count. However, the strategy is not as efficient as it could be because it takes longer to count this way. Eventually, the child will need to learn other strategies to increase speed. This is not to say it is a waste of time to teach children to keep track by putting the objects, one at a time, in a cup. The children learned a way to successfully and accurately count. But targeting instruction means always looking for the next step. The next step, in this case, is increasing the efficiency (reducing the time it takes to complete the task) without losing the accuracy or the child's feelings of satisfaction and engagement. The teacher needs to balance success and challenge. Maybe she'll go back to smaller quantities to help the child retain accuracy while learning more efficient strategies. Good teachers know how to help children be successful as they learn new concepts and face new challenges.

Cardinality

Cardinality is the number of elements in a set. With cardinality comes the understanding that the last number you say when rational counting is the quantity of objects in the group. As the NCTM (2000) notes, "Children should learn that the last number named represents the last object as well as the total number of objects in the collection" (79).

Not too long ago I was working with a kindergartner, Eric, who was counting lima beans. Each time I asked him how many beans, he recounted the set without telling me that there were eight beans. We repeated the exchange several times—I watched and listened to him count, and when he finished I asked him how many beans. He responded by recounting the beans. Each time Eric accurately counted eight beans without being able to name the quantity of the set. Eric did not yet have cardinality of some numbers. When I reduced the number of lima beans to five, he was successfully able to count and tell me that there were five lima beans. In this situation, I found the instructional level and began working on extending Eric's scope of cardinality.

In another classroom, first grader Tia worked with six counting bears. Tia was able to use rational counting forward and backward. After the 6, 5, 4, 3, 2, 1 count, the teacher asked the how-many question. Tia announced "one." Tia's response indicated that she used the last number said to name the quantity of the set. Like Eric, Tia does not yet have cardinality, but she is working at a different instructional level.

Bermejo (1996) suggests that there are six levels of cardinality. A child working at the first level shows no understanding. A child working at the second level answers the how-many question with a number-word sequence (the child responds "1-2-3" instead of "3" when answering the how-many question). A child working in the third level answers the how-many question by recounting, as Eric did with the lima beans. A child working at the fourth level answers the how-many question by repeating the last number said during counting—even if the items are counted backward, as Tia did. A child working in the fifth level shows some understanding when detecting errors in cardinality. A child working at the final level exhibits cardinality. Not all children go through each level, but the levels do give us information about children's understanding of cardinality.

Interestingly, cardinal numbers were first defined by mathematician Georg Cantor. The fact that Cantor (1915) was the first to define cardinal numbers is somewhat amusing because the famous Cantor's Theorem actually refers to the existence of *infinity of infinities*. Understanding cardinality is connected to understanding infinity—who would have thought that a child knowing that there are six objects in a set is related to the very abstract concept of infinity? Math is so cool!

Conservation of Number

Conservation of number, another concept connected to counting, involves understanding that the number of objects remains the same regardless of how the objects are arranged (Piaget 1964, 1970). Piaget believed children develop through stages and that conservation of number is at the core of a child's development of understanding numbers. While Piaget's theory has given us numerous insights to work with in the field of early childhood education, we need to realize that most of Piaget's work focuses on what children *can't* do. In some ways Piagetian theory offers a pessimistic view of children's abilities. We really do not want to limit children. But we need to find the level of instruction by learning what children know and uncovering what they need to learn next. Conservation of number gives us a great place to focus. We can uncover what a child knows about numbers while keeping in mind that it is common for young children to think that the quantity changes when the arrangement changes. Suppose a prekindergartener counts four buttons for her and four buttons for me. If I spread out her four buttons and I push together my four buttons, the child may announce that she now has more buttons (see Figure 2–1).

Figure 2–1

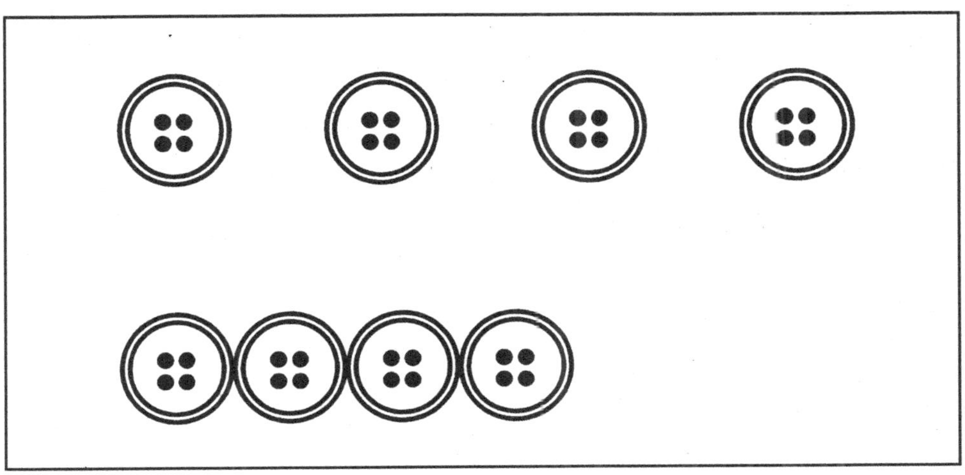

In this case, the change in arrangement causes the child to think that there are more buttons in her set. To the child, it looks like there are more because more space is used to display the buttons. The child interprets the change in arrangement as a change in quantity. It is through experience that we learn that the quantity remains the same even if the arrangement changes. Knowing that the child does not yet conserve number does not mean we should stop instruction. We shouldn't use Piagetian theory as an excuse to wait until the child is older. Instead we should use what we know about the child's abilities to continue targeted instruction. We can ask questions. We can give more opportunities for the child to experience changes in arrangements. We can make sure those experiences are meaningful.

Our goal is not to try to convince the child to believe the quantity remains the same when the arrangement changes. If we say, "See, they are the same. Right? You believe it, right?" the child will most likely agree with us. Not because the child understands, but because the child wants to please us. Trying to convince a child to conserve numbers is not effective. We need to give direct and embedded opportunities to children so that they can construct deeper knowledge of numbers through conservation of number.

Subitizing

Subitizing is related to counting, but does not involve counting. To subitize means to identify the number of objects in a set without having to count the objects. When you subitize you can quickly, accurately, and confidently judge the number of items in a small set. For those interested in its origin, the term *subitize* was coined by Kaufman, Lord, Reese, and Volkman (1949) in their famous study of dot displays, although early work with the idea is traced back to Freeman (1912). The word *subitize* comes from the Latin word *subitus,* which means sudden. When subitizing, you suddenly or immediately know the quantity—without counting.

Small quantities do not need to be counted. When you look at the squares in Figure 2–2 (yes, these are squares, not diamonds), you know that there are three. You don't have to count them. You don't really have to think much about it. You just immediately know, with complete confidence, that there are

Figure 2–2

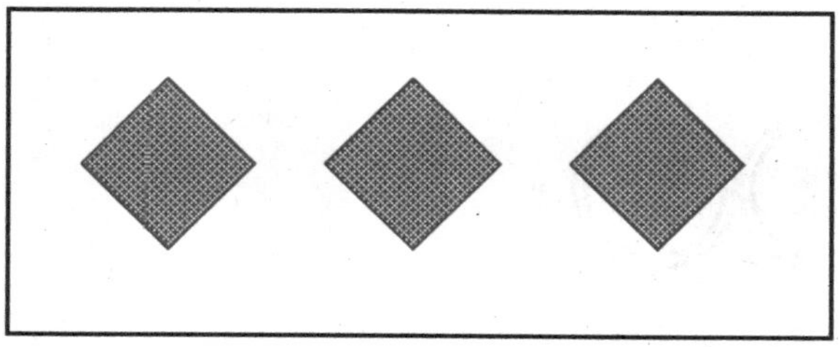

three. As the quantities get larger, the ability to subitize can be enhanced by familiar arrangements.

To many of us the arrangement of the five circles in Figure 2–3 is not new. We have seen dots arranged this way on dice and dominoes. Or perhaps we know it is five because there is one circle at each corner and one in the middle. In both cases, we subitize because we can quickly and accurately state the quantity.

Children subitize quantities with which they are comfortable. Some studies show that very young children subitize even before verbal counting (Starkey and Cooper 1995; Wynn 1992). The more opportunities children are given to subitize, the better subitizers they become. Children who play games with dice and dominoes learn to subitize because they become familiar with the arrangements and are, often, highly motivated to quickly and accurately know the quantities. For example, children playing dice games often learn what six looks like because their desire to roll a six is elevated. As they anticipate the excitement of rolling a six, they visualize what the arrangement of six looks like. Teachers can encourage this type of motivated visualization by making any of the arrangements the desirable outcome in the game. Perhaps the game revolves around how many fours you roll or how close your roll is to five. The beauty of classroom games is that the teacher can design them to meet the exact needs of the children.

Some children take longer to subitize some quantities. I've worked with many children who count the dots on dice, even when they have seen and counted that same quantity multiple times beforehand. In these cases, the children are not yet confident with their accuracy, wanting to make sure they know the correct amount. Again, the teacher's role is not to convince the child, but

Figure 2–3

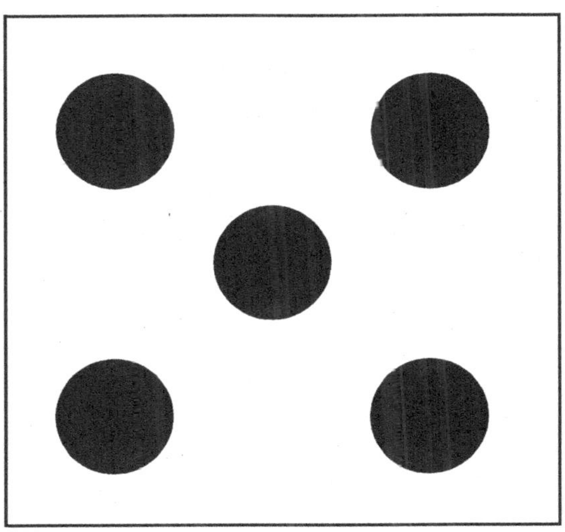

rather to give more implicit and explicit instruction through increased experiences with the arrangements.

Most quantities cannot be subitized without using grouping. For example, it is difficult to subitize the row of smiley faces shown in Figure 2–4. All of the smiley faces look the same, and the arrangement does not help us because it lacks grouping. When faced with this situation, it is natural for us to estimate or count the number of smiley faces, because we are not quick enough and confident enough to subitize. Yet when the arrangement includes grouping, we can subitize the groups and therefore subitize the set. Clements (1999) refers to using units or groups as conceptual subitizing.

The arrangement of groups of threes (see Figure 2–5) is not the only way to group this set of smiley faces. We can group the smiley faces in other familiar arrangements.

Because we can subitize five and four, as shown in Figure 2–6, we can subitize the set of nine.

Groupings can also include colors or patterns, as in Figure 2–7.

Figure 2–4

Figure 2–5

Figure 2–6

Figure 2–7

Notice that all nine smiley faces are lined up in a row. The arrangement is the same as the original row of nine smiley faces. However, groupings are present because there are three different color shadings, which help us subitize.

There are many manipulatives that help with subitizing. The ten frame (Wirtz 1980) is one of the best. The ten frame is a grid that includes two rows of five. Children place counters on the grid (one counter inside each small rectangle) to show various quantities (see Figure 2–8).

We can subitize quantities on the ten frame because each row includes a subitizable amount.

Notice that the first row is filled and there is one in the second row in Figure 2–9. We can subitize six using the groupings provided by the ten frame grid. Young children need to have experience using the ten frame to enhance their subitizing. Teachers may want to start with a five frame (just the first row of the ten frame) for many prekindergarten and some kindergarten students, depending on where the children are in their understanding of number and subitizing abilities.

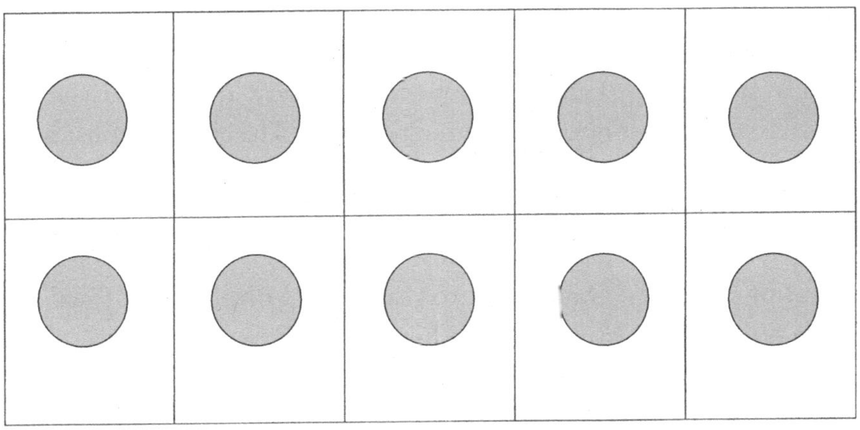

Figure 2–8

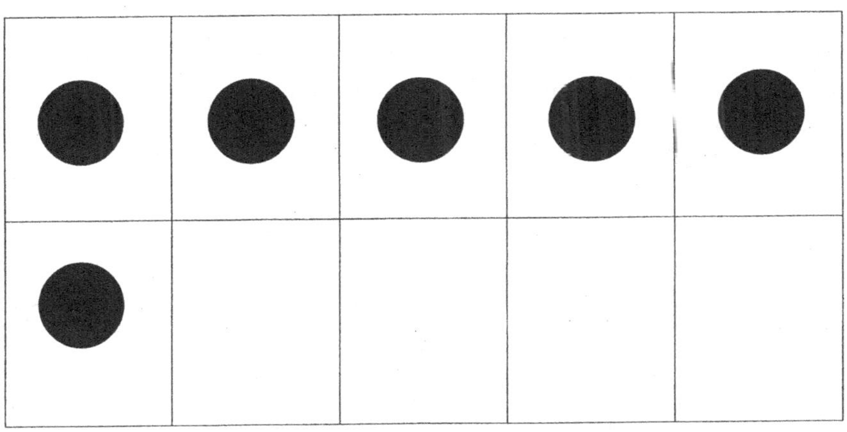

Figure 2–9

Representing Numbers

Numbers are represented in a variety of ways. Children can show numbers with real objects, pictures of real objects, manipulatives, pictures of manipulatives or sketches, number symbols, and number words. The most basic way for a young child to represent numbers is by showing quantities with real objects. The child holds four blocks. The child places three apples in a bowl. The child puts the eight crayons into the pack. Using real objects to show quantities enables young children to understand the numbers that they are representing.

Pictures of real objects are the next best thing, particularly if these pictures are cutouts so that the child can manipulate them. The child can use the pictures to represent numbers by showing quantities. Six pictures of teddy bears are arranged together to represent the number six. Seven pictures of basketballs are collected to show seven. If the pictures are the same, the task is simplified for the child. If the pictures are different, the task becomes more complex.

Manipulatives are essential in the early childhood mathematics classroom. As teachers, we understand that young children need to touch, move, and experience objects as they learn to represent numbers. Sometimes, however, manipulatives may not make tasks simpler. For example, a teacher tells a story of a child who has three cookies and gets two more. The teacher asks the children to use cubes to answer the how-many-now question. Even though the cubes are concrete objects, they aren't cookies. The children must represent the cookies with the cubes. Some children may need to use the actual object (cookies) to represent the quantity. Others may be ready for the representation with manipulatives. The point is to know what to do if the child has difficulty representing numbers. Going back to real objects or pictures of real objects can be an effective strategy to use with some children.

Pictures of manipulatives or sketches are another way to represent numbers. When asked to show three, a prekindergartener may sketch three circles. When asked to show seven, a first grader may draw ten stars. While working with a second grader, the teacher may draw fifteen squares on the dry erase board. Using drawings or sketches of objects to represent numbers requires the child to move from the concrete to a more abstract, two-dimensional representation.

Tally marks are a common way to represent numbers. Because tally marks involve making groups of five, smaller quantities can be subitized and larger quantities can be skip counted. We need to keep in mind that tally marks are symbols. Although the one-to-one correspondence is present in tally marks (four straight lines with the fifth line overlapping the group in a diagonal position creating the five-bar gate), tally marks are representations of objects. Sometimes teachers introduce tally marks to children too early. The teachers (or the curriculum the teachers use) assume that tally marks are concrete objects. This assumption is not accurate. Tally marks do not represent numbers in the same concrete way real objects represent numbers. This is not to say we shouldn't teach tally marks; we simply need to be aware of the abstractness involved with tally marks and children's readiness for them.

Unfortunately, some early childhood programs and teachers give too much attention to recognizing, reading, and writing the number symbols for 1, 2, 3, 4, 5, 6, 7, 8, 9, and 10. From numbers written with puff-paint to numbers cut from sandpaper, we bombard young children with abstract ways to represent numbers. When so doing, we assume that if a child can recognize, read, or write the number symbol, the child understands that number and knows how to represent it. Likewise we assume that if a child cannot recognize, read, or write a number symbol the child does not know that number or how to represent that number. These assumptions are erroneous. There is no point in teaching how to write a number if the child does not understand that number, much like learning how to spell the word *hippopotamus* is rather futile if you do not know what a hippopotamus is. When or how would you write the word in a meaningful way if you do not know what it is?

Of course, we need to teach children to recognize, read, and write numbers and number words. Children need to learn how to communicate numbers in efficient ways. But we need to make sure we are not teaching number symbols at the expense of teaching number concepts. There are many ways to represent numbers, and we want children to understand the numbers that they represent. We can help children represent numbers using real objects, pictures of real objects, manipulatives, pictures of manipulatives or sketches, number symbols, and number words.

Composing and Decomposing Numbers

Composing and decomposing numbers involves building numbers and breaking apart numbers. These terms come out of eastern philosophy where students are taught in ways that enhance their comfort with working with the parts of numbers (Ma 1999). Decomposing is breaking into pieces and composing is assembling the pieces.

Decomposing a number can take multiple forms. The number 15 can be composed and decomposed in many ways, as can be seen in Figure 2–10.

We do not have to limit the composing and decomposing to only two parts. Fifteen can also be composed and decomposed in many other ways.

3 + 3 + 3 + 3 + 3
4 + 4 + 4 + 3
5 + 5 + 5
6 + 4 + 5
7 + 4 + 4

These are just some of the possibilities children can find to represent 15 through composing and decomposing.

Children who compose and decompose numbers easily have a stronger number sense because they can use numbers more fluently and flexibly. Knowing that 15 can be decomposed in many ways gives so much information about

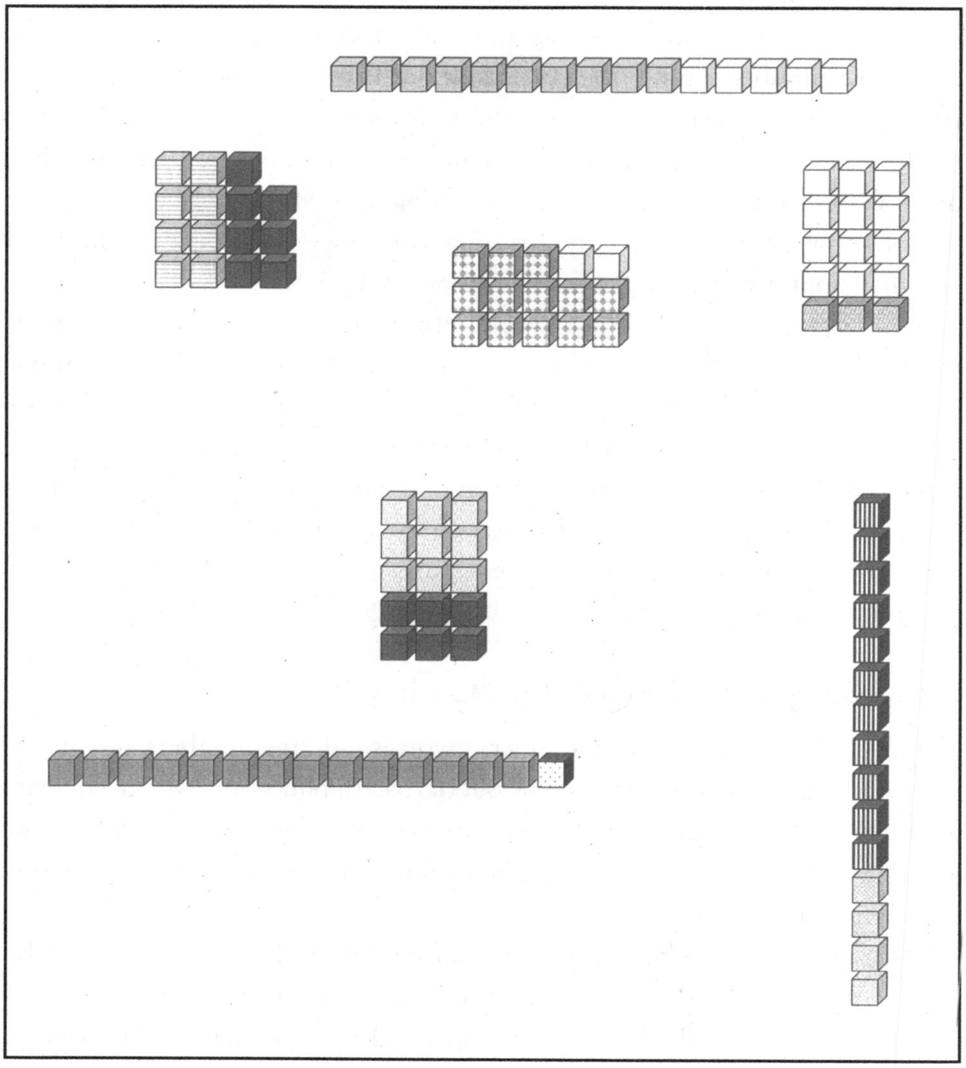

Figure 2–10

15 that it opens the door to working with operations with ease. Children need experiences building and breaking apart numbers.

A host of manipulatives enable children to compose and decompose numbers in a concrete way. Colored linking cubes allow children to make towers that are made of various parts represented by colors. Colored chain links can offer the same kinds of experiences.

The ten frame (Wirtz 1980) is also an excellent tool for visualizing and describing how numbers are composed and decomposed. Traditional use of the ten frame involves filling the first row (from left to right) and then filling the second row (see Figure 2–11).

Teachers can flash partially completed ten frames to students and ask them what number is represented on the ten frame. The students can explain why they know the ten frame shows a specific number. A student may say, "I know it is eight because the first row is full and there are three more." Another child may say, "I know it is eight because you need two more to make ten." These children have comfort with the ten frame and are describing ways to compose and decompose the number eight.

Children can show how numbers are composed and decomposed using blocks. When working with the number 25, children may show various ways the number is composed and decomposed, as in Figure 2–12.

Sometimes teachers encourage students only to compose numbers as is shown in the first example with two tens and five ones. While it is important for children to understand the groups of ten in the number 25, it is also important for them to see other ways the number 25 is composed and decomposed. Knowing that 25 consists of one ten and fifteen ones is a powerful foundation for later computation with regrouping. Likewise, knowing that 25 is also composed of 25 ones or five groups of five will help with computational proficiency.

Figure 2–11

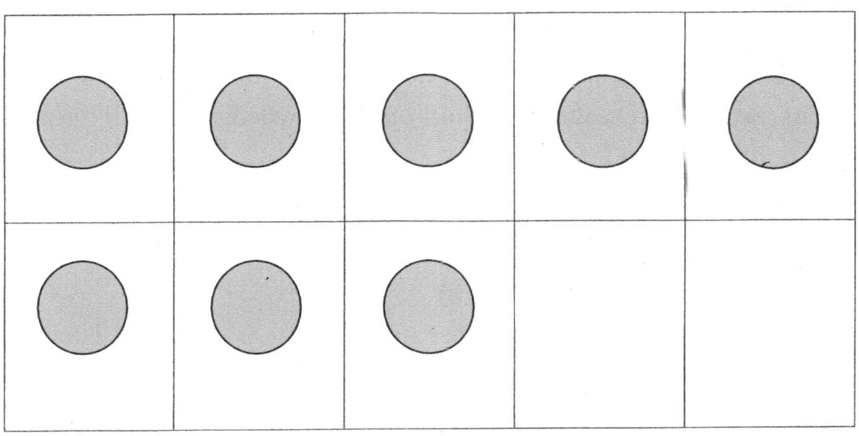

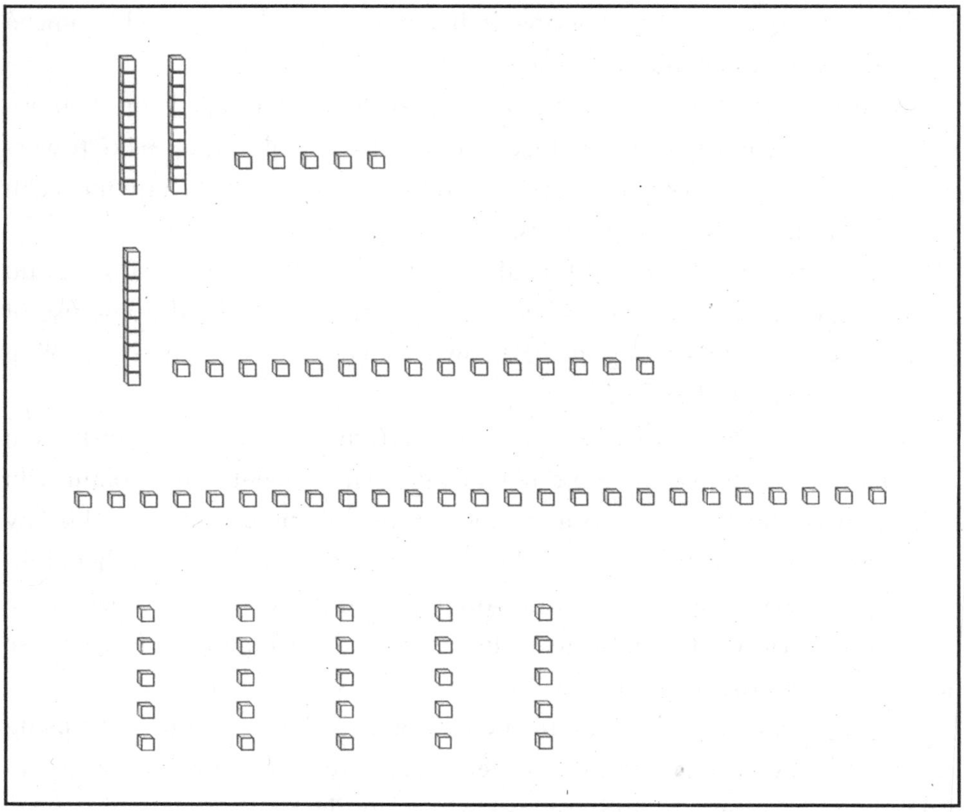

Figure 2–12

Teachers can also represent numbers by showing sets of objects—then covering up part of the set. Students try to name the part that is hidden using their understanding of how numbers are composed and decomposed. The how-many-are-hiding game can provide valuable information to the teacher. Sometimes students can quickly say how many objects are covered. Other times they seem to visualize each object that is hidden before announcing the hidden quantity. Still other children cannot identify the hidden quantity. In each case, the teacher learns more about what the child knows about how the specific number is composed and decomposed. In this way, we can really get a sense of to what degree the child *owns* knowledge of each number.

Relative Position and Relationships of Numbers

Number sense also involves understanding the positions of numbers and how numbers are related to each other.

Ordinal numbers tell us where numbers are positioned. They are used to express order. Anyone who has worked with children can attest that *first* is, by far, the most popular of all ordinal numbers. The first one to line up. The first one to draw a picture. The first one to share her answer. Children spend a lot of time trying to be first. Using this desire to help children understand ordinal numbers can be very effective.

When teachers model the use of ordinal number names, children gain further experiences with ordinal numbers. Taking turns in groups gives children opportunities to use ordinal numbers. Working with the calendar gives children multiple occasions to experience ordinal numbers. The goal is to teach children that numbers not only have size, but they also have position.

As one kindergartener shared with me, "They [ordinal numbers] are almost like real numbers. You just put an extra sound at the end." The child gives an interesting perspective of many of the ordinal numbers, such as fourth, fifth, sixth, seventh, eighth, ninth, and so on. It was exciting how he analyzed the connection between ordinal numbers and cardinal numbers. Interestingly, several minutes later, the same child came over to me with a question: "Why don't they just call it *oneth* and *twoth*, and *threeth*? That would make everything match better." I couldn't agree more! I also wish we could change eleven, twelve, thirteen to *one-teen*, *two-teen*, *three-teen* to more accurately represent the patterning of numbers in sequence leading to fourteen. But since our ordinal and cardinal number names are set, we need to use them accurately. However, discussing these ideas with children when we are musing about numbers helps them understand and appreciate numbers and sequencing more completely.

More, less, and equal are concepts that help children understand number relationships. More, less, and equal are only relevant when comparing two or more numbers or quantities. For example, five cannot be *more* unless it is being compared to a smaller amount. More is an idea, much like first, in its high popularity. Children often want more. They think more is better, unless we're dealing with brussels sprouts or something that is less desirable.

Many children come to school understanding more. Perhaps this is because they are often asked if they want more. Imagine the child in the highchair during meal time. The parent or caretaker commonly asks, "Do you want more?" It is rare to hear a child being asked, "Do you want less?" Perhaps due to these and other experiences, children tend to understand *more* before they understand *less*. However, more is only understood in relation to less, even if the word *less* is not used. Using this information to teach more and less can be very productive. In any given situation less can be depicted as *not more*. Understanding what something is not helps us more completely understand what it actually is.

The concept of less can also be described as fewer. Likewise, more can be described as greater. Fewer and greater are more complex terms because of the comparative ending (*er*) on the words. Greater is even more complex because *great* can refer to either large or wonderful. This doesn't mean we should not use *fewer* and *greater* when we teach children to compare sets. It means we need to be aware of the degree of difficulty involved. If a child is struggling with attaching meaning to the word *fewer*, we may want to try conveying meaning of the concept using the word *less*.

Teaching *more* and *less* involves comparing sets. Given two sets, the student is asked to identify which set is more and which set is less. Identifying more and less is simplified when the quantities are small. For example, a kindergartener is given five crayons on one tray and three crayons on another tray. The teacher could ask, "Which tray has fewer crayons?" or "Which tray has more crayons?" Identifying more and less is easier than creating more and less. Suppose a child is given two trays and some crayons. The teacher could ask the child to show more crayons on this tray and less crayons on the other tray. When the child is required to construct the sets to be compared it is more complex than identifying existing sets as more and less. As children successfully identify and create sets of more and less, we can offer challenges as we increase the quantities and increase the number of sets to be compared.

Equal is a concept largely connected to algebra, but the concept is rooted in number relationships and operations. Children need to learn that equal means *the same as* or *the same quantity as*. This understanding is imperative. I often ask students, "What does equal mean?" The answers they give are very interesting. Some say, "Equal means the answer will be next." Some children say, "Equal means two lines." These explanations show a lack of understanding of equality. As noted by many researchers (Behr, Erlwanger, and Nichols 1980; Falkner, Levi, and Carpenter 1999; Senz-Ludlow and Walgamuth 1998), "children often have serious misconceptions about the meaning of the equals sign. Children tend to perceive the equals sign as a stimulus for an answer" (Molina and Ambrose 2006, 111). Without meaning, the equal sign is useless.

Children need many experiences working with equality. As with more and less, identifying equality is easier than constructing equality, particularly when the items in the set can be manipulated. Consider this scenario.

> First graders Mark and Shianne are learning about equality. The teacher gives Mark five cubes and gives Shianne seven cubes, asking the children if they have an equal amount of cubes. Neither child is sure, so the teacher asks, "What could you do with the cubes to find out if you each have the same amount?" Prompted by the teacher, the children line up the cubes (see Figure 2–13).

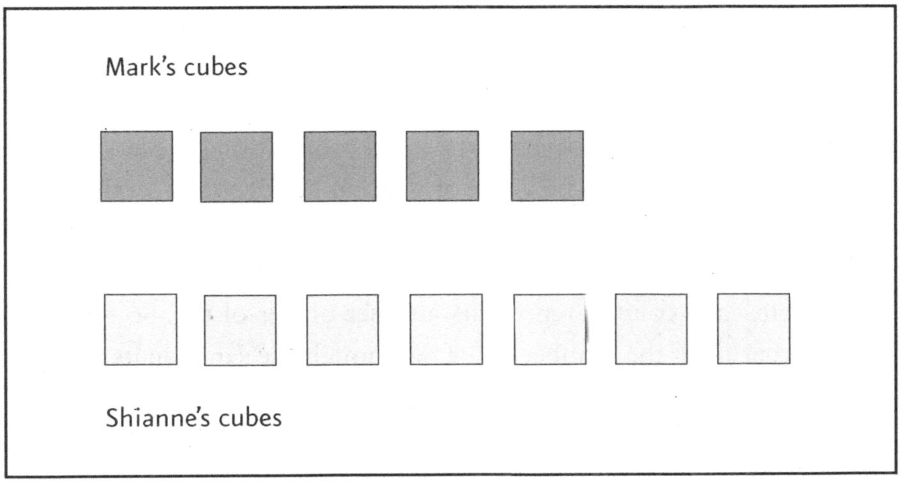

Figure 2–13

Shianne announces, "I have more cubes." Mark agrees and adds, "We don't have equal." The manipulation of the cubes in this way enables the children to see how the sets compare one to one. Now that the children have identified the lack of equality, the teacher moves to constructing equality by asking, "What could you do to make the sets equal?" The children are unsure. The teacher prompts thinking by asking, "Do you want to change the amount of cubes you have?" Mark replies, "Well, if I had more, we would have equal." The teacher asks, "How many more do you need?" Mark and Shianne are able to see that Mark will need two more cubes to make the sets equal. The teacher then asks, "If we didn't use any other cubes, is there still a way to make the sets equal?" Mark and Shianne think about the question. Shianne says, "I could drop two of mine on the floor." The response indicates that Shianne understands that the sets would be equal if she subtracts two cubes from her set. After affirming their thinking, the teacher continues, "What if you used all the cubes on the table. Is there a way to make the sets equal?" After a few attempts, Shianne and Mark conclude that they could take one of Shianne's cubes and add it to Mark's set, making each child have six cubes. With the teacher's guidance, the children are able to successfully construct equality in several ways because they are able to identify equality and manipulate the sets. The concepts of addition and subtraction were embedded within the construction of equality.

Place Value

Place value is the value of a digit's location in a numeral. Place value plays a critical role in understanding numbers and number relationships. According to the NCTM (2000), "It is absolutely essential that students develop a solid understanding of the base-ten numeration system and place-value concepts by the end of grade 2" (81). Learning multiples and understanding the patterns in rational counting help children build foundations in place value.

In our base-ten system, the value of the number depends on the position of the digits, which is why our number system is sometimes referred to as a *positional system*. Of course, the digit on the right represents the ones and moving to the left, each column represents another power of ten. So the number 142 is different from the number 421 even though the same digits are used.

Place value is difficult for some students because the value that they thought a digit had changes to a different value when the digit is in a different place. Often these difficulties occur because the children do not actually understand the numbers they are trying to represent with digits. Children need to have many experiences with quantities to make learning to recognize, read, and write numbers meaningful.

First graders Erin, Mathew, and Troy count twenty-six letters in the alphabet. To record the quantity, Erin writes 206. Mathew writes 62. Troy writes 2-6. These errors are common along the path toward understanding place value. Erin's use of 206 to represent 26 stems from her knowledge of how to write 20. She uses this knowledge and simply attaches the digit 6 in a way she thinks indicates 26. Mathew knows the digits that are needed to communicate 26, but he has reversed the order because his understanding of place value is still developing. Troy's use of a hyphen with the digits to show 26 may be connected to learning to write the number 26. He is simply applying what he has learned. Children learn how to communicate numbers using place value by trying out various representations until they learn the patterns and sequences associated with our positional base-ten number system.

There are various manipulatives that help children learn place value. Some of the staples include base-ten blocks (originally designed by Zoltan Dienes; Dienes 1960; Dienes and Goldring 1971), Digi-Blocks (originally designed by Kohlberg; see Kohlberg and Dacey 1999), ice cream sticks in bundles, colored chips, number lines, and hundred charts. The key to understanding place value is using many different models to represent the same quantities.

Base-ten blocks include ones units, tens rods, hundreds flats, and thousands cubes. Students show place value using the various blocks. Base-ten blocks are powerful because the manipulatives are size correlated and easy to use. Even though one ten rod is the same size as ten units, we cannot assume that children know this just because we tell them or show them. Similarly, we cannot assume they understand the relationships between the tens, hundreds, and thousands simply because we point it out to them. Children need to experience lining up and counting the units, rods, and flats as they come to know the values of the base-ten blocks.

Digi-Blocks are unique in that the blocks pack into one another. The tens block actually holds ten ones. The hundred block actually holds 100 ones inside 10 tens. Likewise, the thousand blocks (which weighs about eighteen pounds) really contains 1,000 ones within 100 tens within 10 hundreds. As the students pack and unpack the blocks to represent various numbers, they gain profound meaning of place value and number relationships.

Ice cream stick bundles are very simple. Each group of ten sticks is bundled together with a rubber band. To show thirty-five, a student may use three bundles of ten and five single sticks. Colored chips are more abstract. To use chip trading to model computation and place value, the students need to understand that the colors represent values. For example, ten white chips (ones) have the same value as one blue chip (tens). Ten blue chips equal one red chip (hundreds), and ten red chips equal one black chip (thousands). It is difficult for some children to understand the seemingly random assignment of value because all of the chips are the same size and shape. For other children the chips serve as a great way to represent numbers using place value.

While the hundred chart and number lines do not show concrete representation of place value, they do provide ways for children to experience the patterning and sequencing associated with place value. For example, a child may notice that on the hundred chart, all of the numbers in a particular row begin with the same digit or all of the numbers in a particular column end with the same digit. These patterns and others help children understand place value.

Fractions

Fractions are used to name parts of a whole or parts of a set. Parts of a whole involve equal regions, as in a single cake that is cut into four equal parts. Fractions of a set involve equal groups, as in twelve cupcakes that are divided into four groups of three. "Although fractions is not a topic for major emphasis for pre-k–2 students, informal experiences at this age will help develop a foundation for deeper learning at higher grades" (National Council of Teachers of Mathematics 2000, 82–83).

Building early experiences with fractions involves clarifying misconceptions. Sometimes children think half is one part. They do not understand that halves are two *equal* parts. This may be due to experiences with inaccurate uses of fraction terminology. How many times do you think an adult has said to a child, "Do you want the bigger half or the smaller half?" The question is erroneous. If the pieces are not the same size, they cannot be halves. Pieces can be different sizes; two halves must be the same size.

Another aspect of fractions that can pose problems for children is the fact that as the denominator digits get larger, the amounts get smaller. When working with one-tenth and one-sixth, the child may think one-tenth is larger because ten is bigger than six. We may be revising their understanding by introducing all these values between whole numbers, which is why we need to give hands-on experiences for children to build foundations in understanding fractions.

Years ago I visited a first grade classroom where the teacher (previously a fourth grade teacher) was introducing fractions to her students. She devoted much of the whole group lesson to teaching the students a mnemonic device for remembering fraction notation. "The *de*nominator is on *dee* bottom," said the teacher. "The *de*nominator is on *dee* bottom," repeated the students. "It is simple," explained the teacher, "Just remember the *de*nominator is on *dee* bottom and the numerator is on the top. That will help you understand fractions."

Sadly, these students did not experience a fractions lesson. They did not engage in learning about fractions. Remembering which is the denominator and which is the numerator is not the same as understanding fractions. According to the NCTM (2000), "At this level [prekindergarten through grade 2], it is more important for students to recognize when things are divided into equal parts than to focus on fraction notation" (82). Fortunately, the teacher and I debriefed after the lesson and discussed how to emphasize equal parts. The students engaged in an exciting, hands-on lesson about fractions dee following day.

Understanding Operations and Relationships of Operations

The hows and whys of math operations

The basic operations in mathematics are addition, subtraction, multiplication, and division. Young children understand these operations more deeply when the operations are given in context. To teach for meaning, our instructional focus needs to be on concepts, not on hollow procedures. This is not to say we cannot teach children *how* to compute. What it means is that we need to teach the *why* along with the *how* to make the math operations meaningful for students.

Addition

If you ask young children, "What is math?" many children respond, "It is putting stuff together" or "It is adding" or, as one child shared, "It is plussing." While we really need to broaden young children's understanding to include all of the aspects of mathematics, we can use their general preference for addition as we help children develop meaning of operations.

Addition involves joining or combining sets. The goal is to compute the sum. Young children begin to understand addition as they connect counting and number sequence. The idea that numerical relationships are embedded within the number sequence is present in the relationship that $n + 1$ equals the number after n in the counting by ones sequence (Baroody 1995). Essentially, children learn that cardinality applies to computing sums.

Addition also involves part-total or part-whole relationships. Understanding that the whole (total) is made up of parts is connected to decomposing and composing numbers. It is also, obviously, connected to addition and subtraction. There are many early childhood educators who successfully teach addition and subtraction simultaneously via the part-whole framework.

Subtraction

Many early childhood teachers use the term *take away* in place of *subtraction* or *minus* because they believe it is easier for young children to understand. The problem is that *take away* is not synonymous with subtraction. Take away is only one type of subtraction. If we only use the term *take away,* we are limiting our students' understanding of subtraction.

Removal subtraction is take away subtraction. Within the math situation, one of the parts of the total is given away, lost, eaten, hidden, crossed out, or in some way removed. The goal is to find out how many are left. For example, I have five pieces of candy. I eat two pieces, how many do I have left?

Missing part subtraction is similar to take away subtraction, but the part that is left is known. We need to figure out the unknown part that completes the total. For example, I have five pieces of candy. I eat some. Three pieces of candy are left. How many did I eat? One of the addends in the related addition equation is missing. The child may use counting on, counting back, and related facts to solve the problem.

Comparison subtraction involves finding the difference. Two sets are being compared. Subtraction tells us how different the two sets are. For example, I have five pieces of candy. You have two pieces of candy. How many more pieces of candy do I have than you have? To solve the problem, you need to compare the sets by finding the difference.

Equal Grouping and Fair Sharing

Equal grouping and fair sharing are the foundational concepts associated with multiplication and division. Even young children can work with these concepts when they are provided with meaningful contexts for doing so. Consider these math situations.

> There are four children. Each child wants three crackers. How many crackers do we need?
>
> There are twelve crackers and four children. How many crackers does each child get if we want to share the crackers equally?

Even young children can solve these multiplication and division situations, given the context and the tools to represent the operations. Children may form equal groups and use repeated addition to solve the multiplication situation. Children could partition the sets by distributing crackers to each child one by one to solve the division situation. The context allows the children to engage in meaningful mathematics operations even if they have not formally been introduced to multiplication and division. We want to teach children how addition and subtraction are related to multiplication and division. We also want to teach the children how multiplication and division are related.

Computing Fluently and Estimating

Accuracy and efficiency in mathematics

Computing fluently involves accuracy and efficiency. Children need to know some equations automatically. But it is important that they understand the operations and the numbers with which they are working. Knowing $8 + 7 = 15$ is meaningless if you do not know what addition is or you do not know the numbers 8, 7, and 15. Computational fluency includes meaning of operations and numbers, as well as number relationships.

Basic Facts

Basic facts are to mathematics as high-frequency words are to reading. Some words are so common that they need to be read with complete automaticity.

For example, the word *the* appears so frequently and is so difficult to decode that it will slow children down and impair their fluency if they have to labor over it every time they come across it. The same is true in mathematics. There are some combinations that students need to know (e.g., plus one, minus one, plus two, minus two, doubles). Because these combinations are so frequent and so interconnected within our number system, it will slow children down if they have to compute these facts every time they come across them. Combinations of ten are another example. Many first graders, for example, know 5 + 5, 10 + 0, and 9 + 1. These basic facts do not have to be computed. Yet many of these same children revert to the more time consuming *count all* or *count on* strategy when faced with 6 – 4, 7 + 3, and 8 + 2 (and the relative facts). All of the combinations of ten are important. Knowing the ways to make ten will help with estimating and with computing larger numbers. Combinations of ten are like high-frequency words. We need to teach children to simply know the facts. All facts (addition and subtraction) up to the sum/minuend of twenty are considered basic facts and play critical roles in computational fluency.

Understanding inverse operations helps children broaden their basic facts repertoire. Learning, for example, that 8 + 4 = 12 is connected to 12 – 4 = 8 is paramount. As the NCTM (2000) notes, "In developing the meaning of operations, teachers should ensure that students repeatedly encounter situations in which the same numbers appear in different contexts" (83). We want students to come to understand how addition and subtraction are related.

Fact Families

Teaching *fact families* offers a way to depict the relationship between addition and subtraction, which helps increase accuracy and efficiency with basic facts. For example, this is the fact family for 2, 3, 5.

$$2 + 3 = 5$$
$$3 + 2 = 5$$
$$5 - 3 = 2$$
$$5 - 2 = 3$$

A fact family comprises two related addition facts and two related subtraction facts. All four facts are part of the same family because they all represent the same part-part-whole relationship. Anyone who has ever taught fact families knows it is difficult for some children. One time I was working on fact families with a first grader, Enrique. Enrique wrote several equations in his math journal.

7 + 3 = 10
3 + 7 = 10
10 + 3 = 13

I said to Enrique, "Tell me about the numbers in your fact family." Enrique replied, "The family is seven, three, and ten." I asked, "What about thirteen?" Enrique shared, "Well, ten plus three is thirteen." "Yes, but is thirteen in the family?" I asked. Enrique responded, "Yep. Thirteen is the cousin."

Amusing as Enrique's response is, he meant it. In his journey toward understanding fact families and the relationships of operations and numbers, he saw that 13 was the correct answer to the equation. He also knew that 13 was not part of the 3, 7, 10 family, but he understood that there was some kind of relationship. He named this relationship through his own experiences by calling 13 the cousin. What a beautiful connection. By using Enrique's existing knowledge of numbers and number relationships, we can further his understanding of fact families.

Strategies for Addition and Subtraction

When faced with an addition situation, young children typically begin by *counting all*. If they have 3 apples on one plate and 5 apples on another plate, they count, "1, 2, 3, 4, 5, 6, 7, 8." To increase efficiency, children learn to *count on*, which means they begin with a number *in their head* and then *count on* by ones from that number. Dealing with the same apples on plates, the child says, "3, 4, 5, 6, 7, 8." Children who are able to *count on* can do so because they can think simultaneously about wholes and parts (Kamii 2000). They see 3 as a whole and 5 as a whole; but at the same time they can see 3 and 5 as parts of another whole (8).

The next level is for the child to *count on from the largest number*, even when the largest number is not first. The child looks at the plates and apples and counts, "5, 6, 7, 8." The task is now performed more quickly. Baroody's (1995) research on the developmental order of *counting on* indicates that we do not have complete clarity about how children progress through and invent *counting on* strategies. Fortunately, we can use the information to teach children more efficient strategies; we don't have to wait for children to invent them. We can also keep in mind that sometimes children use or go back to less efficient strategies (such as count all) out of the desire to gain confidence with the accuracy, particularly when the math situations become more complex.

Teaching *key words* as a strategy for solving problems was common years ago. However, we now know that teaching key words does not help students understand how and when to use number operations to solve problems. Teaching that the word *altogether* means "to add" is not teaching for understanding. We do not want children to memorize rules like *altogether means add* because we want to empower them to think about the math. Consider this problem. Altogether there are eight balloons. Five balloons popped. How many balloons are left? If the child is taught that the key word *altogether* means add the numbers, the child may erroneously add 8 + 5 to solve the balloon problem because the word *altogether* appeared in the word problem and 8 and 5 are the only numbers given.

Problem Types

Other strategies for addition and subtraction include identifying word problem types. Each problem includes the start, the change, and the result. Any of these parts can serve as the unknown in an addition or subtraction situation (Fennema et al. 1999). Consider the following examples for joining and separating:

Start unknown addition: Geneva had some pencils. Her friend gave her 4 pencils. Now she has 9 pencils. How many pencils did she start with?

Unknown + 4 = 9

Change unknown addition: Geneva had 5 pencils. Her friend gave her some more pencils. Now she has 9 pencils. How many pencils did her friend give her?

5 + *Unknown* = 9

Result unknown addition: Geneva had 5 pencils. Her friend gave her 4 more pencils. How many pencils does she have now?

5 + 4 = *Unknown*

Start unknown subtraction: Geneva had some pencils. She gave 4 to her friend. Now she has 5 pencils. How many pencils did she start with?

Unknown – 4 = 5

Change unknown subtraction: Geneva had 9 pencils. She gave some pencils to her friend. Now she has 5 pencils. How many pencils did she give to her friend?

9 – *Unknown* = 5

Result unknown subtraction: Geneva had 9 pencils. She gave 4 pencils to her friend. How many pencils does she have now?

9 – 4 = *Unknown*

Identifying which aspect is the unknown can really help children tackle contextual problems. Knowing the problem types helps the teacher provide a variety of problems to students, avoiding overemphasis on result-unknown types at the expense of start-unknown and change-unknown problem types. Children need multiple opportunities with all problem types.

Computing Beyond Single-Digit Numbers

Computing with larger numbers involves using operations in ways that enhance concept development. We do not want to focus only on procedures. We want to combine procedural understanding with conceptual understanding. It is not enough to know what to do. Children also need to know why. When computing 56 + 25, children may address the problem in a variety of ways. They may use the traditional algorithm in this way:

$$\begin{array}{r} {}^{1} \\ 56 \\ \underline{+\,25} \\ 81 \end{array}$$

Or they may use an alternative strategy such as partial sums in this way:

$$\begin{array}{r} 56 \\ \underline{+\,25} \\ 70 \\ \underline{+\,11} \\ 81 \end{array}$$

Or they may use the facts that they know in this way:

$$\begin{array}{c} 5 + 5 = 10 \\ 10 + 1 = 11 \\ 50 + 20 = 70 \\ 11 + 70 = 81 \end{array}$$

When computing 63 – 19, children may use the traditional algorithm in this way:

$$\begin{array}{r} {}^{5\ 13} \\ \cancel{63} \\ \underline{-\,19} \\ 44 \end{array}$$

Or they may use an alternative strategy such as equal addition in this way:

$$\begin{array}{rcr} 63 & +1 & 64 \\ \underline{-\,19} & +1 & \underline{-\,20} \\ & & 44 \end{array}$$

Or they may use facts that they know in this way;

$$13 - 9 = 4$$
$$50 - 10 = 40$$
$$4 + 40 = 44$$

It is important to encourage students to share the strategies they use to solve problems. They may find that their strategies are more accurate and efficient than the traditional algorithm. They also learn new computation strategies from each other. Engaging in math discourse on why each strategy is effective allows children to synchronize procedural and conceptual learning.

Estimation

Estimation plays an integral part in computational fluency. When you estimate, you use your judgment to approximate quantity, size, position, or value. There are different types of estimation—including true approximations, overestimating, underestimating, and range-based estimating (Taylor-Cox 2001). True approximations are typically used with very large numbers. Things like population statistics, the national deficit, and the distance between planets involve very large numbers. It makes sense to estimate. The problem associated with estimating with young children is that they do not typically deal with such large numbers. Sometimes it *does not* make sense to estimate.

> A second-grade assessment requires children to estimate the sum of 27 + 32. The problem is that the assessment scoring guide indicates that the only acceptable answer is 60 because the goal is estimation. Yet for some children it is easier for them to just compute the actual sum. If they record the actual sum (59), the answer is marked incorrect and the assumption is made that they do not know how to estimate. This is a problem because children who accurately and efficiently compute the sum may in fact be using estimation in context to find the actual sum. We need to ask what makes sense: reporting an estimate or an actual sum? In most cases, when working with small numbers, it makes more sense to report the actual answer, rather than to estimate. If we want to find out if children are using estimation to compute, we need to ask them how they solved the problem, not ask them to report an estimate when it does not make sense to do so.

Sometimes overestimating is a good idea, like when you are shopping and you want to make sure you have enough money to pay for everything.

Sometimes underestimating is a good idea, like when you estimate the amount of gas you have in the car to make sure you arrive at your destination without having to walk the last few miles. We need to teach children what type of estimation is needed given the real-life context.

Using range-based estimation can be very beneficial. "Range-based estimation involves thinking about quantity in terms of the upper end and the lower end that encompass an estimate" (Taylor-Cox 2001, 209). When estimating, our goal is to establish a good range, not necessarily to estimate the actual amount. To teach range-based estimating, we can use the idea of a sandwich. The top slice of bread is higher than your estimate and bottom slice is lower than your estimate. Your estimate is sandwiched between the two slices of bread. This metaphor helps young children learn about establishing a range when estimating.

Making reasonable estimates increases computational fluency *and* computational fluency increases the ability to make reasonable estimates. Computing fluently goes hand in hand with making reasonable estimations. Good estimations help increase accuracy and efficiency in working with numbers and operations. Sharing strategies and otherwise engaging in mathematics discourse enables children to see the connections and benefits associated with estimation and computational fluency.

The three *big ideas* of number and operations are very connected. Understanding numbers and number relationships is intertwined with understanding operations and relationships between and among the operations. Computing fluently and making reasonable estimates are tied to understanding numbers and operations. Understanding these interconnections is valuable and necessary for meaningful mathematics.

CHAPTER 3

Targeting Instruction

Targeting Instruction Using Strategies

Ready. Aim. Teach.

Targeting instruction involves differentiating instruction by content. The teacher uses ongoing assessment data to direct instruction to small groups of students. The teacher focuses on the overt academic needs of the students. Some students may need instruction of preceding concepts, while others may need instruction geared toward subsequent concepts. Still other students need instruction directed between these two levels. There are many strategies that can be used to target mathematics instruction, including back-mapping and forward-mapping, scaffolding, compacting, tiering, and activating prior knowledge.

Back-Mapping and Forward-Mapping

Back-mapping is tracing back to the concepts that came before the current concept of study. Forward-mapping is looking ahead to the concepts that follow the current concept of study. Back-mapping and forward-mapping are best conducted within the same mathematics topic. Moving on to the next unit with some students while concurrently teaching a previous unit with other students—while also teaching the current unit for yet other students—is not viable because the units may be completely different topics. It is simply too disjointed to have some students studying geometry, for example, while others are studying number operations and still others are studying measurement. We need to be studying a common concept, but we can study various levels or aspects of that common mathematics concept. For example, a first-grade class is working with two-digit numbers. The on-grade-level objective is reading, writing, and representing two-digit numbers. Reading, writing, and representing one-digit numbers (kindergarten objective) comes before and reading, writing, and representing three-digit numbers (second grade objective) comes after. Effective use of back-mapping and forward-mapping is a way for teachers to use their command of the content to target the mathematics instruction.

Scaffolding

Scaffolding involves the teacher supporting learners as they construct knowledge. Scaffolding is "a process that enables a child or novice to solve a problem, carry out a task, or achieve a goal, which would be beyond his unassisted efforts" (Wood, Bruner, and Ross 1976, 90). It is likened to the real-life scaffolding that we may see next to a tall structure. The purpose of the scaffolding is to allow the workers to improve the structure. The workers may be adding something new or repairing a section. The educational scaffolding a teacher provides helps the learner move from the current level of understanding to a new or improved level of understanding. The scaffolding next to a building may change from one day to the next, depending on which part of the structure needs attention. When the building is complete or can stand on its own, the scaffolding is removed. So it is that educational scaffolding involves changes in the areas of focus and the gradual withdrawal of the teacher's influence and support. Eventually the temporary scaffolding is removed and what remains is a strong level of understanding held by the student.

Sometimes scaffolding involves doing part of the task for the students because they are not ready to complete the task independently. Yet as we scaffold we do not want to do too much, because our focus is on the learner's academic growth, not our own. It is a balancing act as we provide just the right amount of support, encouragement, and challenge.

Scaffolding is a strategy that is rooted in the work of Lev Vygotsky (1962), who presented the notion of the zone of proximal development (ZPD). A child's ZPD is the distance between the actual development level and the level of potential development (Vygotsky 1962). It is the exact location at which the instruction needs to be targeted. As teachers scaffold instruction, they are revealing learners' ZPDs and supporting learners based on their ZPDs.

Teaching students about the ZPD is beneficial. Each child's ZPD in any given context is the space between what they know and what they can know.

Teachers should talk about the ZPD with their students because it helps the students describe the learning process and focus on learning progress. With young children, I use the term *zone* to communicate the idea of the ZPD. I ask students these and other questions: "Where's your zone?" "How can I help you find your zone?" "How would you describe your zone?" "Has your zone moved?" Several years ago I was targeting instruction for a small group of first graders. One child looked at me, wide-eyed and announced, "I am so in my zone!" What she was communicating was that she was learning and she knew it! The instruction was targeted to the right place because we had found her ZPD.

Compacting

Compacting involves revealing small gaps in a student's understanding and planning accordingly. When compacting, the teacher uses a preassessment to determine what the student knows and does not know, and plans for instruction that will be meaningful and challenging to the student (Tomlinson 1999).

Sometimes students already know a great deal about the concept that the teacher is getting ready to teach. Sometimes this knowledge needs just a small piece to make it more complete. Perhaps the student knows the concept, but does not know what it is called. Perhaps the student understands how to work through the problem, but needs to learn how to report the results. Perhaps the student knows how and why to use a mathematical procedure, but is unclear how to connect it to real life. In these cases (and many other similar situations), it is appropriate to use compacting to differentiate mathematics instruction.

Compacting is a strategy that was originally presented as *curriculum compacting* by Renzulli and Smith (Reis, Burns, and Renzulli 1992; Renzulli and Smith 1978; Renzulli, Smith, and Reis 1982) for gifted and talented students. The students identify their academic strengths, document their content mastery, and engage in alternative activities. The instructional technique was designed to help teachers make appropriate adjustments in the curriculum for high-end learners.

But this is not to say that compacting is a strategy that can only be used with high-end learners. Sometimes it is appropriate to compact with other students. It all depends on what the preassessment indicates. Compacting means taking the bulk of the information and compressing it together (because the student already knows it), so that the focus can be on the small portion of knowledge that the child does not currently have. The caution here is that if you try to compact a lot of unknown information, the students will most likely become confused, even frustrated. Compacting is successful when much of the knowledge is already owned by the child. Compacting allows the students to devote time to learning something new!

Tiering

Tiering is a strategy that provides students with lessons, tasks, and assignments that are leveled. The focus of the activities is the same, but the avenues have varying degrees of difficulty (Tomlinson 1999). Tiering is an excellent strategy for differentiating instruction in mathematics because it allows all children to engage in meaningful and productive learning.

Some educators understand tiering as the creation of multiple lesson plans for the given topic of study. Some of these educators say, "I don't have time to create and implement so many different lesson plans." I understand and appreciate this statement; teachers are busy and time is precious. Some supervisors, who demand multiple lesson plans for mathematics each day, may end up with more tearing (as in crying) than tiering (as in leveled instruction).

The beauty of differentiating instruction on the fly is that we do not need multiple lengthy lesson plans. What we need to do is identify the concept and *bump it up* for some students and *tone it down* for other students. Doing so gives us three levels to work with at any given time. We can use the levels of cognitive demand (discussed in Chapter 5) to implement the tiered activities or we can use back-mapping and forward-mapping, scaffolding, or compacting (discussed previously in this chapter). We can also vary the levels by implementing different degrees of abstractness and open-endedness (Tomlinson 1999).

Tiering can be utilized in lessons, tasks, and assignments. The teacher may meet with small homogeneous ability groups to instruct at different levels; give independent or dependent tasks that are aimed at different levels; tier tasks that serve as classroom centers; and tier in-class or homework assignments. Yes, there may be a lot of tiering going on! To avoid the feeling of being overwhelmed with all of the possibilities, I encourage teachers to begin with the time the students are working directly with the teacher. The time students spend with the teacher is very valuable; therefore differentiating the direct instruction students receive is a great place to concentrate efforts. After a level of comfort is reached, the teacher may concentrate on offering dependent tiered tasks related to the direct instruction. What naturally follow are independent tiered tasks or tiered centers. Then the teacher may decide to give some attention to tiered homework. The point is for the teacher to focus attention on one aspect of differentiation at a time so that the multiple features of differentiated mathematics instruction are not a colossal undertaking, but a natural progression.

Activating Prior Knowledge

Activating prior knowledge is a great strategy for targeting mathematics instruction. Prior knowledge is the personal knowledge a child brings to any given learning situation. This knowledge is a combination of the child's experiences, beliefs, and all the previously learned information. *Experiences* include ordinary and extraordinary activities, situations, and events that the child has encountered in and out of school. *Beliefs* include the awareness a child has of her strengths and weaknesses, her culture, and her motivation. *Previously learned information* includes knowledge that is currently owned by the child. The brain combines all of these aspects to form a framework of understanding that serves as an individual's prior knowledge.

The idea of *hooking* to students' prior knowledge is not new. Good teachers attempt to help students make connections between prior knowledge and new information. These connections enable the students to give meaning to and take ownership of the new information.

Teachers attempt to activate prior knowledge in multiple ways. One way is by using the KWL strategy (Ogle 1986). KWL is recorded on a chart with three category titles; what I *know* (K), what I *want* to learn (W), and what I *learned* (L). The information in the first two columns is recorded before the unit and the last column is recorded after the unit. The idea of gathering information about what children already know, what they are interested in learning, and then recording the knowledge acquired is sound; however, many teachers gather this information in a whole class setting, which means the KWL information is *only* from the children who responded. Yet the information is often interpreted as the prior knowledge of the entire class, desired areas of study, and newly acquired knowledge. To avoid this problem, children need to use personal KWL charts. In this way, the students' prior knowledge can be utilized to target mathematics instruction.

Another way to activate prior knowledge is to use graphic organizers. Graphic organizers are frameworks for organizing information in ways that reveal patterns and connections. Graphic organizers come in a variety of forms, but all are aimed at "giving information a base of context for better understanding and meaning" (Jensen 1998, 97).

As with KWL charts, we need to make sure the graphic organizer is not *one-size-fits-all*. If the goal is to use graphic organizers to activate prior knowledge as a way to differentiate instruction, we cannot assume that the same graphic organizer is optimal for all students. Some children may understand better when using a sequence-oriented graphic organizer. Other children may have greater comfort with a more random-oriented graphic organizer. Some children may prefer sophisticated weblike drawings, while others may learn best with less distracting, more simplistic depictions. Some children may prefer linear graphic organizers, others may not. Some children may need the big picture idea given as a way to activate prior knowledge, while other children may need details to trigger prior knowledge.

The first step in differentiating the graphic organizers used to activate prior knowledge is to stop assuming that the graphic organizer we prefer is the one that is the best for all of our students. Children need exposure to many types of graphic organizers so that they can begin to identify which graphic organizers allow them to activate prior knowledge and develop greater understanding.

Activating prior knowledge also involves appraising the knowledge that is being activated. We cannot assume that all knowledge that the student owns is accurate knowledge. Sometimes children have misconceptions. The inaccuracies held by students can be understood as "pitfalls" that are deeply rooted misconceptions resistant to change (Barnett-Clarke and Ramirez 2004). Teachers need to be on the lookout for misconceptions. Simply telling students that their misconceptions are errors is not the way to solve the problem. We need to address the misconceptions through targeted, differentiated instruction.

Targeting Instruction Using Index Questions

Index questions give an index

An index question is one of the easiest ways to informally assess where students are in their understandings of specific mathematics concepts. The index question or problem gives an *index* of where each student is in terms of their level of understanding. The index questions used need to be purposeful and specific. To create index questions, teachers need to begin with the end in mind. Thinking about the goal and the steps to reach that goal allows us to create indexes that reveal valuable information. To learn more about how to develop and utilize index questions we will analyze four different teachers' implementations of this type of informal assessment. While each grade level can and should teach all of the components of number and operations, this chapter offers a snapshot of different number and operations concepts presented to prekindergarten, kindergarten, first-grade, and second-grade classes.

Spotlight on Representing Numbers in a Prekindergarten Classroom

How do you show numbers?

Ms. Vogel teaches a class of twenty-three prekindergarteners. To gain information about how well her students can represent numbers, Ms. Vogel uses a simple informal assessment. Each child takes a piece of paper, which is clipped to a clipboard and a pencil. The students are asked to find places in the classroom where they can work independently. Some children work at tables, others at the dramatic play center, block corner, small group table, or comfortable places on the floor. When the children are settled, Ms. Vogel gives the verbal directions, "Show four." One student asks, "Anyway we want to?" Ms. Vogel responds, "Yes. Show four anyway you want to." The students record their responses.

See:
Algebra, p. 19
Data, p. 32
Geometry, p. 32
Measurement, p. 29

Explanation of the Representing Numbers Index Question

The task is somewhat complex, in that showing a number with pictures, number symbols, and words is more difficult than showing a number with real objects. To deal with the complexity, Ms. Vogel uses a meaningful number. Four is a really important number to her students because they are all four years old. Ms. Vogel uses a significant number to find out what her students know about representing numbers.

Student Responses

Luis' Response

In response to the directions *show four*, Luis drew seventeen circles (see Figure 3–1). Notice that four of the circles are a little bit darker. These are the circles that Luis drew first. Ms. Vogel saw Luis' original response, which had only four circles on the page. When Luis brought his paper to Ms. Vogel, he saw some of his classmates' work. Viewing others' work prompted him to take his paper back to the table and add more circles. He originally had the correct answer, but apparently doubted his answer when he saw some other students' work. Because Ms. Vogel combined observation with the written response, she has a better understanding of Luis' abilities. He knew the answer, but lacked confidence when he saw some other (incorrect) answers.

See:
Algebra, p. 19
Data, p. 34
Geometry, p. 34
Measurement, p. 30

Other children drew more than four objects (circles, Zs, lines, flowers, etc.) on their papers. Most of these students filled the page as Luis did. Ms.

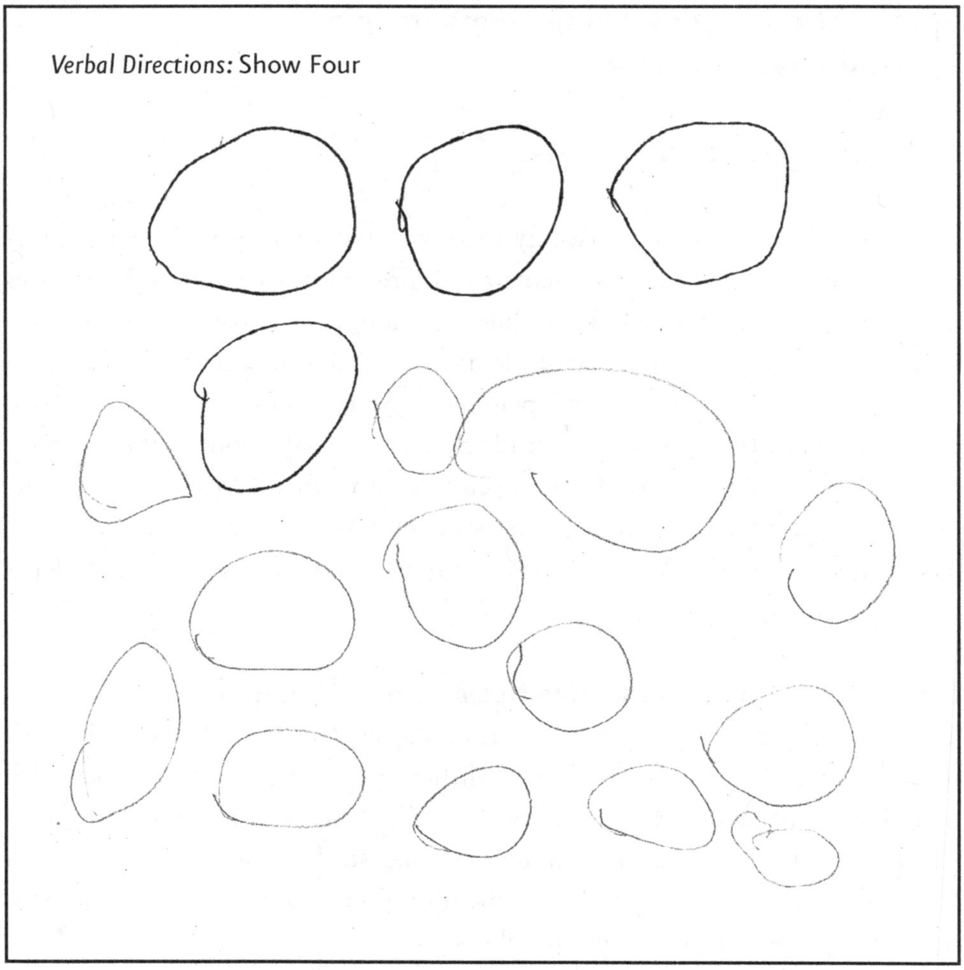

Figure 3–1

Vogel grouped these students with Luis for on-grade-level instruction. While Luis' initial response indicates that he knows a little more than the others, Ms. Vogel plans to start him with this group to give him more experiences with representing numbers to build his confidence. She may provide an additional challenge for Luis within the current group or move him to another group for more challenge. That is the wonderful thing about flexible grouping. Purposeful changes can and should be made at any time.

Musukula's Response

Musukula's response is exciting. At four years old, she can write the numbers one through ten (see Figure 3–2). Even though the ten is written between the six and seven, Musukula knows the sequence of the numbers as evidenced by the fact that Ms. Vogel saw her write ten in the leftover space when she ran out of room after the nine. Musukula also understands that *4* represents four because

Figure 3–2

she put a ring around the number 4 in the sequence. Clearly, Musukula and the other children who wrote the number 4 are ready for some challenge. They do not need the same level of instruction as the rest of the class.

Phuc Lam's Response

Phuc Lam wrote seven letters in response to the verbal directions *show four*. The letters in Figure 3–3 include the first and last letters of his name and a few other letters. Phuc Lam is just learning how to communicate through writing. He is learning how to write his name. It makes sense that when given writing paper and a pencil, Phuc Lam decided to write some of the letters in his name. The teacher assumed Phuc Lam did not understand how to represent four. However, an interesting thing happened when Ms. Vogel asked Phuc Lam about his response. Phuc Lam explained, "Phuc Lam is four." This response indicates that Phuc Lam identifies with the number four because he knows he is four years old. What appeared as random letters in response to the *show four* directions is actually not random at all. Phuc Lam represented four by attempting to write his name because he is four years old. Phuc Lam has some understanding of the number four because the number has meaning to him! The next step is for Phuc Lam to learn how to represent four with objects. Ms. Vogel grouped Phuc Lam with the other children who gave responses that indicate that they should work on representing small numbers with objects.

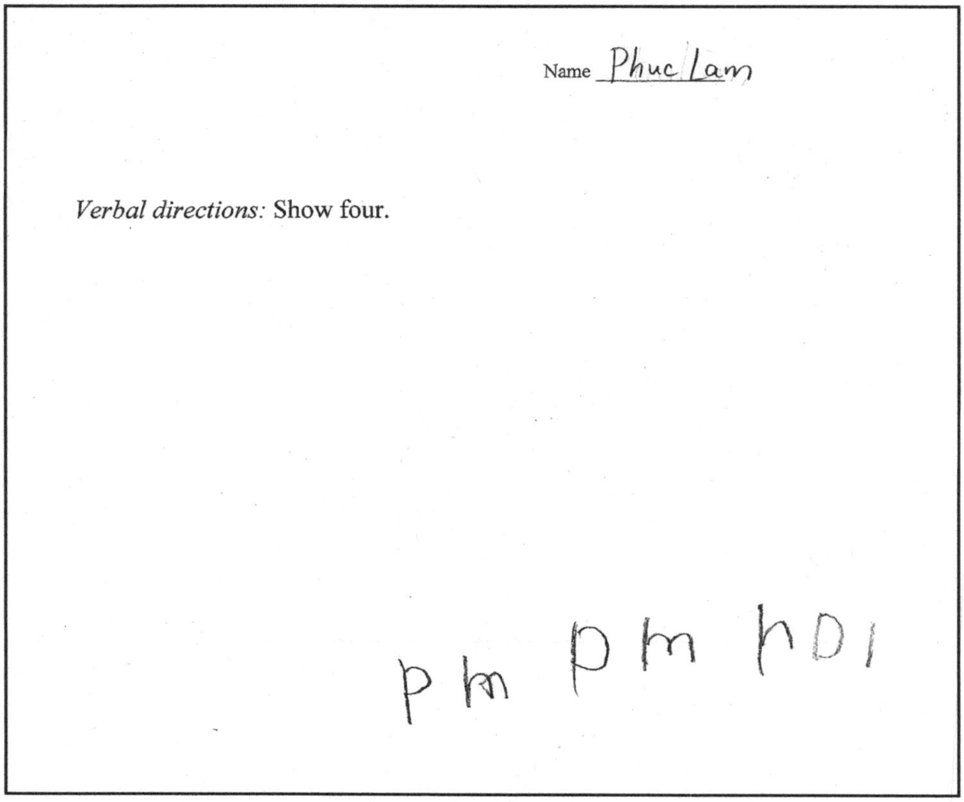
Name Phuc Lam

Verbal directions: Show four.

Figure 3–3

Using a simple index question allowed Ms. Vogel to form groups based on student needs. The preassessment took the students about five minutes to complete (including the time it took to distribute supplies and find work places). Ms. Vogel was able to do a quick sort of the indexes and form her purposeful groups for the day's instruction. Now Ms. Vogel can focus her attention on targeting instruction to meet the students' academic needs.

Small Group, Targeted Instruction

See:
Algebra, p. 25
Data, p. 37
Geometry, p. 37
Measurement, p. 34

There were three distinct levels revealed in the responses given on the preassessment Ms. Vogel gave to her prekindergarteners. Ms. Vogel plans to meet with each group to target instruction while the rest of the class works with center activities. The small group instruction will be distinguished as first group, second group, and third group. The categories in no way imply degree of importance or stagnant order. The ordinal numbering of the groups is simply a coherent way to present the teacher's targeted instruction.

The First Group Works with Representing Numbers

The middle group (including Luis) appears to have some general understanding of how to represent quantities, but they need to work on connecting the representations to specific numbers and keeping track. Ms. Vogel has this group focus on using objects to represent numbers. To help the students *keep track*, Ms. Vogel introduces five frames (one row of the ten frame) to the students to use as they represent numbers. The students explore with bingo chips. They sort and stack the chips. After a couple of minutes of explore time, Ms. Vogel asks the students to examine the five frames. The children look at their five frames and talk about what they see. Ms. Vogel asks, "How many chips do you think we will need if we put one chip in each rectangle?" The children are not sure. "Let's try it," suggests one of the children. The children in the group count as they place one chip at a time to fill the five frame. A couple of the children watch other children and Ms. Vogel for clues about what to do. Ms. Vogel prompts a discussion about what the full five frame looks like and then poses this question: "What do you think it will look like if we show four?" The children think about this question. Several children take off all the chips and begin counting and placing chips one at a time. Luis takes off one chip leaving four on the frame. When everyone has four chips out, Ms. Vogel asks them to explain how they represented four. One child says, "I counted." Another child says, "Like this, one, two, three, four." Other children point to their chips. Luis says, "One is gone." John agrees with Luis as he points to the empty rectangle on the five frame. Ms. Vogel has the children show and discuss other numbers using chips on the five frame.

To continue the learning, Ms. Vogel teaches the children a *show and say game*. One child closes his eyes while his partner represents a number on the five frame. The child showing the number says "Ready," at which time the other child opens his eyes and says the number. The two children verify the quantity and then switch roles. This activity helps children learn more about representing numbers and subitizing. Ms. Vogel differentiates the game within the small group by giving Luis and John a ten frame and ten bingo chips to use to play the game. This provides Luis and John with an appropriate challenge without requiring Ms. Vogel to spend a lot of time explaining a completely different game.

The Second Group Works with Representing Numbers

The responses given by this group of students (including Musukula) indicate that they already understand how to represent numbers with number symbols. In essence, this group already knows how to communicate with number symbols, which is beyond the prekindergarten expectations. Because they deserve instruction aimed at their level, Ms. Vogel meets with this group to provide targeted instruction through forward-mapping.

Ms. Vogel introduces a set of double-six dominoes to the group. (A complete set of dominoes includes all possible combinations of two numbers, from zero [blank] up to the highest number of dots in the set. Each combination of dots occurs only once in a set. A standard double-six domino set consists of twenty-eight tiles.) The children explore with the new math manipulatives. They stack and arrange the dominoes. They discuss the dots on the dominoes. After a few minutes of explore time, Ms. Vogel asks the students to slide the dominoes to her. She holds up one domino and asks the students to describe it.

The children discuss the dots on the domino seen in Figure 3–4. The children conclude that one region has five dots and the other region has four dots, making a total of nine dots. Ms. Vogel asks, "Are there any other dominoes in the set that have a total of nine dots?" The children look through the dominoes. The process of looking encourages them to recognize various ways to represent numbers, see how numbers can be composed, and to subitize quantities. The children find one other domino that has a total of nine dots (three dots in one region and six dots in the other region). Ms. Vogel asks, "How many dominoes do you think have a total of *six* dots?" The children predict that there will be two dominoes that represent six, just as there are two dominoes that represent nine. Ms. Vogel encourages the children to look through the set to find out. The children find all four of the dominoes that represent six (0 + 6, 1 + 5, 2 + 4, 3 + 3) and discuss how the dots are arranged. Ms. Vogel encourages the students to predict and then search for other number representations. The children engage in math discourse as they work on the task. Ms. Vogel helps the students display their findings in a quite sophisticated line plot, shown in Figure 3–5.

The targeted instruction Ms. Vogel provided to this group is well beyond the typical prekindergarten level. Ms. Vogel forward-mapped the instruction to

Figure 3–4

The Domino Ms. Vogel Asked Her Class to Describe

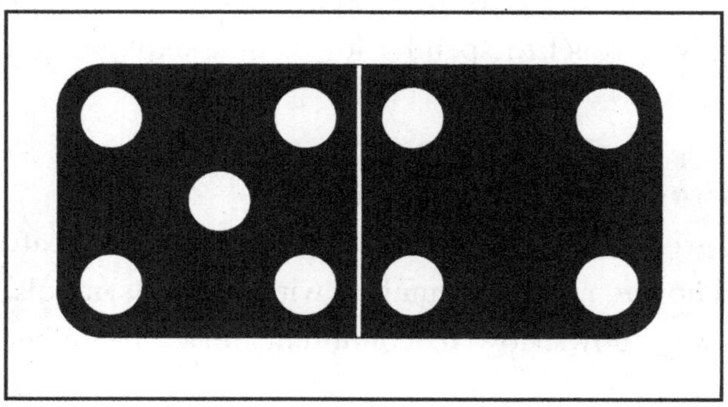

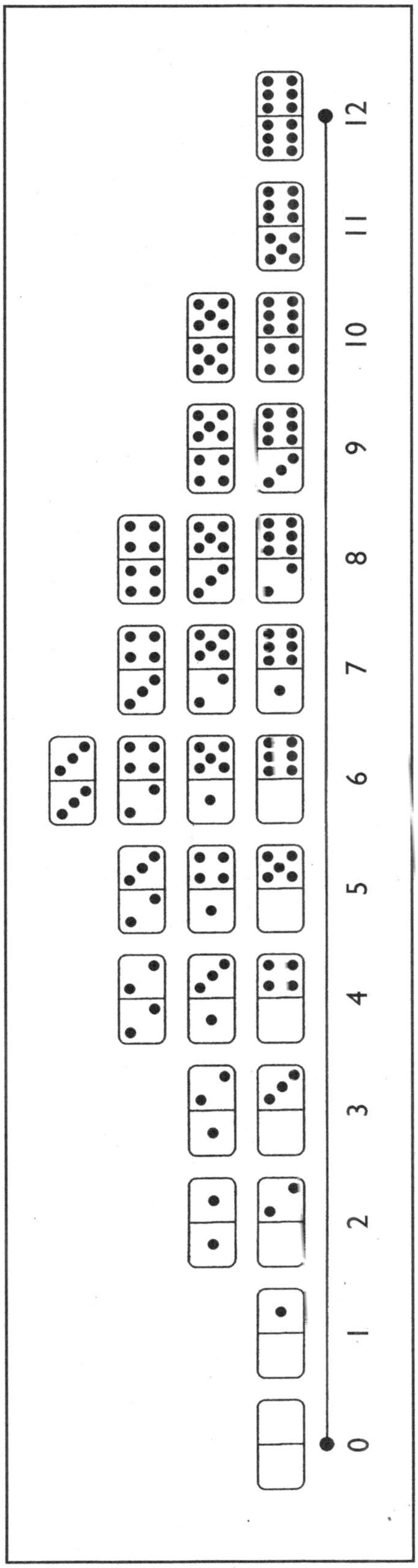

Figure 3–5

include appropriate challenges for this group of students. It is very exciting to see how much young children can accomplish when the instruction is targeted to meet their academic needs.

The Third Group Works with Representing Numbers

These students (including Phuc Lam) gave responses that indicate that they are not yet able to represent numbers with sketches of objects. Ms. Vogel uses back-mapping and scaffolding with this group. She knows that working with real objects will allow the children to be more successful. She focuses the instruction on one-to-one correspondence and rote counting to teach the children how to rational count up to four.

Each child is given a cup and a crayon. The children explore with the cup and crayon, placing the crayon in the cup and dumping the crayon out of the cup. After a few minutes of explore time, Ms. Vogel asks the group to tell how many cups and then how many crayons each person has. Ms. Vogel demonstrates and the children participate. Everyone places a cup on the desk and says, "One cup." Everyone places a crayon inside the cup and says, "One crayon." Everyone empties their cups and repeats the exercise.

After a few rounds, Ms. Vogel collects the cups and crayons and helps the children focus their attention to the center of the table where she places two cups and asks, "How many cups?" The children respond, "Two." Ms. Vogel asks, "What if I want to put one crayon in each cup. How many crayons will I need?" A couple of the children respond, "Two." Ms. Vogel asks one of the children to demonstrate counting by placing one crayon in each cup. The other children join the verbal counting. Ms. Vogel repeats the task with three cups and chooses a different child to demonstrate counting and placing the crayons in the cups. The other children join in the verbal counting.

At this point, Ms. Vogel explains to the children that they will work with partners (in dyads) to count cups and crayons. One child will place the cups out and the other child will put crayons in the cups. Each child will participate in the verbal counting. Ms. Vogel helps each dyad sit so that the children are facing each other with a space between them for the cups. Ms. Vogel says, "OK cup people. Are you ready?" The children say, "Yes." Ms. Vogel continues, "Show three cups." The children display three cups for their partners as they count each cup. Ms. Vogel says, "OK crayon people. Are you ready?" The children reply, "Yes." Ms. Vogel continues, "Show three crayons by placing one crayon in each cup." The children place one crayon in each cup as they count. Ms. Vogel asks the children to switch roles and try the number four. At this point most of the dyads are able to accomplish the task on their own. Ms. Vogel helps those who need assistance. The children repeat the activity with other numbers. Ms. Vogel walks around helping those who need assistance and giving more cups and crayons to the dyads that are ready to try slightly larger numbers. The back-mapping and scaffolding allowed the children to be successful. After the small group session, the crayons and cups became a center activity for children to use independently.

In this targeted mathematics lesson, Ms. Vogel differentiates the instruction for each group. This is not *the* way to differentiate instruction, but it is *a* way to differentiate instruction. There is not a single correct path, but rather many options when differentiating instruction. The path Ms. Vogel chose was very successful because the instruction was targeted to meet the academic needs of the children. Everyone learned more about how to represent numbers.

Spotlight on Composing and Decomposing Numbers in a Kindergarten Classroom

Build up numbers and break apart numbers

Ms. Morris teaches kindergarten. She has twenty-five students in her class. Many of her students are ELLs (English Language Learners). All of her students have diverse needs and various levels of mathematics understanding. Ms. Morris is beginning a unit on composing and decomposing numbers. She uses a simple preassessment to gather information about what her students know about composing and decomposing numbers using the ten frame.

See:
Algebra, p. 26
Data, p. 40
Geometry, p. 41
Measurement, p. 38

Explanation of the Composing and Decomposing Numbers Index Question

The index question Ms. Morris uses is a picture of a ten frame that contains nine circles (see Figure 3–6). The students are familiar with the ten frame because Ms. Morris uses the ten frame for instructional purposes and the ten frame is used by the students during center time. The students are asked to tell how many circles are in the ten frame and then explain how they know. The how-do-you-know question is aimed at revealing how the number nine can be composed and decomposed. The question allows the children to use their knowledge of the parts that make the total of nine.

Student Responses

See:
Algebra, p. 26
Data, p. 41
Geometry, p. 41
Measurement, p. 41

Makayla's Response

Makayla accurately indicates that there are nine circles on the ten frame, as shown in Figure 3–7. She is able to write the number symbol for nine. To

Name ______________________

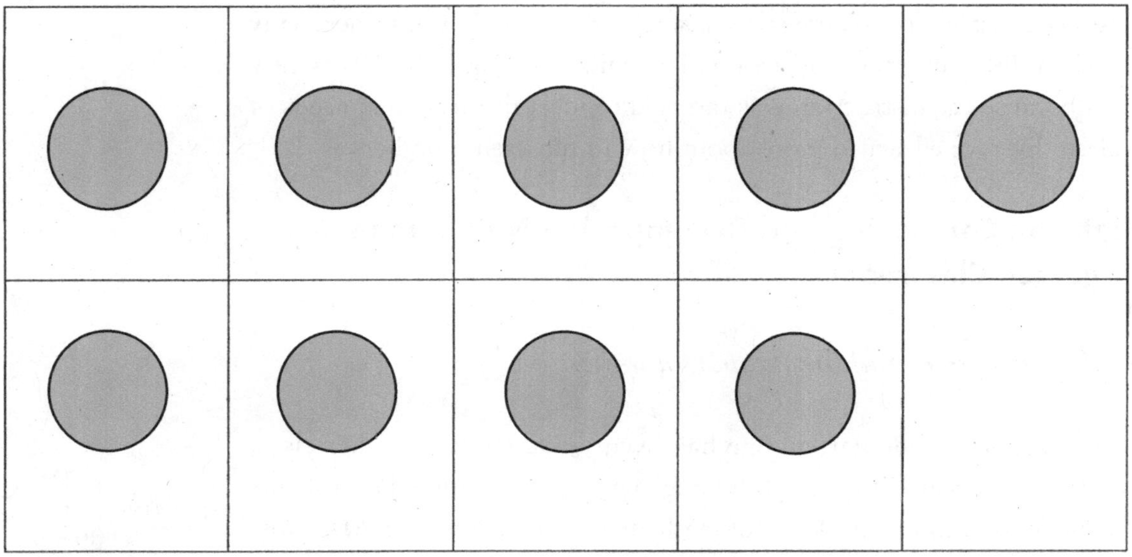

How many circles do you see?

How do you know?

Figure 3–6

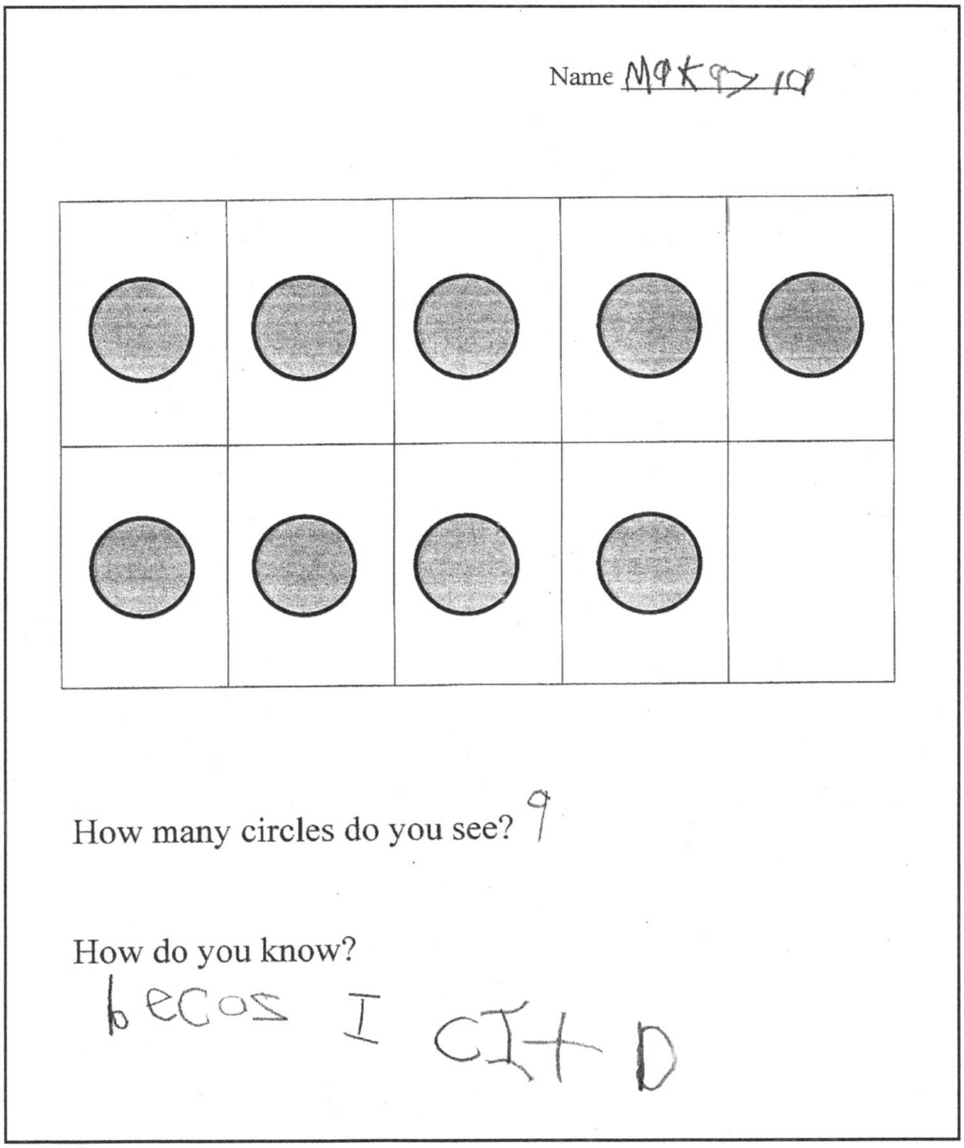

Figure 3–7

answer the how-do-you-know question, Makayla writes *because I counted*. This indicates that Makayla knows how to rational count at least up to nine. While her explanation is sound, it does not include any indication that she used any composing or decomposing strategies. Evidently the ten frame did not prompt Makayla to think about the parts of nine, nor did the ten frame prompt her to use subitizing. She simply (albeit accurately) counted each circle and reported doing so.

It is exciting that Makayla and the other students who gave similar *I counted it* responses can accurately count the nine circles. Ms. Morris formed a group of these ten students and focused on teaching them how to compose and decompose numbers. She also included some subitizing experiences as she targeted instruction for this group of students.

Ramzi's Response

Ramzi's response in Figure 3–8 indicates that he is comfortable composing and decomposing the number nine. Ramzi shares with the teacher that *I know there are five in the first row and one is missing in the next row.* While Ramzi only writes the first part of his answer, the teacher knows that he is using his knowledge of the ten frame and his knowledge of the number nine. His answer indicates that he may be subitizing the quantities in each row and combining this with knowing that nine is made of five and four. Ramzi already knows the on-grade-level concepts associated with composing and decomposing numbers. Ms. Morris understands that Ramzi and the other students who gave similar responses will need a challenge. They will work with other ways to compose and decompose numbers and more complex tasks. Ms. Morris does not want to waste the time of these students by making them sit through a whole group lesson on a topic that they already understand.

Maricamen's Response

Maricamen responded in Figure 3–9 that there are ten circles. She writes *that is what I know.* Maricamen has made great progress using index questions. She started the year not being able to write numbers, let alone any type of explanation associated with her answer. While these skills are not directly related to composing and decomposing numbers, they are important foundational steps in learning how to communicate math thinking. Maricamen and the other students who gave incorrect responses will work in a small group with Ms. Morris. She will scaffold the math with these students by going back to rational counting and smaller quantities.

Ms. Morris' use of the index question allowed her to reveal the different levels of understanding of her students. Using a simple index question allowed Ms. Morris to form groups based on student needs. The preassessment took the students only a few minutes to complete. It took Ms. Morris a couple of minutes to do a quick sort of the indexes and form her purposeful groups for the day's instruction. Now Ms. Morris can focus her attention on targeting instruction aimed at meeting the students' academic needs.

See:
Algebra, p. 31
Data, p. 44
Geometry, p. 46
Measurement, p. 42

Small Group, Targeted Instruction

There were three separate levels revealed in the responses given on the preassessment Ms. Morris gave her kindergarteners. Ms. Morris plans to work

How many circles do you see? 9

How do you know?

I NO ThеRƷ PA The FORST ROW

Figure 3–8

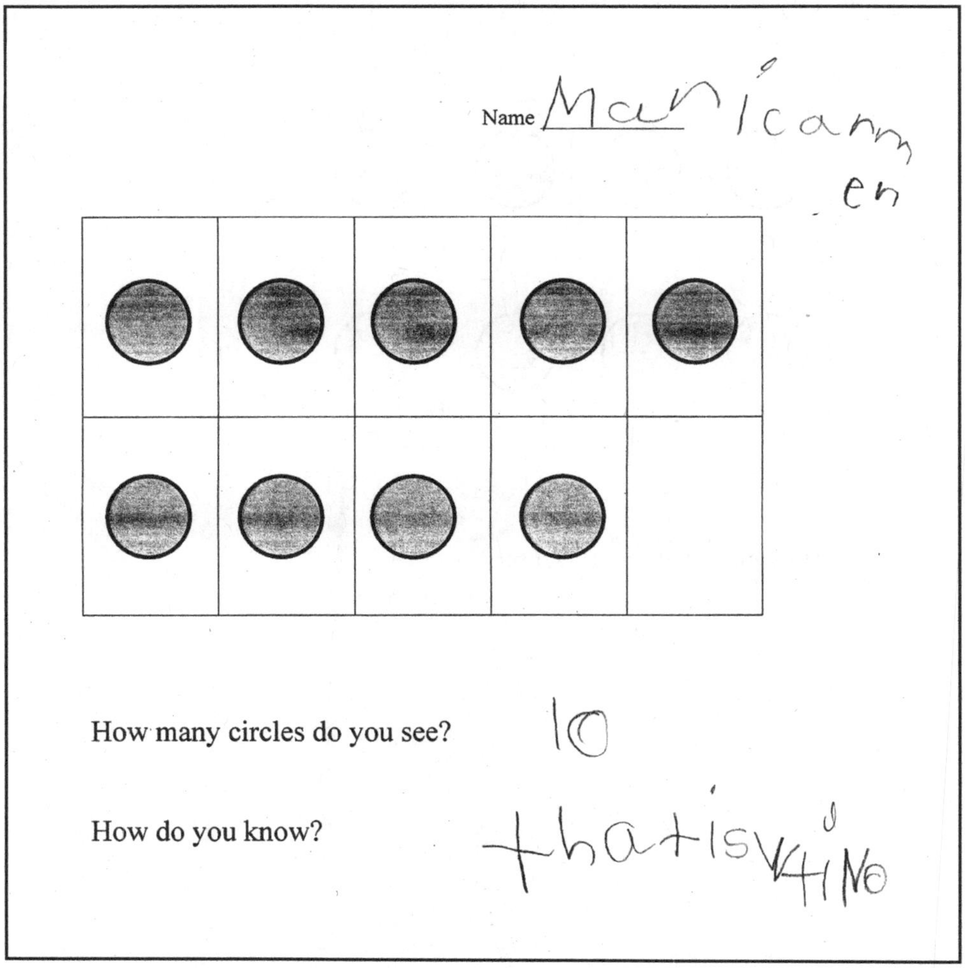

Figure 3–9

with each group to target the instruction. One group will work with Ms. Morris, one group will work with center activities, and one group will work at their desks writing and drawing in their math journals. Ms. Morris will let the students know when it is time to switch groups (about every ten or fifteen minutes).

The First Group Works with Composing and Decomposing Numbers

The middle group (including Makayla) appears to have a solid understanding of rational counting through at least nine, but does not yet understand how to explain composing and decomposing strategies. Ms. Morris uses activating prior knowledge and scaffolding to teach the group of children about composing and decomposing numbers. The students explore with linking cubes for about one minute. Ms. Morris then asks the children to each make a tower of five using all the same colored cubes (so that they can focus on the two parts of the tower rather than parts within parts of the tower). The children compare their towers to confirm that everyone has a tower of five. Ms. Morris uses her tower to prompt the students to think about how five can be decomposed. Ms. Morris says, "I have a tower of five. I put it behind my back and break it into two parts. I will show you one part. Your job is to figure out how many cubes are in the part that is still behind my back."

Ms. Morris breaks the tower behind her back and shows the children part of the tower (this part has three cubes). As evidenced by their quick responses most of the children subitize the quantity. To figure out the missing part, some of the children use their own towers to think about the parts of five. Other children seem to be visualizing the missing part of the tower. The children decide the part that is behind Ms. Morris' back has two cubes in it. Ms. Morris affirms the answer by showing them. Ms. Morris asks, "How did you figure it out?" One student shares, "I knew it wasn't one because that would only be a four tower." Another student says, "I know three and two make five." Another student adds, "Five is made of three and two."

Ms. Morris invites partners to take turns trying the activity. She monitors their progress and decides after only a couple of rounds that they are ready to try other numbers. Ms. Morris invites the children to try the same task with a tower of nine. The students actively engage in the activity. The group then discusses all the different ways to break apart (decompose) a tower of nine.

The Second Group Works with Composing and Decomposing Numbers

These students (including Ramzi) gave responses that indicate that they already know how the number nine is composed and decomposed. Because they understand at a level beyond the rest of the class, they are ready for a challenge. Ms. Morris has options for how to challenge these students. She can target instruction by increasing the size of the numbers the students work with. But Ms. Morris opts for compacting some information and forward-mapping to a more complex idea within the range of zero to ten. She uses a similar activity that she used with the previous group—but this time the towers are composed of three parts.

After the children explore with the linking cubes for a minute, Ms. Morris has them each make a tower of ten cubes using any cube colors. She hides her tower of ten under the table and breaks off one part of the tower, displaying it (three cubes) on the table. Then she breaks off another part of the tower and displays it (two cubes) on the table. She asks the children to figure out how many cubes are in the part that is still in her hand under the table. The students are intrigued. They have not yet worked with decomposing numbers into more than two parts. The task is further complicated by the fact that the different colors do not represent the parts, but instead the colors are parts within the parts. Ms. Morris skipped the step of making each part represented by a specific color because she wanted to make the activity more challenging for the students.

The students are able to solve and explain that the part of ten that is under the table is five. As she did with the previous group, Ms. Morris has the children work with partners to take turns breaking the towers into parts and using the known parts to figure out the unknown part. Ms. Morris has the students discuss and record the various ways ten can be decomposed into three *or more* parts.

The Third Group Works with Composing and Decomposing Numbers

This group of students (including Maricamen) gave responses that indicate that they need additional support with rational counting to build the foundations for composing and decomposing small numbers. Ms. Morris targets the instruction for this group of students by using some of the same techniques she used with the previous groups, but she incorporates specific back-mapping and more scaffolding. After a couple of minutes of explore time, Ms. Morris asks each student to make a tower of five using two green cubes and three blue cubes. The students each make a tower and Ms. Morris encourages the students to talk about how five is composed of two and three. The different colors help the students better see the parts that comprise the whole tower. Ms. Morris then asks, "Is there another way to make a tower of five?" The students respond to the question by linking cubes together. One student shares, "I can make five with four red and one yellow. See? One, two, three, four, and one. That's five." Another student says, "I can make five with three orange and two brown cubes." Another student says, "I can make five with one purple and four pink cubes." All of the students successfully count and show how five can be composed. The children compare their towers of five. Ms. Morris asks the students to look at all the towers of five and discuss how they are alike and different. She also introduces the idea of five being composed of five and zero. After the exchange of mathematics ideas, Ms. Morris invites the children to try the same activity using a different number. They make towers of seven and then make towers of nine. Ms. Morris helps the students use rational counting as they explore ways to compose numbers.

In this targeted mathematics lesson, Ms. Morris successfully challenges and supports each of the groups through differentiated instruction. Ms. Morris had many options for how to target the instruction. She chose to tier the lesson, use back-mapping, use forward-mapping, scaffold, compact, and activate prior knowledge. All of the students gained further knowledge of how to compose and decompose numbers.

Spotlight on Computational Fluency in a First-Grade Classroom

Strategies for computing

Mr. Samuel has a class of twenty-three first graders. The students range in ability and mathematics expertise. The students have learned about addition and are currently working on increasing computational fluency. The next mathematics topic Mr. Samuel's class will be learning about is addition with more than two addends. Before beginning instruction, Mr. Samuel developed a preassessment aimed at revealing the different levels of knowledge of the students.

See:
Algebra, p. 32
Data, p. 49
Geometry, p. 52
Measurement, p. 48

Explanation of the Computational Fluency Index Question

Mr. Samuel wants to give a preassessment to the students to find out what they know about adding several addends. He intentionally uses an equation (shown in Figure 3–10) that includes four related addends because he wants to see the computational fluency strategies his students use. Using an equation that includes doubles (2 + 2 and 5 + 5) opens the door for students to use facts that they already know to solve the equation.

Student Responses

Jessica's Response

In Figure 3–11, Jessica incorrectly solves the equation by writing 10 as the sum. However, Jessica shows some understanding of the need to include 2 + 2 because she writes 4 under that part of the equation. Jessica's explanation is *I really know how to do this. I know 5 + 5 = 10 because I have been learning how to do that.* Her explanation is adorable; she gives a literal response of how she knows the answer. While her answer does not reveal a lot about her math thinking, the 5 + 5 = 10 part indicates that she is trying to use facts that she knows to solve new problems and increase her computational fluency. Mr. Samuel forms a group including Jessica and the other students who gave similar responses to target instruction.

See:
Algebra, p. 34
Data, p. 51
Geometry, p. 52
Measurement, p. 50

Nancy's Response

Nancy's response in Figure 3–12 is exciting. She accurately and efficiently solves the problem. She also gives an excellent depiction of how she solved the

Name ______________________________

Solve.

$$2 + 2 + 5 + 5 =$$

Explain your answer with words, pictures, and/or numbers.

Figure 3–10

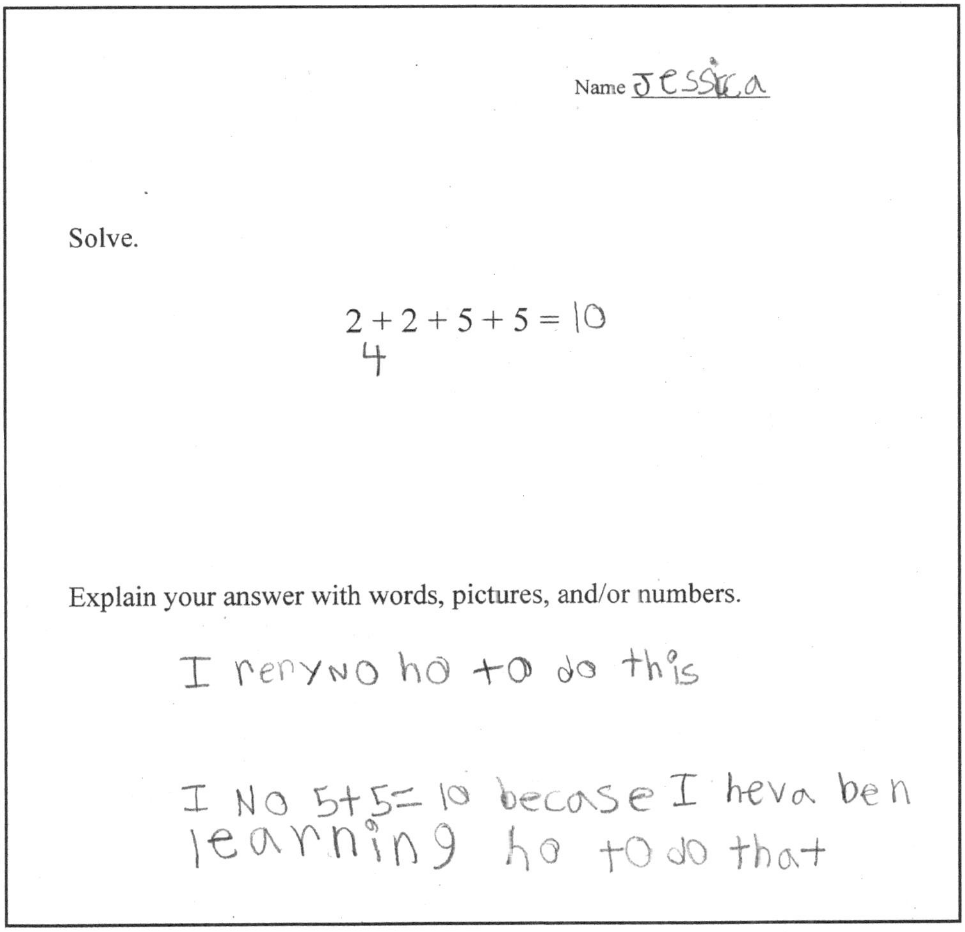
Name Jessica

Solve.

2 + 2 + 5 + 5 = 10
4

Explain your answer with words, pictures, and/or numbers.

I renyno ho to do this

I No 5+5=10 becase I heva ben learning ho to do that

Figure 3–11

equation. She grouped the doubles and added the partial sums. The picture of the five fingers plus five fingers gives additional information about what she did first to solve the problem. Although the second part is not illustrated, the equation she writes with the grouped addends clearly indicates she used an efficient strategy that allowed her to achieve computational fluency with this equation. Mr. Samuel understands that Nancy and the other students who gave similar responses will need a challenge. They will need to work with higher-level equations and more complex tasks. Mr. Samuel values his students' time and, consequently, wants to provide them with instruction that is aimed at their specific levels.

Kevin's Response

Kevin's response in Figure 3–13 is delightful. Although he inaccurately solves the equation, he does have some thinking attached to it. He solves part of the

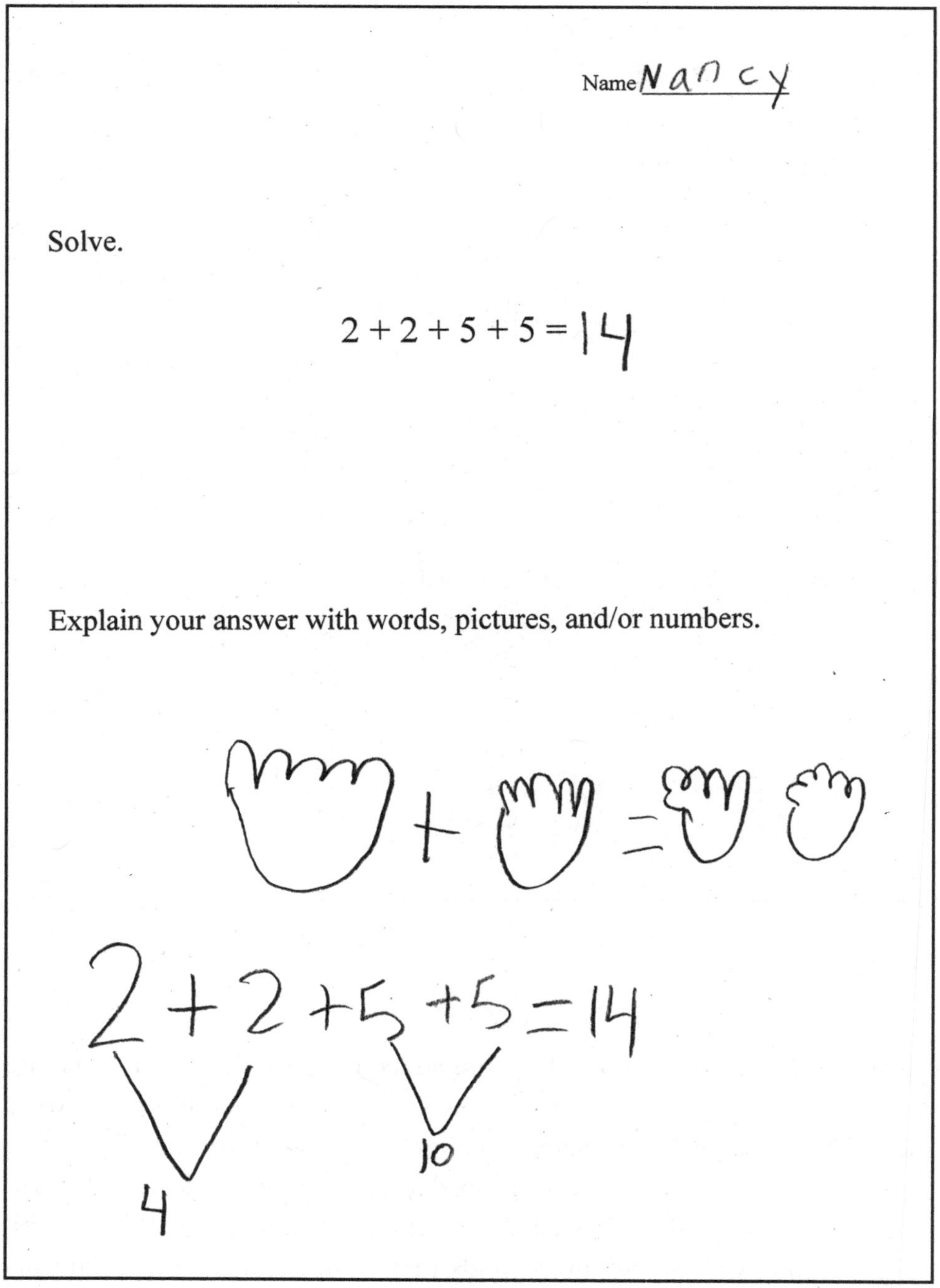

Figure 3–12

equation (2 + 5). To explain that he used his fingers to solve the equation, he cleverly traced his hand. Yet the picture only shows one hand with five fingers, so the explanation picture does not match his answer to the equation. Mr. Samuel knows that Kevin's level of understanding is not high. Kevin and the other students who gave similar responses needed some additional work with

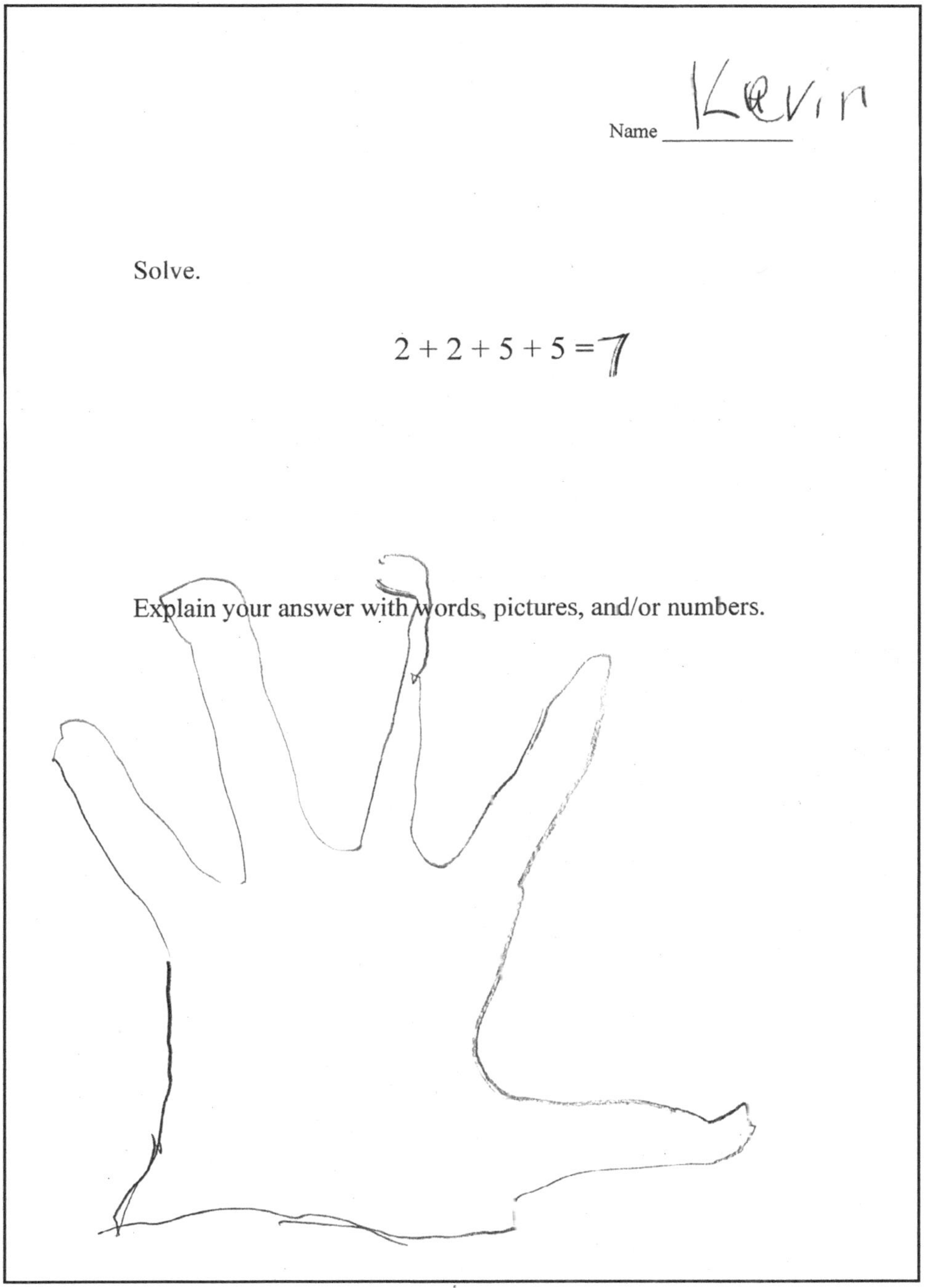

Figure 3–13

computational fluency and working with more than two addends. Mr. Samuel needs to provide some scaffolding to help this group gain a more solid foundation.

Mr. Samuel's use of the index question allowed him to reveal the levels of understanding of his students. The index question served as a preassessment

See:
Algebra, p. 37
Data, p. 54
Geometry, p. 56
Measurement, p. 53

for adding more than two numbers *and* as an ongoing assessment for computational fluency. It only took the students a few minutes to respond to the index question and just a few more minutes for Mr. Samuel to quickly sort the information, which helped him form his groups for targeted instruction.

Small Group, Targeted Instruction

There were three levels revealed in the responses given on the preassessment Mr. Samuel gave to his first graders. Mr. Samuel uses tiering as he provides adjusted equations for each of the groups. While Mr. Samuel meets with each group to target instruction, the rest of the class works on the tasks in their math folders. These tasks include designing a board game that involves addition and finishing any uncompleted work from the previous day.

The First Group Works with Computational Fluency

This group of students (including Jessica) appears to have some strategies for computational fluency, but these strategies are incomplete and lack meaning. With this group, Mr. Samuel focuses on activating prior knowledge, scaffolding, and compacting. The goal is to teach the students to use strategies such as *find the doubles* when working with several addends. The students have some knowledge of how to do this, so parts of the instruction can be compacted. Yet the students need help understanding when to use the strategies and why these strategies work. Thus Mr. Samuel plans to help the students connect to this prior knowledge and scaffold to greater levels of understanding.

Mr. Samuel presents an equation similar to the one used in the preassessment. He writes $4 + 5 + 5 + 4 = ?$ on the dry-erase board and asks, "What would you do first and why?" Mr. Samuel invites the children to *think, pair, share, and show*. The students think about the question, turn to the person beside them, discuss the question with that person, and use manipulatives (in this case, colored chain links) to show what they talked about. The students then share with the rest of the group. One student holds up two chains of five blue links and says, "We would put the fives together first." Another student shows one chain of ten red links and says, "We made ten, too." One student says, "I saw 4 + 5 and 5 + 4 as 9 + 9," showing the corresponding chain links. Another student says, "I put the fours together first, but my partner put the fives together first. Does it matter?"

Mr. Samuel is thrilled with the question. He poses the question back to the group saying, "What do you think? Does it matter what you do first?"

After some thought, one student responds, "I don't think it matters." Another student adds, "But you have to make sure you have it all." Mr. Samuel asks, "What do you mean by *have it all*?" The student responds, "Everything must be in it. You can't forget something." Mr. Samuel asks, "Why?" The student replies, "Because it will be wrong if you forget something!"

Mr. Samuel smiles and responds, "Yes. All of the addends are part of the equation." He then asks, "So if the order does not matter, what is the point of changing the order?" The students think about Mr. Samuel's question. One student replies, "Because changing the order makes it faster." Another student says, "Yes. You can solve it quickly." Another student says, "It also makes it easier." "And you have a better chance to get it right," adds another student.

Through the math discourse facilitated by Mr. Samuel, the students have uncovered the components of accuracy and efficiency associated with computational fluency. They have also given purpose to the strategies. They are not simply following procedures in isolation. Instead they are giving meaning to procedures and strategies, which increases their computational fluency. They have also learned another way to explain their thinking by using relevant representations such as the chain links.

The Second Group Works with Computational Fluency

Mr. Samuel focuses his attention on the next group. The students in this group (including Nancy) need a challenge. The students already know what Mr. Samuel's curriculum guide indicates that he should teach. Therefore Mr. Samuel needs to *bump up* the content for these particular students. One simple yet effective way for Mr. Samuel to increase the content level is to use more and larger addends. Mr. Samuel chooses to do both. He asks the students to work with partners to solve $12 + 10 + 25 + 7 + 8 + 5 = ?$ Additionally, Mr. Samuel instructs the students to depict how they solved the equation using their dry-erase boards. He invites the students to try more than one way to solve the equation. Mr. Samuel is forward-mapping to a higher level of content for these students. The students increase their accuracy and efficiency with computational fluency strategies by working together to solve a complex problem and by sharing depictions of how they solved the equation. Mr. Samuel has the students share their depictions with the rest of the group (see Figure 3–14). The rest of the group interprets the depictions. The sharing group verifies the interpretation and explains why the strategy is effective. The students describe how to use compatible numbers in the various combinations as powerful strategies of computational fluency.

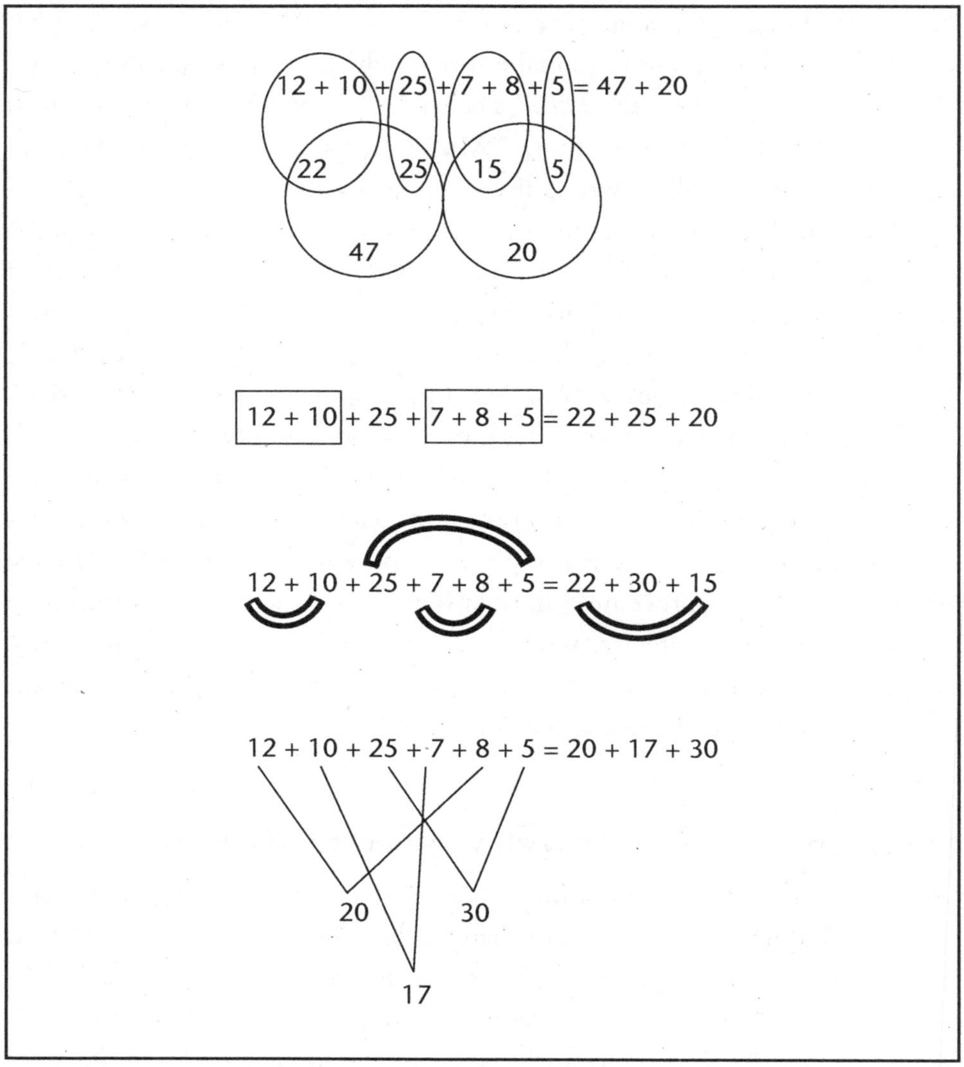

Figure 3–14

The Third Group Works with Computational Fluency

Mr. Samuel works with the third group (including Kevin) as well. He will use back-mapping to smaller numbers and scaffolding to teach the students how to add three addends and how to give explanations that represent the thinking. The children in the group explore with number cubes. These number cubes were created by Mr. Samuel. They look like dice, but they do not show the quantities from one to six as standard dice do. Instead each number cube has these numbers: 5, 5, 2, 2, 3, 3. Mr. Samuel uses these number cubes to provide more opportunities for the students to make five and work with the doubles.

After a minute of explore time, Mr. Samuel explains the activity by demonstrating one round. He tosses three number cubes. The numbers 5, 2, and 3 are displayed. Mr. Samuel asks the group to explain how they would add the displayed numbers. One student says, "I would say *five* and count, six, seven." Mr. Samuel asks, "What can you do to include the three?" A different student says, "You could say, *seven* and count, eight, nine, ten" as he shows the counting on his fingers. Mr. Samuel says, "Great. Is there another way?" One student asks, "Can you put the 2 and 3 together?" "Yes. Tell us how you would do that," replies Mr. Samuel. The student explains, "Two and three make five, so it is like five plus five."

Mr. Samuel then demonstrates to the students the second part of the activity. When the number cubes are rolled, popsicle sticks are placed by each number. Two of the sets of popsicle sticks are then grouped into a combined set and the other set is added on. One of the students asks, "Are the popsicle sticks like our fingers?" Mr. Samuel responds, "Tell us what you are thinking." The child explains, "Putting five popsicle sticks together is like all the fingers on one hand." Another student adds, "I get it. You count them like you count your fingers."

Mr. Samuel groups the students into dyads (groups of two) and encourages them to begin the activity. One person rolls the number cubes and the other person shows the popsicle sticks. Together they make the grouping decisions and find the sum. Afterward, the students switch roles and begin again. As the students engage in the activity, Mr. Samuel encourages the students to talk about the strategies as they explain their thinking.

In this targeted mathematics lesson, Mr. Samuel successfully challenged and supported each of the groups through targeted instruction. Mr. Samuel had options for how to differentiate the instruction and chose to tier the lesson, use back-mapping, use forward-mapping, scaffold, compact, and activate prior knowledge. All of the students increased their levels of computational fluency.

Spotlight on Operation in a Second-Grade Classroom

Addition and subtraction

Ms. Burger currently teachers twenty-five second graders. The school has a high mobility rate. About one-third of the students will leave and the same amount of new students will join the class by the end of the year. Teaching in a high mobility school is difficult, but differentiated instruction helps all students make progress during the time they are in the class.

See:
Algebra, p. 40
Data, p. 57
Geometry, p. 59
Measurement, p. 56

Explanation of the Operations Index Question

Ms. Burger is working on addition and subtraction with her students. She wants to find out the level of understanding her students currently have. The index question is aimed at revealing the students' understanding of addition and subtraction with regrouping. Ms. Burger gives an index question with two equations that are inaccurately solved (see Figure 3–15). The students are to indicate whether the equations are solved correctly or not and explain why. Using incorrect examples can be very motivating for students. It encourages them to evaluate someone else's answer. The explanations associated with the evaluation open the door for students to explain what they know about the mathematics.

Student Responses

Lily's Response

See:
Algebra, p. 41
Data, p. 58
Geometry, p. 60
Measurement, p. 57

Lily's response (see Figure 3–16) is interesting. She writes, *I think that it is wrong because 9 plus 3 is 12.* She shows the regrouped ten in the equation, but then incorrectly adds it to the ones, indicating that the answer should be 73. Lily writes, *It is right because 93 – 46 is 53* for the subtraction problem. In these responses, Lily shows that she knows something about addition and subtraction with regrouping, but she needs more instruction with these types of problems. Ms. Burger grouped Lily with ten other students who had similar errors, but showed some sparks of understanding. These students worked on the on-grade-level objectives for addition and subtraction of two-place numbers.

Taylor's Response

Taylor accurately solves the two equations in Figure 3–17. For the addition problem she explains *the person put the number wrong*, meaning the sum should be 82 instead of 72. In the subtraction equation, Taylor draws a place value mat and base-ten blocks to represent the computation. She regroups one of the tens, showing 93 as 8 tens and 13 ones. Then she subtracts 46 by crossing off 6 ones and 4 tens. Taylor writes *He didn't regroup* to explain why the answer is not correct. Obviously Taylor understands how to add and subtract with two-place numbers. She can find errors and explain the process. Her picture gives meaning to the operation. Taylor, and the seven other students who gave similar responses, will need instruction at a higher level than the rest of the class. They need to be challenged.

Yuliana's Response

Yuliana's response in Figure 3–18 (p. 82) indicates that she needs more instruction on addition and subtraction with regrouping. She checks the answers

Name ________________________________

Do you think these answers are correct?

Explain why or why not.

$$\begin{array}{r} 53 \\ +\ 29 \\ \hline 72 \end{array}$$

$$\begin{array}{r} 93 \\ -\ 46 \\ \hline 53 \end{array}$$

Figure 3–15

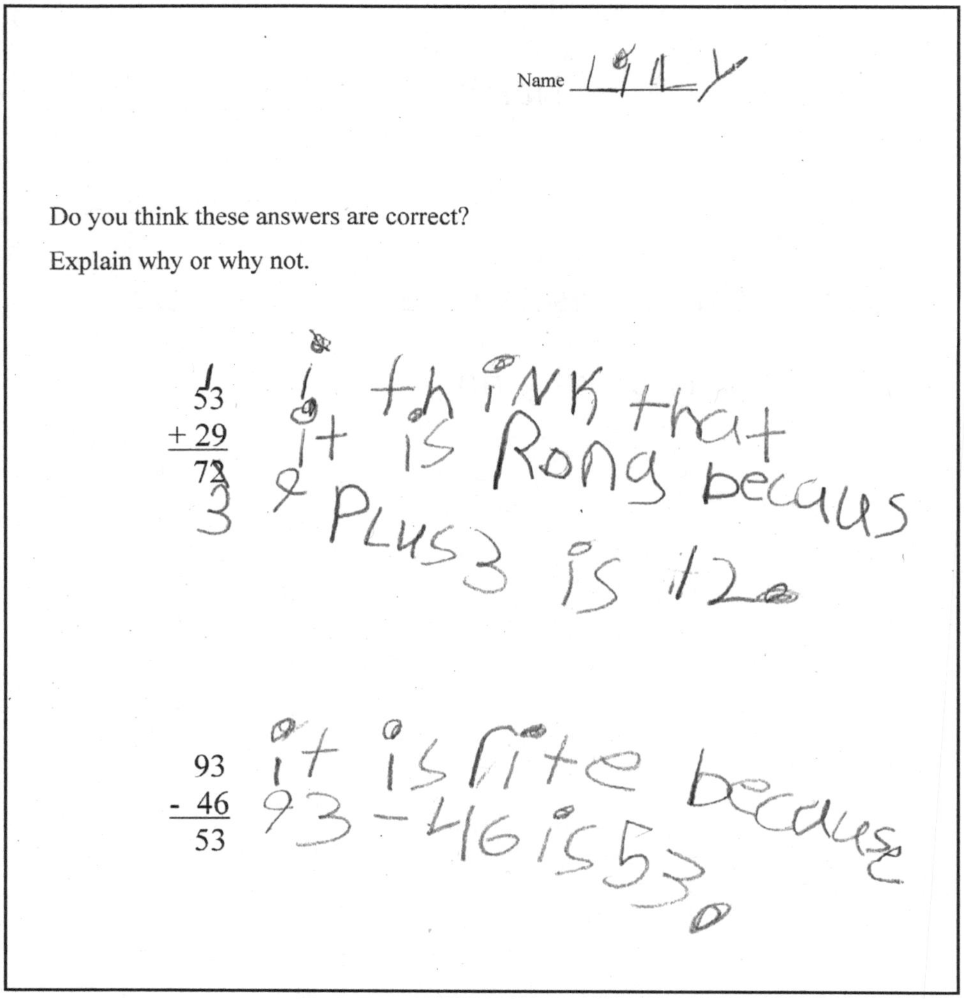

Name LiLY

Do you think these answers are correct?

Explain why or why not.

  1
  53
+ 29
  72

i think that it is Rong becaus 9 PLUS 3 is 12.

  93
- 46
  53

it is rite because 93-46 is 53.

Figure 3–16

and writes, *Those are correct.* Ms. Burger knows that Yuliana needs to work with more basic addition and subtraction to build her experiences with and knowledge of computation. Ms. Burger groups Yuliana with the seven other students who agreed that the answers given in this preassessment were correct. Ms. Burger will employ some back-mapping and scaffolding as she targets instruction for this group of students.

The index question Ms. Burger used provided her with valuable information. Based on the evidence, Ms. Burger adjusted the level of cognitive demand and targeted instruction for three groups of students. She knew that the students working at a high level needed challenge and the students who did not yet understand this concept needed additional support and scaffolding. Ms. Burger met with each group and was able to gear her teaching strategies to meet each group's specific needs.

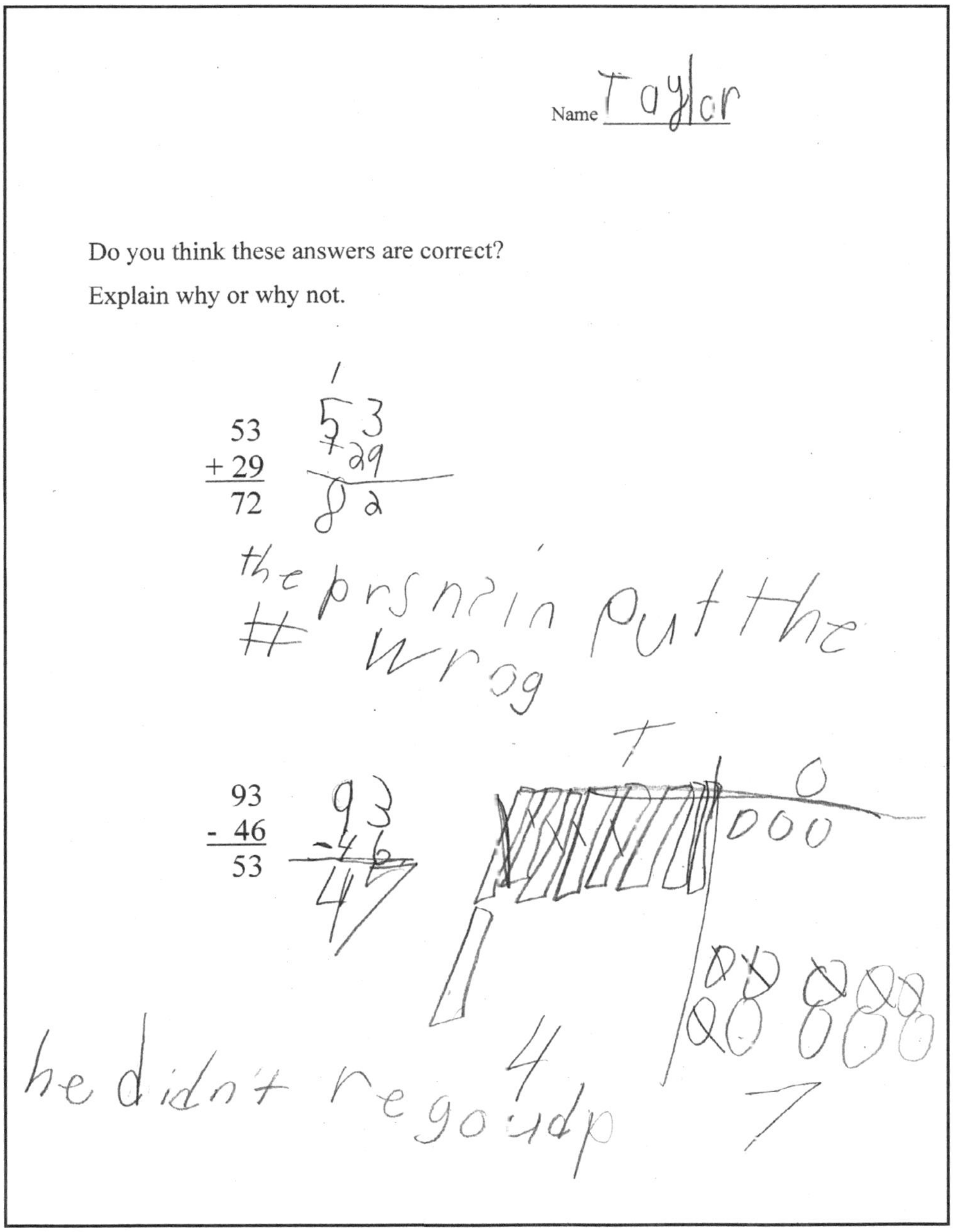

Name Taylor

Do you think these answers are correct?

Explain why or why not.

53
+ 29
72

the prsn?in put the # wrog

93
- 46
53

he didn't regoudp

Figure 3–17

Small Group, Targeted Instruction

There were three levels revealed in the responses given on the preassessment Ms. Burger gave to her second graders. Ms. Burger uses tiering to provide different levels of instruction for the groups. While Ms. Burger meets with each group to target instruction, the rest of the class works on an anchor activity. Anchor activities are ongoing tasks that students work on independently.

See:
Algebra, p. 46
Data, p. 62
Geometry, p. 62
Measurement, p. 61

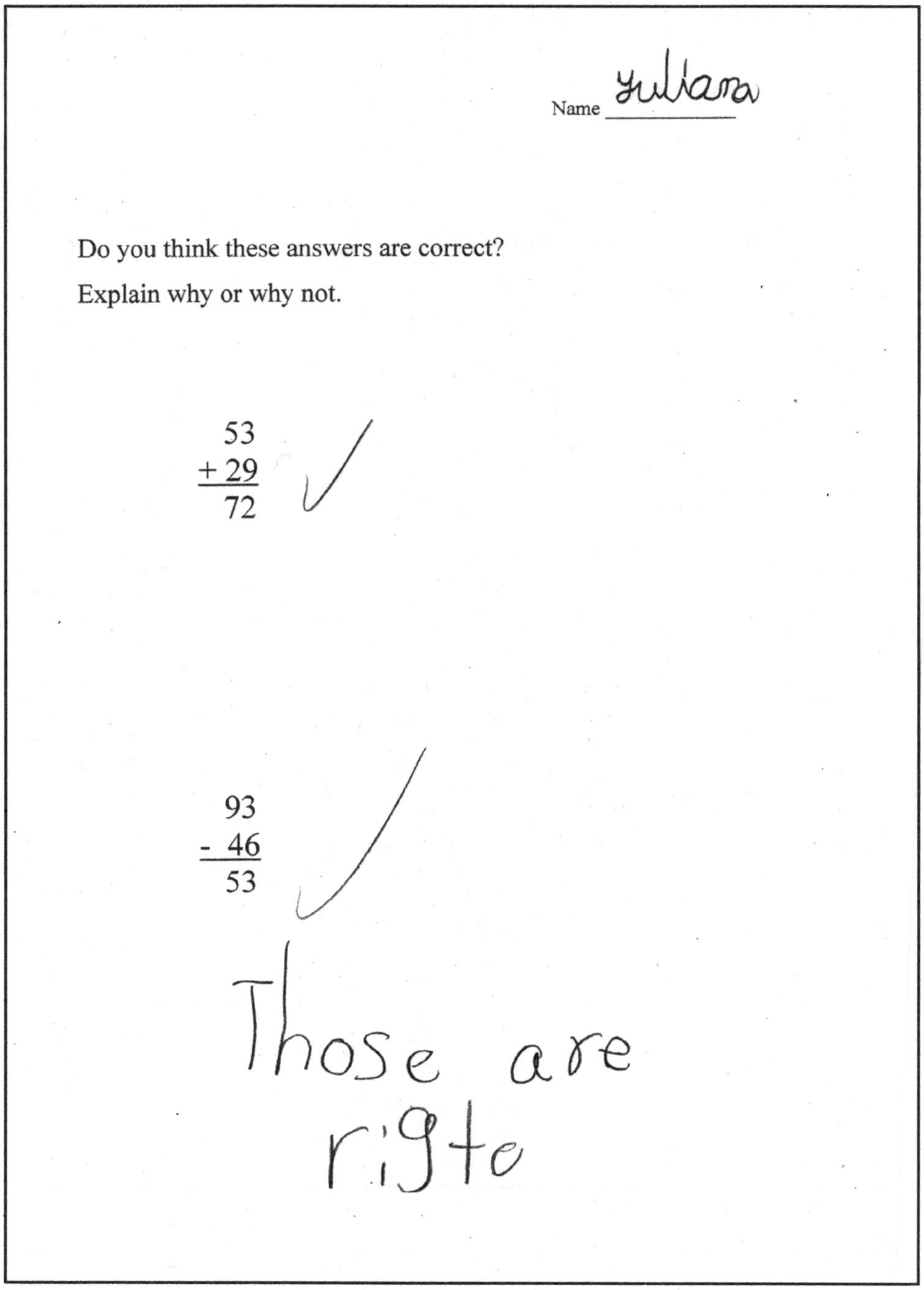

Name Juliana

Do you think these answers are correct?

Explain why or why not.

$$\begin{array}{r} 53 \\ +\,29 \\ \hline 72 \end{array}$$

$$\begin{array}{r} 93 \\ -\,46 \\ \hline 53 \end{array}$$

Those are rigto

Figure 3–18

The beauty of anchor activities is that they are designed to engage students in active learning without direct guidance from the teacher. While initially the teacher devotes some time to teaching students how to work on these tasks, anchor activities serve to productively engage students while the teacher targets instruction for small groups.

The particular anchor activity that Ms. Burger's class is currently working on is a math autobiography. For the last two weeks, the students have been writing (and drawing pictures) about personal life experiences with mathematics (see Figure 3–19).

The First Group Works with Operations

This group of students (including Lily) works with Ms. Burger on the on-grade-level objectives of addition and subtraction using two-digit numbers. Ms. Burger invites the students to explore with Digi-Blocks (Kohlberg and Dacey 1999). The students pack and unpack tens as they explore. Each digi ten-case holds exactly ten ones. The lid on the ten-case will not stay closed if there are not ten ones inside. The same holds true for the hundred-case and even the thousand-case. The lids only close properly when the cases contain the correct number of blocks.

After a couple of minutes of explore time, Ms. Burger asks each student to work with a partner to show 64 – 16. The exciting thing about using digi-blocks is that you do not have to *trade in* blocks. You simply open up a ten when more ones are needed. In this situation, one of the tens in the minuend (64) is opened to allow the subtrahend (16) to be more easily subtracted. You do not have to borrow anything! The students work on solving this and several other subtraction problems using the digi-blocks. Some of the subtraction problems involve regrouping and some of the subtraction problems do not involve regrouping.

Ms. Burger encourages the students to talk about the math in ways that combine procedural understanding with conceptual understanding. To do so she asks questions to invite the students to think about how and why. The students talk with their partners, asking questions like, "Do you think we will need to open up a ten for this problem?" Questions like this prove that the students are analyzing the math situations and giving meaning to procedures as they solve the problems.

The Second Group Works with Operations

This group of students (including Taylor) has a solid understanding of the hows and whys of addition and subtraction with regrouping. Ms. Burger knows that these students already understand a great deal about addition and subtraction. She can compact the information her curriculum guide indicates should be taught and forward-map into a more challenging task for the students. Ms. Burger decides to *bump up* the level by teaching this group of students how to add and subtract with three-digit numbers because they are ready to learn how to do so.

Math Autobiography

Write a Math Autobiography.
This will be the story of your life experiences with mathematics. The autobiography needs to include four sections. You may add illustrations.

Part 1: Early Math

Think about your early experiences with math. Did you like doing math when you were young? Did you play with math toys? Did you count and sort objects? Did you create patterns? Did your family share math ideas with you? How were your early math concepts shaped?

Part 2: First Math in School

Think about when you started school. What kind of math experiences did you have? Who shared math concepts with you? How did you learn some of the math you now use? Recall mathematics experiences in the classroom and outside of the classroom.

Part 3: Math Now

Think about your current experiences with math. What kind of math do you like? Why? Which activities give you challenge? Why? How do you use math in your everyday life? Where do you do math? When is math applicable?

Part 4: Math in the Future

Think about the kind of math you want to learn in the future. Where and when will you learn this math? How will you use math in the future? Which job do you plan to pursue and how will math help you in this job?

Figure 3–19

The students explore with digi-blocks and base-ten blocks (ones, tens, and hundreds) for a couple of minutes. Ms. Burger writes two equations on the chalkboard: *352 + 258 = ?* and *453 – 198 = ?* The students are asked to work with partners to solve the equations. They are invited to choose which manipulatives, if any, they would like to use to solve the two equations. As the four dyads of students work on the problems, Ms. Burger moves from dyad to dyad monitoring progress—directing, facilitating, and coaching as needed.

One dyad uses base-ten blocks to represent the addition problem. The students successfully trade in 10 ones for a ten rod, but face some difficulties when the 10 tens need to be traded in for a hundred flat. Ms. Burger directs the students through the difficulties by modeling a think aloud approach to problem solving. Afterward, the students are able to accurately solve the equation.

Two of the other dyads solve the problems using digi-blocks. They are able to successfully pack a ten block and a hundred block in the addition equation. With some coaching from Ms. Burger they are also able to unpack a ten block and a hundred block to help them solve the subtraction equation.

The students in the other dyad successfully use the traditional algorithm to solve the addition equation. Afterward, they show the process with the base-ten blocks to verify their answer. When working with the subtraction equation they actually use an alternative algorithm by adding 2 to the minuend and the subtrahend (453 – 198 = 455 – 200) to solve the equation. Afterward, they verify their answer using the traditional algorithm. Ms. Burger facilitates math discourse asking, "Why did you decide to add 2?" One of the students replies, "Because that makes the numbers easier to work with." The other student adds, "Yes. You can just subtract 200 in your head." Ms. Burger asks, "Why did you solve the problem again using a different way?" One student replies, "We wanted to check it." The other student adds, "Just to make sure." Ms. Burger asks, "What did you find out?" One of the students says, "That we were right." The other student says, "And we found a way to do it faster."

Ms. Burger has each of the dyads share with the rest of the group how they solved the equations. The students moved to higher-level content in this differentiated small group learning situation because the instruction was targeted to meet their academic needs.

The Third Group Works with Operations

Ms. Burger works with this group of students (including Yuliana) on building foundations for addition and subtraction with regrouping. Ms. Burger will use scaffolding and activating prior knowledge by going back (back-mapping) to decomposing numbers with this group of students. The students explore with digi-blocks and base-ten blocks. After a couple minutes of explore time, Ms. Burger asks the students to work with partners to show 54. She helps them connect to their earlier work with place value and representing numbers. All of the students show 54 with 5 tens and 4 ones. Ms. Burger scaffolds from this level of understanding to the next by asking the students to *open up* or *trade in* one of the tens in 54. Ms. Burger asks, "What number are you showing now?" Most of the students begin to count. One of them says, "It is still 54." Ms. Burger asks, "How do you know?" Another child responds, "But it doesn't look the same." Another student replies, "Yes. It looks different, but it is still 54." The others agree that 54 can be represented as 4 tens and 14 ones.

Ms. Burger writes *54 – 16 = ?* on the flipchart and asks, "How can you use what we just learned to solve this equation?" The students examine the problem. A few students look at their digi-blocks. One of the students answers, "It will be easier to subtract if we use 54 that is made of 4 tens and 14 ones." Ms. Burger asks, "Why?" Another child answers, "Because you can get all the ones." The other students agree. Ms. Burger offers the group two more subtraction problems to solve. She works with the students as they enthusiastically tackle the problems.

In this targeted mathematics lesson, Ms. Burger differentiates the instruction for each group of students. She activates prior knowledge, compacts, scaffolds, tiers, and uses back-mapping and forward-mapping. The lessons are designed to meet the needs of all of the students. The tasks are similar, yet they address different levels of understanding.

Using various strategies to target the instruction, the teachers in each of the classrooms differentiate the instruction for the students based on the evidence revealed in the index question responses. In many of the small group lessons, the students were grouped in dyads. This grouping within the small group is beneficial for several reasons. Working with a partner gives more opportunities for math discourse than working alone does. Working with smaller groups within the small group structure also gives more hands-on time for each student. The dyad structure also allows for the teacher to further target the instruction for the students.

While each teacher had many options for how to differentiate and there is not one single strategy that is best for all students at all times, the teachers implemented highly effective lessons. Children are at different levels of understanding and each child deserves to have appropriate instruction. Kathy Richardson (2004) highlights the task at hand for teachers:

> Being a good teacher is not about getting all of your children to perform at a particular level at a particular time. Being a good teacher is about know-

ing what your children already know and what they are still grappling with. (324)

We need to know and appreciate where our students are and what they need next. Targeting instruction is a powerful way to teach because it propels students to higher levels of understanding.

CHAPTER 4

Grouping Students

Finding the Right Grouping Structure

Grouping students is key for successful differentiated instruction in math. Differentiated instruction requires moving away from the perpetual whole group math lessons. Honestly, we don't teach reading with continuous whole group lessons anymore—why do we continue to do this in mathematics? Good educators know the reason we have reading groups is so we can meet the precise and immediate needs of each student within the small groups. If you think about it, the lack of use of small group structure may be the major reason differentiated instruction is less common in mathematics than literacy. In math, we're working with an outdated, unproductive structure when we teach whole group all the time, no matter who needs what or when.

Questions arise when considering grouping students. Should students be grouped together by similar abilities or by different abilities? Should teaching occur in whole group or small group settings? How should groups be formed? Should students stay in the same group or switch groups? Which groupings of students are the most productive? What should the role of the teacher be? To begin to answer these and other questions, we need to examine homogeneous and heterogeneous grouping, flexible ability grouping, small group and whole group structuring, purposeful grouping, strategic and random grouping, flexible and fluid grouping, the nature of adjustments, and the role of the teacher amid various group structures.

Heterogeneous Grouping Versus Homogeneous Grouping

Which grouping structure is best?

As is often the case in educational research, the issues connected to academic grouping practices are controversial. Most of this research stems from many years ago when we began to face the great debate of tracking versus detracking. Tracking refers to the practice of grouping together entire classes of students by similar academic ability, commonly called *homogeneous classes*. *Detracking* refers to the practice of grouping together entire classes of students by mixed academic abilities, commonly called *heterogeneous classes*.

Interestingly, some research supports grouping students together by likeness in ability or homogeneous grouping (Kulik 1992; Kulik and Kulik 1992; Gentry and Owens 1999; Goldring 1990; Brewer, Rees, and Argys 1995; Gallagher 1993). Other research supports the practice of grouping students by differences in academic abilities or heterogeneous grouping (Slavin 1987a, 1987b; Oakes 1985, 1988, 1990; Kagan 1997; Wheelock 1992; Smith-Maddox and Wheelock 1995). Researchers from both sides of the fence have data to support their positions. These opposing positions are held strongly by their respective commanders. In one camp, there is Robert Slavin—revered challenger of tracking. In the other camp, there is James Kulik—respected supporter of some forms of tracking. Both researchers have conducted large-scale reviews of multiple studies (i.e., meta-analyses) on grouping practices. Findings differ based on which studies are included and which studies are omitted. Kulik asserts that tracking promotes achievement and harms no one. Slavin declares that tracking is a nonfactor and regards it as "anti-democratic" (Loveless 1998). Thus the opposing positions remain at polar ends.

The complexity of this issue begins to unravel when you take a look at which students are the point of interest. We have learned over the years that if we place low-achieving students in homogeneous classes, they typically make less progress. The National Education Longitudinal Study (NELS) data give credence to this finding (Loveless 1998)—but more importantly, it actually makes sense. By grouping struggling learners with other struggling learners we give them little of what they need. They need to hear what a good answer sounds like. They need to see peers modeling solid problem solving techniques. They need to encounter the excitement that comes with understanding. They need to engage in student-to-student mathematics discourse. If struggling students only work with other struggling students, they receive few opportunities to experience these important aspects of learning mathematics. To compound the problem further, when low-achieving students are constantly grouped together, the educators who work with them tend to emit low expectations and turn to memorization and drill techniques that do not help students truly understand the math. Struggling learners make the least progress when they are in homogeneous math classes.

And so the call for the mixed-ability class was born. The merits of heterogeneous grouping practices are sound. Many schools only group classes heterogeneously, which makes sense given the potential gains for previously low-achieving students. The problem is that this perspective does not include all students. Some students, particularly high-achieving students, need a different type of academic setting. As Olszewski-Kubilius (2003) reports (using Kulik's research as support), "Finally, sophisticated analyses across hundreds of studies involving homogeneous grouping of gifted students shows that ability grouping or 'homogeneous grouping' for acceleration or enrichment results in significant gains in achievement for gifted students (not so for other students)" (2003, 3).

As educators, we understand that high-end learners need to be challenged. Like struggling learners, they also need to hear what a good answer sounds like and see models of exemplary problem solving approaches from their academic peers. They too need to encounter the excitement that comes with understanding and to engage in student-to-student mathematics discourse. High-achieving students make more progress when they are grouped homogeneously. Herein lies the conundrum. High-ability students fare best in homogeneous settings. Lower-ability students fare best in heterogeneous settings. This poses a huge problem for teachers because our job is to educate all learners. One type of group structure is not best for all students. Yet there is a way to meet all needs—differentiated instruction using flexible ability grouping.

Flexible Ability Grouping

Ability grouping is the practice of grouping students together by similar ability within a heterogeneous class. This practice is found most commonly during reading instruction in elementary schools. Small homogeneous group instruction is associated with increased achievement (Lou et al. 1996). Again, the research makes sense. When teachers work with small groups of students who are at similar levels, the focus can be on exactly what the students need to learn.

Unfortunately, the traditional approach to ability grouping is too stagnant. Students are placed in groups based on test scores and remain in the same group for the entire school year. Because of the immobile nature of the structures, this practice resembles tracking. Students are stuck in a particular group regardless of current performance.

To alleviate this problem, we need to make ability groups flexible. Flexible ability groups change based on which students have similar specific academic needs during any given lesson. The teacher has an opportunity to focus instruction on addressing the specific gaps in understanding or posing challenges to extend knowledge. It is difficult to engage in this type of targeted instruction using a whole group structure.

Whole Group Versus Small Group

Effective group configurations

The need for small group instruction is not to imply that we should never work with the whole group at the same time in mathematics. The whole group structure has its place in differentiated instruction. If the preassessment indicates that all students are at the same level within any given topic, it makes sense to teach the whole group; however, this situation occurs less frequently than many educators assume it does. Most of the time students are at various academic levels. We need to stop kidding ourselves that all students are always at the same point in their learning journeys.

A whole group structure is important for some things. Introductions, directions, closure, building community, and helping students to be comfortable with where they are in their learning journeys can all occur quite productively in a whole group setting.

Introductions and directions that are applicable to everyone should be shared in a whole group setting. It makes sense to begin the math class with something that is appropriate for everyone. An introduction that piques their interests in the day's mathematics topic or otherwise engages students to set the stage for learning is likely to be a productive use of whole group time. Likewise, directions that everyone needs should be given in a whole group setting. If all the students will be writing in their math journals that day, then it makes sense to talk about those particular directions with the entire class at the same time. However, if the teacher has leveled math writing tasks with varying directions, it would be better to save these directions for the specific small groups so as not to create confusion about the tasks. There are many classroom tasks that every student completes that can be introduced and explained in the whole group setting to save time. If the teacher repeats the *same* directions to three different groups of students, then the teacher has spent thrice the amount of time needed. The idea is to be as efficient as possible, so that the majority of time can be spent on differentiating the instruction.

Closure of the lesson is also a great time for a whole group structure. Students can reflect on the learning of the day. The teacher can guide the students toward making connections with other math topics and other curricular areas during lesson closure. Whole group lesson closure brings the class back together in a way that helps strengthen learning and commitment toward learning.

Students need to feel a strong sense of classroom community. They need to know that they can take risks and admit when they do not understand something. They need to know that the classroom is a safe and comfortable place. Building classroom community is well suited for whole group structure.

Targeted instruction, however, is best carried out in a small group setting. Small group instruction is where real teaching and learning are at their best. Even if the targeted instruction is for a mere five minutes, the time spent is extremely valuable. Five minutes of exactly what a small group of children academically needs is better than sixty minutes directed too far above or below the specific needs.

There are many reasons why small group instruction makes a positive difference. First, small group interaction often includes more opportunities for children to assimilate and accommodate new information. The teacher can modify and adjust the instruction to meet the specific needs of the students in the group. Second, small group interaction often includes more opportunities for students to construct knowledge through hands-on approaches and active engagement in learning. The number of students working with the teacher is smaller, which allows the students to have more teacher attention. Third, small group interaction can serve to empower students through the intrinsically rewarding nature of collaborative and cooperative work. The teacher can more easily foster this type of motivation within the small group. Given these reasons and others, small group instruction serves to increase achievement, increase persistence, and increase interest for students.

When deciding how much time should be devoted to small group instruction, the teacher needs to consider many factors. We should consider the needs of the students. We also need to think about what the rest of the class is working on while we meet with small groups. We want everyone to experience as much productive time during mathematics as possible.

If the teacher is working with a small group of students, the rest of the students need to be engaged in tasks that they can work at without the teacher. The tasks may be independent, with the students working completely on their own. More often the tasks are dependent, but the dependence is student-to-student rather than student-to-teacher. The classroom environment must match these expectations. We can't require students to solve problems by asking each other if we have rules such as *no talking*. We can't require that students seek the answers to their questions if we have rules such as *you must stay in your seat*. We need to think about what we want for our students and then make sure we are not imposing classroom contradictions with our rules.

We have to teach students how to work productively even when they are not working with the teacher. Think of how many times you have heard a student say, "I don't know what to do." This statement is full of so many potential messages. The message could be, "I am confused." The message could be, "I don't know how to solve my problem." The message could be, "It is your job, teacher, to direct me." The message could be, "I'm afraid I might make a mistake." The message could be, "This work is too hard for me."

Let's look at some of the possible messages and figure out how we can help students work productively while we are working with other students in a small group situation. What can students do if they are confused? How can students solve their own problems? The student could ask another student. The student could look for the answer somewhere in the classroom (chalkboard with directions, model of task hanging on the front board, books, folders, work baskets, etc.). The student could try to skip that part of the task and move on to the next part. The student could think about what we worked on during small group time or during the whole class introduction and directions period. These solutions rarely come naturally to students, but even young children can seek solutions if we require it and give them the tools to be successful.

As the teacher, I want to set the students up for success. Therefore, I am not going to leave them to fend for themselves for long periods of time. I get my small groups going and then may take a strategic walk around the room. I'm checking to make sure the students are working on the tasks and I am available for questions. But if a student says, "I don't know what to do," I always ask, "What have you done to try to find out what to do?" This question helps the students realize that it is their responsibility to do something to try to solve the problem. The method is not flawless. I still have students who have a difficult time taking the initiative to solve their own problems, but most of my students try to figure it out. I commend them for their efforts, which propels them to continue to keep trying.

The message involving fear of making a mistake is connected to classroom community. We want students to feel safe. We need students to understand that our classroom is a place where people can make mistakes and not feel humiliated. It is a normal feeling to be embarrassed when you don't understand something, so we have to work hard to create an environment that allows children to know that others will not intensify this feeling. As the teacher, I even point out my mistakes, so that the students understand that it is acceptable to make mistakes. I am also modeling how to handle the situation.

If the work is too difficult for the student, it is the teacher's job to give direct instruction and support. We can't give difficult tasks to students and expect them to complete these tasks on their own. This does not mean we can't challenge students, but we need to facilitate or in some way support the students. When facing a challenging task, the student may need to discuss some options with the teacher or with peers. The student may need to ask some questions (by the way, "I don't understand" is not a question). When we encourage students to ask questions about the task, we are teaching them to think about the situation and come up with an initial step toward solving the problem.

Small group instruction is deeply intertwined with classroom management. If we meet with one group of students without setting the boundaries and expectations for the rest of the class, we may have a disaster on our hands. Students need to know what to do, how to solve problems if they become perplexed, and that the teacher will offer support and guidance at particular times. What we don't want is for students to interrupt the small group with questions. My students understand that when I am working with a group, I do not want to be interrupted (unless it is an emergency). Yes, this is difficult for some students. They want answers to questions or support or affirmation immediately. But I have to teach them not to ask me when I am working with a small group. I do this for several reasons. One, it validates the importance of what we are doing in the small group setting. Two, it teaches them that there are other ways to find answers and seek support. Three, it empowers them to solve their own problems. Four, it helps them to learn how to be productive without direct guidance from the teacher. However, I only work with small groups for short increments of time. It may be just ten minutes before I am up and moving around the classroom to answer students' questions or provide guidance. With some classes, we have to work our way up from two to ten minutes of successful, uninterrupted small group time. Each day we succeed, we increase the small group time by one minute. Students typically enjoy working toward increasing the small group time because they take pride in experiencing the small steps of success and they understand how meaningful the small group time can be.

Purposeful Groups

The small groups need to be purposeful. The teacher should have a reason to put specific students together in a group. If there are five first graders struggling with subtraction, the teacher can offer direct instruction to these students in a small group. If there are six other students who already understand basic subtraction and are ready for a challenge, the teacher can work with these students accordingly. The point is that the groups are formed according to specific needs.

Sometimes the groups are formed heterogeneously for a purpose. The teacher purposefully groups together students by mixed ability. The instructional goal is related to a particular mathematics process. For example, the teacher may focus on math communication. Some students may be working at higher levels of communication than others and these differences may or may not be related to math content ability. For example, a kindergarten teacher groups together six students to concentrate attention on increasing math talk. Three of the students are very verbal and three are somewhat quiet. The teacher pairs the students by differences in math communication and offers direct instruction related to using math vocabulary to explain and justify answers. The teacher wants to encourage less verbal students to use more mathematics words and explanations by allowing them to hear their peers do so.

Other times the academically heterogeneous group may work together because they have particular interests in common. Say eight students in the class collect baseball cards. These students may be working at different levels of understanding computation. But the teacher groups them together because the task is related to baseball statistics. The students benefit from each other because they have high motivation and involvement in the task.

In another situation, the academically heterogeneous group may have a particular learning style in common. If there is a small group of visual learners, they may work together creating pictures of word problems. Even though the students' abilities may be different, they are able to participate in the group together because the teacher uses a specific learning preference as the way for the students to understand (and express) the content.

Similarly, the teacher may meet with a small group to focus on the concept of addition. The students are at different levels of understanding, but they are all tactile learners. The teacher uses the learning style to help the students manipulate the addends with counting chips. The students, guided by the teacher, help each other explain and record the processes and outcomes.

A great deal of learning can take place in small heterogeneous groups. The group cooperates as they tackle the math task at hand. Cooperation and collaboration are beneficial. This is probably why "cooperative learning" is a strong influence in the elementary school classroom. Those who subscribe to the theories of cooperative learning believe in the power of heterogeneous grouping.

Cooperative learning involves placing students in small academically and culturally heterogeneous groups and providing the group with tasks that encourage all students to work toward a common goal. Students working in successful cooperative groups have positive interdependence, individual accountability, equal participation, and simultaneous interaction (Kagan 1997). The idea is that as the students work together and rely on each other, their motivation and productivity increase. Roles can be assigned to group members to ensure participation and influence group learning. As one first-grade teacher explained, "You put two high-end learners, two average learners, and two lower-end learners together in one group. Everyone has a job. Everyone is accountable because they share the final grade. They help each other."

Who does this type of grouping help the most? As we have discussed, struggling learners typically fare best when they are in heterogeneous groups. Average learners fare well when they work with higher-end learners. But high-end learners potentially learn less when they are in a heterogeneous group. So who does the heterogeneous cooperative group help the most? The teacher! In many heterogeneous situations that are not teacher-directed, the high-end learners spend most of the time explaining and instructing the rest of the group—which may help the teacher a great deal, but it may not necessarily help the high-end learners. Some say that when you teach someone else, you come to understand the subject matter more deeply; therefore, it is a productive thing for high-end learners to spend time tutoring other students. However, it is not fair to high-end learners if they spend the majority of their time teaching others what they already know. We owe them instruction on their level, just as we owe all of our students targeted instruction.

The answer is not to dismiss cooperative, heterogeneous grouping structures. There are times when students need to work with academic peers and times when students need to work with peers of different abilities. A balance can be met by using some heterogeneous grouping and using some homogeneous grouping. We need both direct teacher instruction and a purpose for grouping students together.

Strategic Versus Random Grouping

In a kindergarten class, the teacher has established small group management. The students are comfortable working in groups. They understand that they need to accomplish certain tasks without the teacher. The students have learned that everyone's group will have a turn. Sounds wonderful, right? Well, the management is instituted. The students understand the expectations and the teacher has figured out how to give optimal time to students in their small group settings. Yet each small group is taught the same thing in the same way. The teacher meets with each of the three groups and repeats the same instruction each time. The materials are the same. The content is the same. The teacher's comments are even the same. Simply repeating the same lesson with three (or any number of) small groups is not as purposeful as it could be because the students are not grouped together for a reason. While there are benefits to small group instruction, we can make the experience doubly meaningful by incorporating strategic, specific planning for each group.

Some teachers use a can of popsicle sticks with individual student names on each stick. The can of sticks is incorporated into various classroom routines. Unfortunately, this device is one of the culprits of artificial randomization in the classroom. There were good intentions behind the can—everyone gets a turn, it is more fair, it will discourage the teacher from choosing the same students to answer over and over again, and so on. As the can of sticks moved up the ranks, it started to be used in forming random groups. Yet random groups, in and of themselves, are not strategic because grouping decisions should be coupled with rationales. The teacher needs to be deliberate when forming small groups. Even if I want a heterogeneous group, I can do a better job forming the groups without the can of popsicle sticks. I know the students and therefore can (and should) make purposeful, strategic decisions about group formation without using randomizing mechanisms.

Flexible and Fluid Groups

Groups that regularly change

Small groups need to be flexible and fluid. Flexibility in grouping means that the students in the groups change based on the needs of the students. Students are not always in the same group since placement in groups is based on the students' performance on the assessment and the goals the teacher has regarding instruction. Adding the concept of fluidness to the definition describes the groups more completely. The groups are fluid because students flow in and out of groups based on needs. There is motion and movement between and among groups.

Making Adjustments

Teachers often say to me, "But what if I put the child in the wrong group?" The answer is that you simply move the child. My students are quite accustomed to changing groups before, during, and after instruction. Given the varying purposes I use to form groups and the different structures, the students are sometimes unaware of how I have grouped them. While it is not my goal to deceive, I really like that I can change the groups around enough to make the group decisions less obvious. I do not want students to feel that one group is "better" or "faster" than another group. By highlighting the fact that the group structures are based on the needs of the students in the specific groups, we can negate some of the self-esteem outcomes associated with having a "cheetahs group" and a "turtles group." No child should have to endure being labeled a turtle compared to a cheetah. Likewise, letter names can be hurtful because the students may think the A group is the best. This is why we need to be cautious when naming groups. Many primary teachers use color names, which can be helpful if the color names periodically change. Because I am always trying to expose children to math language, I often use content vocabulary to label small groups.

Using Number and Operations Vocabulary to Label Small Groups

See:
Algebra, p. 48
Data, p. 67
Geometry, p. 69
Measurement, p. 67

Using content vocabulary to identify small groups offers a twofold benefit. The group names help with classroom management and offer opportunities for exposure to content vocabulary. Because the groups are always changing, we want the names of the groups to change as well. Using specific content vocabulary as the group names encourages the students to see and hear more math. These lists contain some of the number and operations vocabulary that could be used for small group names.

Understanding Number and Number Relationships Words

Accurate	Eighty	Five frame
Cardinal numbers	Eleven	Forty
Compose	Equal	Four
Count	Even	Fourteen
Decompose	Fifteen	Fourth
Digit	Fifth	Fractions
Eight	Fifty	Half
Eighteen	First	Least
Eighth	Five	Less

Match
Model
More
Most
Nine
Nineteen
Ninety
Ninth
Number
Number line
Odd
One
One hundred
Ordinal numbers
Parts
Place value
Position
Quantity
Relationship
Second
Sequence
Set
Seven
Seventeen
Seventh
Seventy
Show
Six
Sixteen
Sixth
Sixty
Ten
Ten frame
Tenth
Third
Thirteen
Thirty
Three
Twelve
Twenty
Two
Value
Whole
Zero

Understanding Operations Words

Add
Addend
Addition
Combine
Compare
Compute
Difference
Division
Equal grouping
Equation
Fair sharing
Greater than
Join
Less than
Minus
Missing part
Multiplication
Operations
Regrouping
Removal
Separate
Solve
Subtract
Subtraction
Sum
Total

Computing Fluently and Estimating Words

Accuracy
Algorithm
Alternative strategy
Basic facts
Change
Efficiency
Equation
Estimate
Fact families
Fluency
Reasonable
Result
Start
Strategies
Unknown

To make the management a little less cumbersome, I use magnetic name cards for the students. Before math time each day, I group the name cards to indicate the groups and activities of respective students. If I am using content vocabulary for group names, I can use icons with the labels to help my students understand which group they are in and which activities they will complete at specific times.

The Roles of the Teacher

The teacher has many roles

OK, I will admit it. When I first started teaching I was the *sage on the stage.* I thought I was serving my students well. I had the knowledge and it was my job to impart the information to my students. As I continued teaching and learning, I came to understand the significance of serving as the *guide on the side.* I learned that I could help students construct their own knowledge by questioning and channeling their inquiry. I have now come to understand that teachers have many roles—designers, directors, facilitators, and coaches. All of these roles can be taken by the teacher in either small group or whole group structures.

The Teacher Is the Designer

The teacher as designer plans the lesson, making sure to think through the needs of the students. She observes and assesses the students constantly. These observations and assessments help highlight the ways in which the plans will be revised. If she is working with a small group and sees that students are using some new math manipulatives in a way that may create misconceptions, the teacher can adjust to include a longer introduction to the new manipulatives. Or she may decide to modify the assignment for those particular students so as to give them more time to explore the new manipulatives.

In a whole group situation, the teacher may notice that the class is having difficulty with a specific concept. He may decide to take a different approach to teaching this concept or perhaps devote more time to building foundations of the previous concepts. The difficult part of designing for the whole group is that the whole group is made up of individuals who frequently need different designs. It is often much easier (and more exact) to arrange and rearrange the learning environment and specific learning situations when working with a small group of students—simply because these needed changes are more easily noted by the teacher working with just a few students as opposed to the whole group. Yet prolific whole group designing comes into play as the classroom environment and management techniques are reconsidered. For example, in a prekindergarten classroom, the students change activities when the teacher signals. However, he notices that the transitions between the activities take too long. He is waiting for groups of students to start their next tasks for over five minutes; the extra time is being devoted to putting away the materials in an organized manner. He does not want the students to slight the cleanup, because organization is helpful—yet he wants more time to devote to direct academic instruction during math. He revises the design by giving the students a cleanup warning several minutes before it is actually time to switch groups. This prompt helps the students prepare for the transition and ultimately increases the time the teacher can spend with the small groups.

The Teacher Is the Director

Much like the director of a play, the teacher as director sets the stage and directs the performance, but encourages the students to take an active part in the learning process. This involves a degree of commanding. In the whole group situation, teachers provide directions and expectations. The attention is focused on the teachers who explain and entertain as they teach. The teacher may use modeling or role-playing as ways to direct students during the whole group structure.

In a small group setting, the teacher's directing can be more specific to the academic needs of the students. If a first-grade teacher notices that some or all of the students in a group are struggling with how to start to solve a math problem, the teacher may decide to offer specific modeling using a think aloud approach to problem solving.

The Teacher Is the Facilitator

The teacher in the role of facilitator uses suggesting, supporting, and questioning to teach the students. In the whole group situation, the teacher poses questions that engage students in learning. In a second-grade classroom, the teacher may offer students an opportunity to study multiplication through experiences with repeated addition. The teacher may suggest that students represent the mathematics situation with numbers, pictures, or words.

In the small group structure the teacher facilitates in much the same manner, yet the support is more geared toward specific students based on the current topic. Because the teacher can work with individual needs within the small group, the questions can be very specific. When working with a small group of students on describing how a particular number can be composed and decomposed, the teacher may ask questions related to how the number can be represented. These questions help the students make connections within and among the parts of the number.

The Teacher Is the Coach

The teacher as coach works to prepare and encourage the children. In a whole group setting, the encouragement is directed toward *we*. The teacher in this important role shares certain sentiments—"we are a team," "we will work together to help each other," and "we will make a commitment to doing our best." When established and appreciated, these and other mottos can be very empowering to students. The coach elicits dedication to learning and excellence.

When the teacher serves as a coach in the small group setting the encouragement is directed toward *you* because it is more individualized. The teacher says other things—"you can do it!" "you almost have it, keep going," and "you have this part right, now focus on this part." The teacher in a small group situation can provide support and then withdraw the support based on the immediate performance of the students.

All the roles the teacher takes are important—and whether designing, directing, facilitating, or coaching the teaching comes alive. Most often teachers move in and out of the various roles to provide high-quality instruction, which produces optimal learning.

The Leader of the Group

Leaders have multifaceted roles

Obviously the teacher's role varies depending on the group structure and the nature of the tasks offered to or required of the students. Every group needs leadership. Sometimes the group is led by the teacher. Other times students lead themselves or each other. There are advantages and disadvantages related to each type of group structure and the associated leadership.

A teacher-led group structure is very beneficial. The teacher is present, knows exactly what is happening, and can adjust or revise the instruction to best meet the immediate learning needs of the students. Whole group structure allows the teacher to pilot the instruction. Yet many students gain only minimally in a whole group situation, especially when the whole group structure lasts for long periods of time. Some students are disruptive. Other students behave appropriately, but they are still not fully engaged in the learning. These students *check out* and let the other students answer questions and guide the mathematics inquiry. Thus, even though it is easier to pilot the class in a whole group situation, the benefits may not outweigh the costs.

To successfully implement small group instruction, the teacher must teach children how to help each other. Like the teacher, the students must also take on roles of designing, directing, facilitating, and coaching. Students learn how to take on these roles by watching the teacher and experiencing the learning situations as steered by the teacher in various roles.

Teachers who use flexible, fluid, purposeful grouping practices consider student goals, instructional activities, and individual needs. Teachers form groups by clustering similarities or differences for specific and varying purposes. Successful differentiated instruction in mathematics relies heavily upon the productivity of students in various group structures. Whether working with the whole group or with a small group, the teacher needs to be clear on the reasons associated with group formation and modifications. The teacher also needs to ensure that the groups are flexible, fluid, and purposeful. The ever-changing roles of the teacher in the various group structures must be illuminated. Successful implementation of differentiated instruction in mathematics is deeply rooted in securing the right group structure at the right time for each student.

CHAPTER 5

Levels of Cognitive Demand

Understanding Levels of Cognitive Demand

Required degrees of thinking and ownership

Differentiating instruction in mathematics requires the ability to adjust the level of cognitive demand (LCD) for students. Cognitive demand is the degree of thinking and ownership required to fully grasp the learning situation. Many mathematics publishers, policy makers, and curriculum experts aspire to offer higher levels of cognitive demand in mathematics curricula to ensure academic rigor and, ultimately, to yield increased student performance. While the intentions are straightforward, the implementation is often unsuccessful because *insisting* that children use a high LCD is not the same as *teaching* children to use a high LCD when it is appropriate. The first step for the teacher is to understand levels of cognitive demand. The second step is to gain comfort with the levels of cognitive demand. The third step is to adjust the levels of cognitive demand for particular students at particular times.

The LCD can range from low to high. "A high level of cognitive demand occurs in classrooms where students are engaged in complex learning activities that involve applying higher level thinking processes to challenging content knowledge" (Kramer 2005). Conversely, lower levels of cognitive demand involve such things as memorization and following explicit instructions.

The mathematics tasks students work on require various levels of cognitive demand. The lowest level involves committing specific facts, rules, procedures, and definitions to memory. Students memorize the information and later recall it. There is a step-by-step, predetermined manner in which the learner approaches a mathematics problem. Often the teacher models what to do and how to do it. A lower LCD is required of the learner when connections are not explored and the emphasis is on finding the correct answer. Less attention is given to enhancing the student's understanding.

Because of the lack of depth associated with low-LCD tasks, many mathematics educators abandon this type of instruction in search of enriching students' understandings. While this aspiration is commendable, the realities of the classroom often oppose the intentions—let alone the anticipated outcomes. Requiring a high LCD of all students at all times is *pie in the sky* instruction. Gearing instruction too far above what is needed does not work. Students need foundations, especially when the material is new or when they are struggling for understanding. Students need something to fall back on when they do not know how to solve a mathematics problem.

For example, rote counting is a beneficial, low-level task. Students need to know how to rote count before they can rational count, much less compute. However, just because students know how to rote count, it does not mean they know how to rational count or add one more—any more than knowing how to say the alphabet means they know how to read. The rote counting serves as a foundation. Rote counting by ones involves memorizing the number names in consecutive order. Hearing and repeating the numbers requires a relatively low LCD. Yet rational counting and computation may require a higher LCD depending on how the task is presented. The point is we cannot discard low-LCD tasks because students need preliminary, background-knowledge-building experiences.

Requiring low levels of cognitive demand for all students at all times is *door in the floor* instruction (the opposite of *pie in the sky* instruction). Gearing instruction too far below the level that is needed will not help students achieve rich understanding. We need to provide students with tasks that enhance connections and encourage students to engage in thinking about, applying, and analyzing mathematical concepts. Higher levels of cognitive demand require thinking. The students need to do more than mindlessly recite facts or robotically perform procedures. Students need to explore multiple ways of solving a math problem and examining mathematical relationships.

For example, engaging in math talk is a beneficial high-level task. No matter what level students are working at, they need to have opportunities and channels to talk about the math. Even if some students do not have extensive mathematics vocabularies, they need to use the words they do know. Even if students do not completely know how to articulate the math process or concept, they need to talk about what they do know and ask questions. They also need to hear others using mathematics vocabulary and verbally explaining or reflecting on mathematical ideas. Math discourse involves a high LCD regardless of the level at which the child is currently working. Math discourse promotes more thinking and reflecting about math at all levels.

Gaining Comfort with the Levels of Cognitive Demand

Knowing the levels of cognitive demand

Not all students learn mathematics in the same manner or sequence or time frame (although many curriculum creators imply that this is true). While it makes sense that students need to engage in rote counting before engaging in rational counting and computation, not all students need to spend the same amount of time building foundations. Some students learn rote counting more quickly. Other students may understand how to join or separate smaller quantities before they have even finished memorizing rote counting to one hundred. Still other students may need to hear and see the numbers from zero to twenty in consecutive order many, many times before they are able to rote count with ease.

Dooming particular students to tasks *only* involving low levels of cognitive demand is not appropriate or beneficial. All students deserve to engage in some tasks that require high levels of cognitive demand. There are some teachers who believe that students who struggle in mathematics should always engage in tasks that require low levels of cognitive demand. But if procedures are memorized rather than being understood, the learning is too shallow. Similarly, if facts are learned in isolation but are never applied to a real-life (or even contrived) context, what is the point of knowing the facts? Tasks that require a low LCD cannot represent the final destination. The ground level is not the finish line, but it may serve as the starting gate for some students in particular math concept areas.

The degree of thinking involved is not the only way to determine the LCD essential to any given task. You can also consider the ownership of learning held by the student versus the teacher. The more ownership the student takes, the greater the LCD. As the ownership of learning moves from the teacher to the student, there is what some refer to as a *transfer of agency*. This type of increase in the LCD "is evident when teachers enable students to focus on an authentic learning problem and guide them [students] in discovering a solution or alternative approach to its resolution" (Kramer 2005). As students face more complex math problems, they may need a decrease in the LCD and less ownership of the learning. This means teachers may need to offer more guidance and direction because the problem situation is foreign to the students. On the other hand, if the goal is to increase the LCD, the teacher may pose a task that is somewhat less complex while encouraging the students to take more ownership of the learning.

Adjusting Levels of Cognitive Demand

Using mathematics processes to adjust the LCD

We need to be comfortable enough with the levels of cognitive demand to know when to use which level with which students at which particular times. There are multiple windows of opportunity for adjusting the LCD as a way to differentiate mathematics instruction. Educators can use the processes of mathematics and levels of questioning to adjust the LCD required in any given task.

The processes of mathematics offer opportunities to increase or decrease the LCD. According to the NCTM (2000), the five process standards include problem solving, reasoning and proof, communication, connections, and representations. While all of the process standards should be interwoven into the fabric of mathematics instruction for all students, each process standard offers a gateway to allow the teacher to increase or decrease the LCD to best meet the immediate needs of specific students.

Adjusting LCD in Problem Solving

See
Algebra, p. 50
Data, p. 69
Geometry, p. 72
Measurement, p. 70

Because "problem solving is an integral part of all mathematics learning" (National Council of Teachers of Mathematics 2000, 52), it is not appropriate to provide problem solving situations to only the students working at or above the average level of instruction. All students need to problem solve. However, the LCD needed to solve problems can range from simple to complex.

A group of first graders works with number relationships using hundred charts. Because the group has had some difficulty with the concept, the teacher uses a lower LCD by modeling a think aloud strategy. The teacher demonstrates on her hundred chart. She asks the children to close their eyes and she uses chips to cover up the numbers 35, 36, and 37. The children open their eyes and the teacher poses the math situation by asking, "How can you figure out which numbers are covered up?" The children are not sure.

The teacher models a think aloud strategy by saying, "To figure this out, I would use the numbers that I can see. I see 34 comes right before the first number that is covered up. I think about the order of the numbers and ask myself, 'What number comes after 34?' I say the numbers to myself to figure it out."

The children respond, "It is 35!" Then they employ the teacher's think aloud strategy to figure out the other two numbers that are covered up. Afterward, they try covering up numbers for each other. They use think aloud strategies to figure out which numbers are covered up.

In this scenario, the teacher did not require an extremely low LCD because the students were not given the answers. There were several possible ways to derive the answer in this problem solving situation. Yet the LCD was not extremely high because the students were given modeling and related questioning. The teacher used the LCD that best fit the needs of the students.

Given the same topic (number relationships) but a different group of students, the teacher may differentiate the problem solving situation in another way.

This group of students understands the basics of number relationships within the hundred chart and is ready to work on problem solving in a way that uses a much higher LCD. The teacher places chips on 35, 36, 37, 45, 46, 47, 55, 56, and 57. She points to the chip that covers 46 and poses the question, "How can you figure out the number that is under this chip?" The manipulatives (hundred chart and chips) are the same ones as used by the other group, but the problem is different. More numbers are hidden—but more importantly, the hidden numbers are clustered in a way that makes the task more complex. The teacher also asks the children to figure out the hidden number that has the least information surrounding it. All the numbers around 46 are covered by chips, which makes the problem solving task more difficult. Notice the students' thinking and the role of the teacher in the following dialogue:

Jennie: We can't see what comes right before it.

Sam: And we can't see what comes right after it.

Liam: But we do know that 44 is before the one that is before it.

Jennie: Yep. So it has to be 46.

Sam: I think it is 46, too.

Teacher: Why do you think it is 46?

Sam: Because 47 is covered up, then we can see 48. So you count back two.

Teacher: Is there a way to use different numbers to solve the problem?

Jennie: Yes. Count on two from 44. Like this [pointing to the chips]—44, 45, 46.

Teacher: Is there a way to use different numbers to solve the problem?

Rosella: You can count by tens.

Jennie: How?

Rosella: Start here [points to 6]—6, 16, 26, 36, 46. All the numbers end with six.

Sam: I get it. You could do the same counting by tens backward [Sam points to 96 and counts, with the other children joining in]—96, 86, 76, 66, 56, 46.

Liam: There are a lot of ways to figure this out.

The group works on additional problem solving using the hundred chart by covering up even more numbers in clusters. Even though there was one correct answer in this problem solving situation, there was a degree of open-endedness because there were many ways to solve the problem. Notice how the teacher did not model how to solve the problem, yet constantly raised the LCD by asking questions that helped the group continue to probe deeper into the math situation. Additionally, the level of ownership moves up a notch when one of the students (Jennie) asks a question that is not directed to the teacher.

The levels of cognitive demand required in math problem solving situations should vary based upon the needs of the students. Adjusting the LCD based on the immediate academic needs of the students is an excellent way to differentiate mathematics instruction.

See:
Algebra, p. 52
Data, p. 73
Geometry, p. 76
Measurement, p. 72

Adjusting LCD in Reasoning and Proof

Reasoning and proof is another process standard that provides a vehicle for increasing or decreasing the required level of cognitive demand. According to the NCTM (2000), "a mathematical proof is a formal way of expressing particular kinds of reasoning and justification" (56). The neat part of mathematics is actually doing the math and discovering patterns and predicting. Mathematicians make guesses and test hypotheses to learn more about the world of math. We can help students better understand mathematics by adjusting the level of cognitive demand required as they reason and analyze.

One of the best ways to help young children reason mathematically is to ask them, "How do you know?" This question encourages children to explain their reasoning and allows them an opportunity to give the proof associated with their answer. Let's look at two classroom scenarios of a teacher adjusting the LCD using mathematics reasoning and proof.

> One of my all time favorite responses to the how-do-you-know question occurred with Xavier, an ELL (English Language Learner) student, several years ago. I was so impressed with how quickly he understood mathematics and how quickly he was learning the English language. One day Xavier was solving *plus ten* equations using base-ten blocks. After representing and solving a few equations, he peered at the next one (76 + 10 = ?) and announced, "It is 86!" Because I wanted to uncover his thinking process, I asked, "How do you know?" Xavier pondered the question and then said, "I just thinked and thinked and the answer pooped right out." Adorably, Xavier mixed the word *pooped* with the word *popped*, but I understood what he meant. He knew the answer, but did not have enough command of English to explain his thinking. So I asked Xavier to show me how he knew the answer. He demonstrated adding a ten rod to the number 76. I affirmed his demonstration and then asked if there was another way he could prove his answer to me. Xavier responded by bringing me over to the class hundred chart and pointing at 76 and 86. Again I affirmed his answer and asked if there was another way to show me how he knew the answer. Xavier brought me to the class number line, where he pointed at 76 with the classroom pointer. He made ten hopping motions with the stick as he moved from 76 to 86. Then he went back to 76 and made one large motion to 86. He then took me a hundred chart on his desk where he placed a bean on 76 and smiled as he moved it down to 86 in one motion. Xavier had multiple ways of showing his reasoning and proof. The answer didn't pop out; he really understood the math. He was able to show his rea-

soning and proof because he was given an adjustment in the level of cognitive demand through questioning and persistence.

In another classroom scenario, the teacher works with a group of students. She asks the students, "Which is larger, 1,000 or 100?" The students respond, "1,000." The teacher asks them to explain how they know. Notice how the teacher promotes thinking about reasoning and proof using levels of cognitive demand in the following dialogue:

Teacher: How do you know 1,000 is larger than 100?

Lorimer: It is just bigger.

Ky: It is really a lot bigger.

Teacher: How could you prove it to someone?

Halona: We could show them.

Teacher: How would you show them?

Halona: We could show them a box of buttons.

Lorimer: Where are we going to find a box of a thousand buttons?

Halona: My mom has some buttons, but I don't think it will be enough.

Yolanda: I would write it. *100* and *1,000*.

Ky: Yeah, 1,000 has more zeroes.

Lorimer: Yep, and 100 has less zeroes than 1,000.

Teacher: Is there another way to prove it?

Halona: We could prove it with digi-blocks.

Yolanda: Yes. The thousand block is a lot bigger than the hundred block.

Ky: We can open it up, too. That would really prove it.

Teacher: Why would you open up the blocks?

Ky: When you open it up you can see the hundreds inside.

Lorimer: You can see the ten hundreds inside the thousand. That really proves it.

> *Yolanda:* I would say "Look at all these hundreds that we have to use to make 1,000." Everyone would have to believe us.
>
> *Lorimer:* Because we explained why with the blocks.

There is a difference between explaining and justifying mathematics thinking. Typically explaining involves *what* you did to answer the question or *how* you answered the question. Justifying often involves a deeper probe into *why* you chose to answer the question the way you did. While both explaining and justifying are important forms of reasoning and proof, it is important to keep in mind that clarifying *why* you did something often requires a higher LCD than explaining *what* you did or *how* you did it. However, we must not reserve clarifying *why* for only our brightest students. All students need opportunities for explaining and justifying. We can use explanations and justifications to offer quick and effective ways to differentiate instruction.

Adjusting LCD in Communication

See:
Algebra, p. 53
Data, p. 74
Geometry, p. 76
Measurement, p. 74

Communication is the third process standard. As the NCTM (2000) notes, "communication is an essential part of mathematics and mathematics education" (60). The levels of cognitive demand associated with mathematics communication come in the form of expressing and receiving information. The vehicles we use to communicate mathematics include words (verbal and written), pictures (diagrams, graphs), and numbers (including equations and expressions).

Too often young children are required to communicate something that they do not yet understand. Weeks are spent in many kindergarten (and some prekindergarten) classrooms teaching children how to form number symbols. To make a *5* children are taught to "come down, go around, go back, and add a hat." This cute little chant is aimed at helping children remember how to form the symbol *5*. The problem is that this is not how you make five; this is how you communicate five. Making five involves showing the quantity, which means you need five objects. While we do need to teach children how to communicate with math symbols, we cannot assume that children understand a number just because they can write the number. Furthermore, why know how to write a number if you do not understand what that number means?

> Years ago, I was working with a kindergartener who was having some difficulties in mathematics. I gave him a cup of counters and asked him to show me four. He reached for the counters one at a time, arranging them on his work mat. I watched him take out seven counters. When he

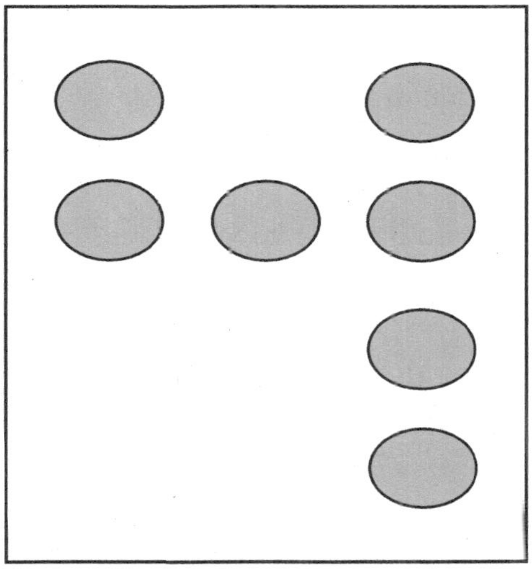

Figure 5–1

announced that he was "done," I asked him to show me. This is how he arranged the counters (see Figure 5–1). The child communicated the number symbol for four without any regard to the concept of the quantity of four. He used seven counters to show the number four. Needless to say, this is problematic. Young children need time and experience to develop an understanding of *number*. It makes more sense for the child to learn how to form number symbols after the child has ownership of the number value.

Communication in mathematics provides another way to adjust the LCD as we differentiate instruction in mathematics. Of course, we want all children to communicate in mathematics, but we can use various levels of sophistication to adjust the levels of cognitive demand.

A group of prekindergarteners works with the teacher on ways to make four. Each child is given the opportunity to make four using objects from the dramatic play center. Krystle finds four plates. Sam finds four cups. Ebony finds four place mats. Nicki reaches for four spoons, but there are only three. The following dialogue takes place:

Nicki: I can't make four.

Teacher: Why can't you make four?

Nicki: Because there are not enough.

Teacher: How many more spoons do you need?

Nicki: Four.

Teacher: How many do you have?

Nicki: Three.

Teacher: Sam and Krystle, do you agree?

Sam and Krystle: Yes.

Teacher: Is three the same as four?

Nicki: No. It is smaller.

Sam: Three is not as big as four.

Teacher: How many plates does Krystle have?

Everyone: Four.

Teacher: What if we match one spoon on each of Krystle's plates to see how many spoons we are missing? [Nicki places one spoon on each plate]

Krystle: Yes. Then we can see it.

Sam: She needs one more.

Nicki: Yeah, this one [Nicki points to the empty plate]. I need one more spoon.

Teacher: Let's draw a picture in our math journals of what we found out.

The students draw various interpretations of the math situation. Nicki's drawing includes four plates with one spoon on each plate. She colored the last spoon with a purple crayon. The teacher says, "Nicki, tell me about the purple spoon." Nicki replies, "That's the one that I need. It is special."

The mathematics communication in this scenario is multifaceted. The students use models to represent and understand the number four. One of the students (Nicki) discovers that there are only three instead of four spoons. The students seem to understand that three is less than four, but they are not sure about the comparison subtraction situation posed by the teacher's question, "How many more spoons do you need?" Like many young children, Nicki focuses on the total she is trying achieve rather than how many more she needs to obtain the desired total. The teacher adjusts the LCD through mathematics communication by helping the students talk about the number, create models of the number, and draw pictures of the number representations. When the teacher asks if the other students agree, she is offering a way for the children to engage in the math thinking and communication (though the question is not high level). The teacher's questions guide the students to further communication. Ultimately the models and corresponding pictures serve as additional communication vehicles. The LCD is adjusted to a lower level to help the group verbally communicate. Asking if others agree, and asking questions to the whole group, helps enhance the mathematics discourse. Encouraging the students to use each other's models (as when the teacher suggests using Krystle's plates and Nicki's spoons) is a way to help the children communicate through the models. When the teacher asks Nicki about the purple spoon in her drawing, Nicki is given the opportunity to verbally express how she illustrated her math thinking.

In another classroom scenario, the levels of cognitive demand are adjusted within the mathematics communication in a different way. These prekindergarten students are investigating how to compose the number four using buttons of various colors. The teacher gives each child a small plate with specific buttons on it. The teacher works with the students to help them communicate the mathematics processes and thinking by raising the LCD. The following math talk occurs:

Josh: I have two blue buttons and two red buttons.

Sandy: I have one green button and three purple buttons.

Henry: I have three purple buttons and one blue button.

Taylor: I have four red buttons.

Kelsey: I have two yellow buttons and two purple buttons.

Mark: I have four green buttons.

Teacher: Who has four buttons? [Everyone indicates that they have four buttons]

Teacher: I want you to be a detective and look really closely at each other's buttons. Try to notice which sets of buttons are alike in some way.

Sandy: Look at Taylor's and Mark's.

Kelsey: They have all the same color.

Mark: Yeah. I have all green and she has all red.

Taylor: We are the same because we don't have any other colors.

Henry: I have three purples. So does Sandy.

Sandy: Yeah. We both have three purples.

Teacher: How would you describe your set of buttons with numbers?

Henry: [pointing to the buttons] Three and one.

Sandy: One and three is the same. Just turn it around.

Kelsey: I have two purple. Who has one like mine?

Josh: I don't have two purple. [Josh pushes his plate of buttons closer to Kelsey's plate] Look at mine.

Kelsey: What is yours?

Josh: Two blue and two red.

Teacher: How are Kelsey's and Josh's buttons alike?

Sandy: Two and two. Two and two. [Sandy points to the buttons]

Kelsey: That's what I think, too.

Everyone: Me, too.

Teacher: Now I would like for you to show the same ways to make four using linking cubes in a tower. Talk to each other and look at the towers.

The children work to construct towers with the linking cubes. They discuss how many of each color and compare and contrast one another's towers. In this scenario, notice how the teacher was strategic in giving out the button sets. The teacher wanted the students to have specific combinations of four to set the foundation for optimal comparisons. The task of *being a detective* offers the children an opportunity to engage in a higher LCD that requires analysis. The question about describing the sets with numbers serves as an invitation to communicate at a higher level. The children in this classroom communicate with each other, asking questions and speaking directly to one another during the task. The final task of showing the same number combinations with towers allows the students to take the communication to an even higher level through the models they construct and the surrounding math discourse. The teacher's role is one of providing challenge by increasing the LCD in multiple ways.

Adjusting LCD in Connections

See:
Algebra, p. 54
Data, p. 75
Geometry, p. 81
Measurement, p. 76

Connections in mathematics involve links both between math and other content areas and links within mathematics among different concepts. "Mathematics is not a collection of separate strands or standards, even though it is often partitioned and presented in this manner. Rather, mathematics is an integrated field of study" (National Council of Teachers of Mathematics 2000, 64).

Number and operations are connected to many topics outside of mathematics such as science, art, literacy, social studies, physical education, music, and technology. Helping students make these connections enhances their understanding and application of number and operations. Number and operations are also connected to all other math content standards in multiple ways. For example, the ties between number and algebra are especially profound. Using math models to represent and understand quantitative relationships is an algebra concept that is completely embedded in number relationships and relationships of operations. Other connections within the standards may appear less direct until one takes a closer look. Geometry, for example, may seem like a very different field of study when compared to number and operations. Yet shapes are distinguished and understood by the number of sides and angles. Measurement is interwoven with geometry, but is grounded in number and operations. Likewise, sets of data are only understood because of the connection to number relationships and relationships of operations. Helping students understand these and other connections provides ways to adjust the LCD when differentiating instruction in mathematics.

In a nutshell, if the connections are simple, the LCD is low. If the connections are complex, the LCD is high. Teachers need to adjust the levels based on the specific needs of the students.

A class of second graders is working on fractions. The teacher has preassessed the students and learned that some need a higher LCD and others need a lower LCD. Yet the teacher plans for all of the students to grow in their understanding of fractions and making connections.

The class is given this prompt: *How did we use fractions and other math concepts in this morning's cooking experience?* All students are to address this question by talking to their cooking partners, writing independently in their math journals, sharing what they have written with their partners, and adding clarifying illustrations to the math writing. While the students are writing, Ms. Hampton meets with five students to provide extra support. Ms. Hampton displays the recipe (see Figure 5–2).

The students look at the recipe and discuss the fractions that they see, focusing on ½ and ¾. Ms. Hampton asks, "Did we use more mini–chocolate chips or more mini-marshmallows?" The students are not sure. Ms. Hampton asks, "How can we use a representation to compare the fractions?" One of the students responds, "Let's use fraction circles," as she gets up to retrieve the box of fraction circles. After she returns with the manipulatives, the children use the fraction circles to show ½ and ¾. Ms. Hampton prompts the students to make connections by drawing a number line labeled 0–1. Ms. Hampton asks, "Where does ½ go on this number line?" The students decide that it goes *exactly* in the middle, explaining that it is halfway between 0 and 1. Ms. Hampton asks, "Where does ¾ go?" The students take some time to think about this. One student says, "Well, it has to go after ½." Ms. Hampton asks, "How do you know that?" The student responds (pointing at the circle fractions), "Because you can see it is bigger than ½." The other children in the group agree and decide it goes *exactly* be-

Sweet Cream Sandwiches

½ cup mini-chocolate chips
¾ cup mini-marshmallows
2 cups whipped topping
1 box of graham crackers

Stir together the first three ingredients in a large bowl. Mix well. Place two spoonfuls of sweet cream mixture onto one graham cracker square. Cover the mixture with another graham cracker (to form a sandwich). Form other sandwiches with the rest of the sweet cream mixture. Put sandwiches into the freezer for approximately 1½ hours or until frozen.

Serve frozen.

Figure 5–2 *Ms. Hampton's Recipe for Working with Fractions*

tween ½ and 1. As one student explains, "It is half more than ½, so it goes halfway between ½ and 1." The teacher adjusts the LCD to allow the children to make connections with the cooking experience and make connections within the mathematics by comparing and ordering the fractions using number sense and measurement.

Before Ms. Hampton meets with the next group, she walks around the classroom checking on the other students' math writing and sharing progress. She offers suggestions, answers questions, and redirects a couple of students. Ms. Hampton now calls the next group to work with her at the back table. This group has a strong understanding of fractions. She offers the group a task that requires a higher LCD by posing more sophisticated connections. Ms. Hampton asks, "If you needed to make three times as many sweet cream sandwiches, how much of each ingredient would you need?" The students discuss the question. Ms. Hampton gives the following task: "Considering that you want to triple the recipe, work together to write an equation for each ingredient. Add illustrations to explain your thinking." The students begin working on the task. Ms. Hampton helps the students connect fractions, number sense, number relationships, and operations to the cooking experience by asking questions and guiding the students through the task. Ms. Hampton teaches the students how to multiply fractions using repeated addition. After the task is completed, the students go back to writing in their math journals.

Ms. Hampton meets with the third group of second graders who showed that they have a mid-range understanding on the preassessment. Ms. Hampton uses a combination of the two previous groups' connections tasks for this group. The students use the fraction circles to double the recipe. Ms. Hampton guides the students through as they use models to add fractions. The LCD required is not too high and not too low—just right for this group of students.

Adjusting LCD in Representations

See:
Algebra, p. 56
Data, p. 78
Geometry, p. 83
Measurement, p. 79

Representation is the way students show their math thinking and develop new understanding. This process standard is closely linked to communication. The representations students use often either become the communication of math thinking or enhance it. "Teachers should analyze students' representations and carefully listen to their discussions to gain insights into the development of mathematical thinking and to enable them to provide support as students connect their languages to the conventional language of mathematics" (National Council of Teachers of Mathematics 2000, 136). Representation offers another way to adjust the LCD as we differentiate instruction in mathematics. Basically, a lower LCD is required when the representation is clearly defined, teacher-initiated, and teacher-directed. A higher LCD is required when the representation is open-ended, student-generated, and student-monitored.

First graders are learning about number relationships and computation with skip counting by tens. When Ms. Dudley works with the whole group, she leads them in rote counting from zero to one hundred. The students clap to the rhythm of the rote count together several times. After some whole class discussion about what it means to count by tens and how skip counting can be applied to specific mathematics situations, Ms. Dudley explains and demonstrates the assignment. The students will work with partners playing a skip counting game.

After getting the dyads (groups of two) started with the game, Ms. Dudley meets with some students who already know how to skip count by tens from zero to one hundred. Ms. Dudley increases the LCD within the areas of representation and computation for this group of students by asking them if it is possible to say the number thirty-one when orally skip counting by tens. After a brief discussion, Ms. Dudley explains that their task is to develop three different ways to show skip counting by tens starting with one. The group decides that they could use the large classroom hundred chart and a small desk-size hundred chart. Ms. Dudley offers a few questions to the group to help them understand that even though the sizes of the charts are different, the representation on the charts may actually be the same. One of the students suggests using base-ten blocks to represent the skip counting. With a few questions from Ms. Dudley, the group discusses how the base-ten blocks could be used. In search of one other way to represent the skip counting, the students decide to go look at the shelf of math manipulatives. One of the children sees the plastic coins and poses an idea of using money. "Which coins should we use to skip count by tens starting with one?" After a brief discussion, the students decide to use dimes and pennies. After the group members display the three representations, Ms. Dudley explains how the game that she introduced to the class will be modified. Instead of skip counting by tens starting with zero, they will play the game of skip counting starting with different numbers (as generated by the 0–9 spinners that she gives to each pair of students). These students go back to the tables to play the modified version of the game that the rest of the class is playing.

After Ms. Dudley checks on the other students, providing direction and guidance, she meets with the group of students who need support in the area of skip counting. She separates the group into dyads and asks them to represent the skip count by tens pattern with translucent chips on number charts (0–50). The students work with their partners to place the chips on the appropriate numbers (0, 10, 20, 30, 40, and 50). Ms. Dudley asks, "How would you describe the pattern? How do you know where the chips should be placed?" The students use the representation to engage in a discussion about the number pattern. Notice that the teacher gives more explicit directions to this group. The students are still working on the same topics (computation and representation), but the LCD is suited to meet the needs of the students within each group.

Later in the day, two of the students approach Ms. Dudley and share, "We found another way to show skip counting. We're going to use towers of cubes. Can we work on it tomorrow?" The LCD has skyrocketed because the students are continuing and broadening the task without any guidance from the teacher. "When students seek new learning experiences in the absence of teacher direction, that is the ultimate transfer agency" (Kramer 2005). Differentiated instruction prompts powerful learning.

Levels of Thinking and Questioning

Good old Bloom

One of the best ways to quickly and effectively adjust the LCD in any math task is to use Bloom's taxonomy of cognitive domain (Bloom et al. 1956) to provide questions and promote thinking. Essentially the taxonomy provides a hierarchical list of what educators want students to learn, from basic to complex. From bottom to top the levels are knowledge, comprehension, application, analysis, and synthesis and evaluation. The original work by Bloom et al. (1956) indicated that the highest level is evaluation. More recent research (Anderson and Krathwohl 2001) indicates that synthesis is actually more complex than evaluation. I tend to agree, and think synthesizing requires a greater LCD because when you synthesize you incorporate evaluation as you create something new.

Using Bloom's taxonomy to adjust the level of cognitive demand in no way implies that some children should always work at the lowest levels. *All* children deserve to have opportunities to think at higher levels. We just need to present the levels of thinking at the right times for students as we differentiate the mathematics instruction.

Clarifying the Levels

Bloom referred to the lowest level as *knowledge* (I prefer to call this level *recall*). At this level students list, label, name, tell, identify, find, and define. Students are working at the most basic level when they learn something by rote and memorization. At the next level, *comprehension*, students describe, summarize, compute, order, and explain. The level of understanding has increased beyond memorization and there is a more solid degree of understanding. At the *application* level students apply, use, show, demonstrate, and solve. Now the level of understanding has moved up a notch because students utilize the information in other contexts. At the *analysis* level students analyze, classify, connect, compare, and contrast. Students begin to manipulate the information in ways that help them reach greater levels of knowing. When students *evaluate* they critique, judge, assess, recommend, prioritize, and justify. They use critical thinking to ascertain higher levels of understanding. When students *synthesize* they create, invent, imagine, redesign, and rearrange. Now the knowledge takes on renewed intensity because students take the known parts and reconstruct the information into something new.

Some educators view the six levels as three levels—grouping recall with comprehension, application with analysis, and synthesis with evaluation. In this view, the levels of cognitive demand are more compact and easier to manage. Years ago I was teaching a graduate-level pedagogy course to math educators and, musing on the levels of cognitive demand, arranged the three levels in a stacked version, as shown in Figure 5–3.

It is interesting to me that when the levels of cognitive demand are viewed in this manner, you readily notice the direct increases in sophistication. Look at the left side of the graphic. Recall is remembering, but not using the information. When you utilize the things that you remember you move to application. When you heighten the application, you synthesize—taking all known parts to create something new. Looking at the right side of the graphic gives you another hierarchical perspective. Comprehension begins the understanding process. When you comprehend more deeply, you can analyze the information. After you successfully analyze, you can move to the greater intensity required to evaluate the information.

Using Questions at Different Levels

Questioning is one of the most important crafts that successful math teachers possess. Asking questions allows the teacher to adjust the level of intensity in

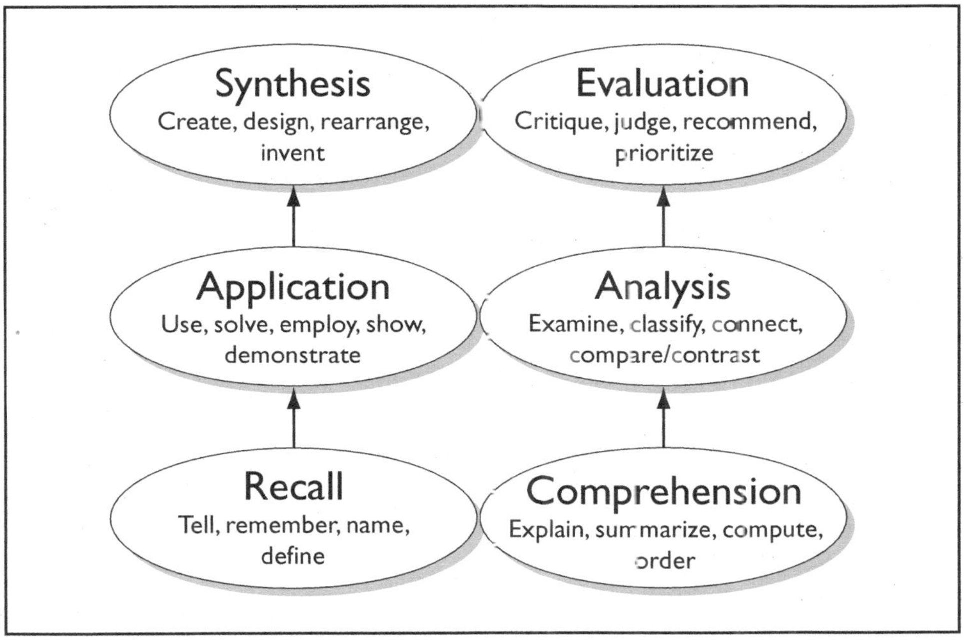

Figure 5–3 *Using Bloom et al.'s Taxonomy to Adjust the Level of Cognitive Demand to Differentiate Mathematics Instruction*

a quick and effective manner. When we notice that students need a challenge, we can give them a higher-level question to chew on. When we see that students are frustrated with the task, we can decrease the complexity by asking a lower-level question. Sometimes questions are posed to the whole group. Many other times the questions serve as a way to differentiate instruction *on the fly* for small groups or even individuals. To do so, we need to be comfortable with the question types, meanings of each type, and possible prompts. I post the list in Figure 5–4 in my classroom.

Unfortunately many teachers ask most of their questions at the basic levels. Recall and comprehension questions are the most common in the mathematics classroom. Why? Well, these kinds of questions are easy to ask. They are less complex, so they take less time. It is easier to assess the answers because of the simplicity. It really is no wonder that in today's fast-paced math class, recall and comprehension questions are so prevalent. The problem is that children need to experience higher levels of thinking. Children need to do more than recall and comprehend—they need to apply, analyze, evaluate, and synthesize! They need to think at higher levels when it is the right time and in the right context. To be able to provide the right level of cognitive demand at the right time, we need to make sure we are comfortable with the levels of questioning. Suppose the teacher is working with a small group of students and thinks, *This is the right time for a synthesis question . . . umm . . . what is a synthesis*

Question Type	Meaning	Prompts
Synthesis	Restructure parts to make new whole	Design, Invent, Rearrange, Imagine, Create, Compose, Reorganize
Evaluation	Judge the value of something	Critique, Evaluate, Recommend, Prioritize, Assess, Judge
Analysis	Understand how parts relate	Analyze, Classify, Categorize, Connect, Compare, Contrast, Examine, Scrutinize
Application	Use knowledge in another situation	Demonstrate, Use, Show, Utilize, Employ, Apply, Solve
Comprehension	Basic understanding	Explain, Summarize, Compute, Order
Recall	Remember something learned	Tell, Recall, Remember, Recite

(Question types are from Bloom et al.'s taxonomy)

Figure 5–4 *Asking Questions to Differentiate Instruction in Mathematics*

question? We need to be ready. Honestly, you may start out by memorizing these prompts, but to own the knowledge you have to understand and use it to make it second nature. While many questions overlap levels, these are a few questions that can be used to elicit specific levels of thinking.

Recall: What is the answer?
Comprehension: How do you know?
Application: How can you use the information?
Analysis: How can you connect the ideas?
Evaluation: What do you recommend?
Synthesis: What if the situation was different?

The *what if* prompt is helpful when it comes to provoking synthesis. What if there were half as many? What if you started with five? What if the pattern changed? What if the number doubled? Using the *what if* prompt pushes the situation to something new and different. Questions such as these prompt thinking and enhance communication. Questions beyond recall help students solidify understanding and think about more than one right answer. The teacher who is a good questioner models when and how to ask questions. Ultimately we want students to learn to ask questions of each other, which will perpetuate and enhance rich mathematics discourse.

Sometimes we ask questions during instruction. Other times we ask questions prior to instruction. Still other times we ask questions after the instruction to help the math thinking continue beyond the lesson. Questions of all levels can be used strategically at various times to differentiate instruction.

Using the Levels to Differentiate Math Tasks

Levels of thinking

Bloom's levels can also be used to design tasks for students. If you know a group needs extra support with a concept, think about a task that helps them recall and comprehend. If you know a group needs a challenge, create a task that encourages them to analyze, evaluate, or synthesize. Again, this is not to say that certain children should only engage in low-level tasks. All children need to experience various levels at different times. However, if teachers are comfortable with Bloom's levels, they have an extensive source of ideas to use to differentiate instruction in mathematics. Let's look at one number and operations concept, *subtraction*, and see how it can be adjusted to the various levels of cognitive demand.

See:
Algebra, p. 58
Data, p. 79
Geometry, p. 84
Measurement, p. 81

Level 1 task: Define subtraction.
Level 2 task: Explain what subtraction means.
Level 3 task: Show how to subtract part of the total.
Level 4 task: Classify the types of subtraction.
Level 5 task: Recommend a way to teach subtraction to someone else.
Level 6 task: Create a new symbol for subtraction.

Using these tasks to differentiate instruction does not mean that all students will proceed through the tasks in consecutive order. Some groups of students may work on the first few levels, others may focus on the middle levels, and yet others may only work on the higher-level tasks. The important thing is that the children are given tasks that are appropriate for their particular level.

The levels of cognitive demand offer many windows of opportunity to differentiate instruction in mathematics. I am always in search of new ways to *bump up* the LCD or *tone down* the LCD to enable my students to better grasp the math that I am teaching. Ultimately my goal is for all students to receive just the right amount of support and challenge as they learn and grow.

CHAPTER 6

Learning Frameworks

Students' Learning Frameworks

Learning frameworks are unique

Learning frameworks provide channels for students to learn based on preferences, modalities, and interests and therefore offer teachers ways to target mathematics instruction. Learning frameworks include learning styles, multiple intelligences, environmental needs, affective needs, and interests. The field is vast and ever-evolving. New ideas and revisions on previous ideas continue to reach the forefront of educational research. Because addressing students' learning needs serves as a powerful tool in planning, implementing, and assessing differentiated mathematics instruction, many books have been written on this topic. Thus I will give here a brief summary of a select few learning frameworks, discuss some misconceptions, and share specific examples of how certain learning frameworks can be used to target instruction in number and operations for prekindergarten through second-grade students.

Learning Styles

Learning preferences are in style

The basic learning styles include visual, auditory, kinesthetic, and tactile. Visual learners prefer to look at something to help them learn. Auditory learners prefer to hear and speak to help them learn. Kinesthetic learners prefer to move around. Tactile learners prefer manipulating objects (Dunn, Dunn, and Price 1985). Using learning styles to target instruction involves knowing which students have which preferences and knowing how to incorporate the ways children learn best into the targeted mathematics instruction. To do so, we need to avoid some common misconceptions about learning styles.

Misconceptions About Learning Styles

Misconception 1: All instruction should include visuals because most children are visual learners. Not true. There may be some classes that have many visual learners, but that is not the case for all classes. Directing instruction toward only one learning style is not differentiating the instruction.

Misconception 2: Everyone has only one learning style. Not so. Some people have more than one learning style. Sometimes a learning style is dominant. Other times learning preferences involve combinations of learning styles that change based on the situation.

Misconception 3: Learning style preference will not change. While it is true that some people have preferences that last a lifetime, it is also true that some people (especially young people) adapt to their surroundings and can change learning styles.

Misconception 4: Kinesthetic and tactile are the same. Even though many publishers combine these two learning styles, they are not the same. Kinesthetic learners learn best by moving and doing—more focus is on gross motor skills. Tactile learners learn best by handling objects—more focus is on fine motor skills.

Misconception 5: Children should learn only through their learning style. We would be creating an artificial reality by having *all* learning occur in one learning style. We would also, as implementers of such plans, set ourselves up for unobtainable goals. Yet we can incorporate learning styles as we target instruction in small groups, when we tutor individuals, and when we offer process and product choices to all students.

Misconception 6: If I teach to all the learning styles, everyone will get what they need. This can lead to an overstimulated environment for some children.

There is no guarantee that each child will be able to pick out the modality that they need to use from all the presented styles. Differentiating instruction means using the learning style preferences that match specific children.

Misconception 7: Children know their own learning styles. Some children may know how they learn. Other children are not yet able to understand, let alone articulate, how they learn. There are many learning styles inventories available (look for the primary-level versions). Teachers should use these inventories to learn how their students best learn.

We can better implement targeted instruction incorporating learning style preferences if we address these misconceptions. To better understand how to use learning styles, we will look at an example concept and ways of modifying the instruction for different learning styles.

Incorporating Learning Styles

See:
Algebra, p. 59
Data, p. 80
Geometry, p. 85
Measurement, p. 83

The following classroom example (pp. 128–131) shows a first-grade class beginning a unit on fact families. The teacher understands that working with fact families helps children understand operations, relationships of operations, and math properties. The teacher has assessment data that indicate the students' learning styles.

Visual Learners Work with Fact Families

When the teacher meets with the students who are visual learners, she displays a part-whole graphic of eight octagons, as shown in Figure 6–1. Five of the octagons are black and three of the octagons are gray. The total number of octagons is eight. The students work with the fact family of 5, 3, and 8 using the arrangement of the octagons to visualize the basic facts in the fact family.

The students use the part-whole display to add the black and gray octagons, recording 5 + 3 = 8. They add the gray and black octagons together and record 3 + 5 = 8. The students visualize the whole (8) and subtract the black part, recording 8 – 5 = 3. Then they subtract the gray part and record

Figure 6–1

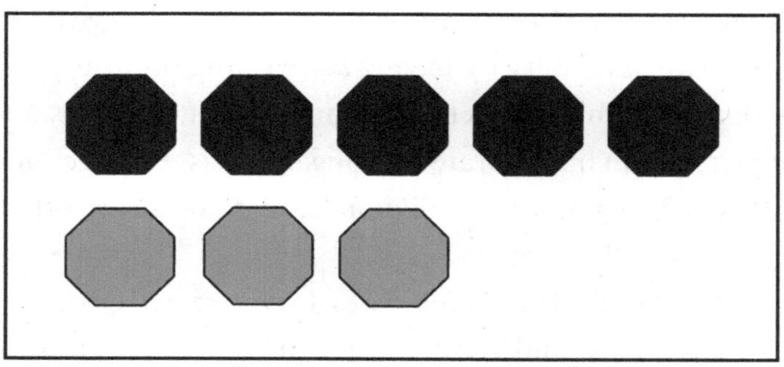

8 – 3 = 5. One of the students shares with the group that the way the octagons are displayed reminds him of the ten frame. He knows that the total is 8 because the first row is filled (5) and the second row needs 2 more to be filled. Several other students agree. The teacher encourages the students to draw other part-whole graphics using different shapes. In this small group lesson, the students are able to use their visual preferences to help them understand fact families.

Auditory Learners Work with Fact Families

When the teacher meets with the auditory learners the focus is on sound, pitch, and voice. Using a template as a springboard (see Figure 6–2), the teacher begins a chant with the students.

> *Teacher:* Who's in the family? Who's in the family?
>
> *Students:* Five and three and eight!
>
> *Teacher (using a high-pitched voice):* What is upstairs? What is upstairs?

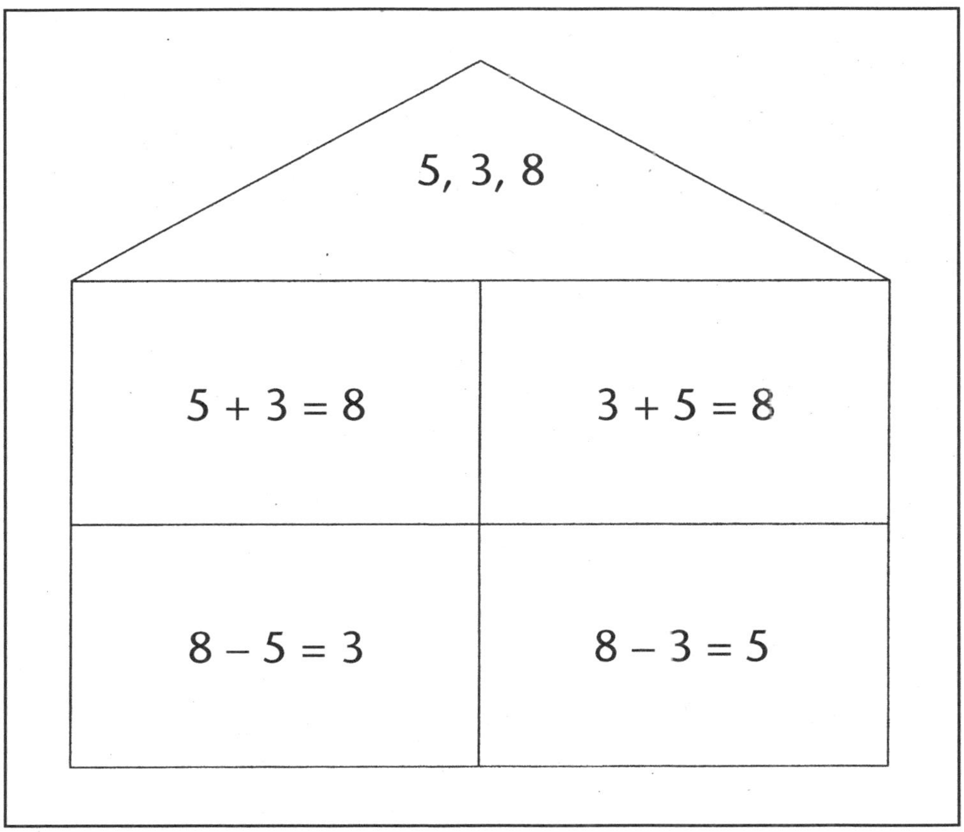

Figure 6–2

Students (mimicking the high-pitched voice): 5 + 3 = 8 and 3 + 5 = 8.

Teacher (using a low-pitched voice): What is downstairs? What is downstairs?

Students (mimicking the low-pitched voice): 8 – 5 = 3 and 8 – 3 = 5.

The chant prompts the students to think about the numbers in the fact family and the addition and subtraction equations that connect the numbers. The different voice pitches help the students hear the relationships of the operations and properties. The students use their auditory preferences to help them understand fact families.

Kinesthetic Learners Work with Fact Families

The kinesthetic learners are asked to show the 5, 3, 8 fact family using chairs. The teacher prompts the students in the group to use their gross motor skills to carry 8 chairs to the center of the classroom. The teacher asks, "How can we show part 5 and part 3 with the chairs?" The students decide to have 5 students sit in chairs and have 3 empty chairs. The students demonstrate each aspect of the fact family.

5 full chairs + 3 empty chairs = 8 chairs
3 empty chairs + 5 full chairs = 8 chairs
8 chairs – 5 full chairs = 3 empty chairs
8 chairs – 3 empty chairs = 5 full chairs

The students in this group use their kinesthetic preferences to understand fact families.

Tactile Learners Work with Fact Families

The tactile learners work with the teacher at the back table using linking cubes to construct towers. The towers are made using five cubes of one color and three cubes of another color. The teacher encourages the students to put together and break apart the fact family. The students use hands-on experiences to understand fact families.

In this first-grade example, the learning style preferences were addressed in ways that helped the children better understand fact families. The instruction was targeted to meet the learning needs of the students. Additionally, each group created a final product that reflected the learning style preference—the visual group created pictures, the auditory group created a chant, the kinesthetic group created a dramatic role-play, and the tactile group created three-dimensional towers.

Multiple Intelligences

My MI

The work of Howard Gardner (1983, 1993) in the field of multiple intelligences has had a profound influence on instructional practices. Gardner opened up the door to understanding intelligence as multifaceted rather than one set of criteria. Currently nine distinct intelligences are recognized. The profile of each learner is like a list of personal ingredients—one part this intelligence, two parts that intelligence, ½ part of another intelligence. This personalized list of intelligences defines each learner's ways of knowing. Understanding students' intelligences in terms of strengths and weaknesses allows educators to target instruction in ways that are most beneficial to students. Each intelligence serves as another way that a particular child may understand or demonstrate new knowledge. The following is a list of the current intelligences in multiple intelligence (MI) theory and a simple *I like* statement for each intelligence:

Word smart (verbal-linguistic intelligence): I like working with words.
Number smart (logical-mathematical intelligence): I like working with number sense and logic.
Picture smart (visual-spatial intelligence): I like working with pictures and drawing.
Body smart (body-kinesthetic intelligence): I like working with my physical skills.
Music smart (musical-rhythmic intelligence): I like working with music and patterns.
People smart (interpersonal intelligence): I like working with others.
Self smart (intrapersonal intelligence): I like working by myself.
Nature smart (natural intelligence): I like working with nature and being outside.
Wondering smart (existential intelligence): I like working with wondering questions.

Using MI theory to target instruction involves knowing which students have which strengths and knowing how to incorporate the ways children learn best into the mathematics instruction. To do so, we need to avoid some common misconceptions about multiple intelligences.

Misconceptions About Multiple Intelligences

Misconception 1: There is no need to implement MI theory in mathematics because logical-mathematical is one of the intelligences. On the contrary, utilizing MI theory to target mathematics instruction opens doors to new levels of understanding. Everyone can learn math even without a high logical-mathematical intelligence.

Misconception 2: Intelligences do not change. This is not true. Intelligences can change. People may have a particular intelligence strength for a while, and then another intelligence may increase. Inventories are helpful, but they serve as a snapshot of how a person learns. Learning profiles can change.

Misconception 3: All children have one dominant intelligence. Not true. MI theory proposes that each learner has a personal intelligence profile that is made up of combinations of some or all of the nine different intelligences. There is not one dominant intelligence for everyone.

Misconception 4: You can't strengthen an intelligence. Yes, you can. By working specific parts of the brain as we engage in particular activities and experiences we can strengthen certain intelligences.

Misconception 5: MI theory just labels kids. The identification of an intelligence strength should be used to empower learners, not to pigeonhole learners by labeling them. Understanding how students learn best opens doors for increased levels of performance.

Misconception 6: MI theory replaces a rigorous curriculum. Not true. MI theory is not a curriculum; it is a theory that can be used in tandem with the implementation of a rigorous, standards-based curriculum.

Addressing these misconceptions and others will help us better implement MI theory as we target mathematics instruction for all students. To better understand how to use MI theory, we will look at an example concept and the different ways of differentiating the instruction.

Incorporating Multiple Intelligences

See:
Algebra, p. 60
Data, p. 82
Geometry, p. 86
Measurement, p. 86

In a second-grade class the students are learning about fractions. The students have participated in a recent inventory of multiple intelligences and the teacher grouped students by likenesses in intelligences. During the lesson the teacher serves as a facilitator, moving from group to group answering and asking questions, advising, assisting, and directing. All groups are given the same three fractions ($1/5$, $2/4$, $3/3$) and asked to explain how they are ordered from smallest to largest. However, each group is asked to solve the problem (*showing the knowing*) in a different way.

Showing the Knowing in the Word Smart Group

Four students show strengths in word smart (verbal-linguistic intelligence). Their task is to create and tell a story about the fractions. The students sketch pictures of the fractions and compare the sizes as they confirm the order and develop the story. Here is the story the group creates, revises, and eventually tells to the class.

> Three little fractions were sitting on a fence. The first one is the smallest. He is one-fifth. The next one is two-fourths. We know she is next because she has a twin sister named one-half. The last one is the biggest. He is three-thirds. He is the whole thing. The end.

Showing the Knowing in the Number Smart Group

Five students are high in number smart (logical-mathematical intelligence). These students work on comparing the fractions. Using fraction circles, they reveal several things.

$1/5$ is smaller than $2/4$
$2/4$ is smaller than $3/3$
$2/4$ is the same as $1/2$
$3/3$ is the same as 1

The teacher offers the students the <, >, and = symbols to incorporate into their answers. The second-grade curriculum the teacher uses does not focus on fraction notation or the < and > symbols, but the teacher knows that these students are ready to try working with these concepts. The students use their logical-mathematical intelligence to successfully display the fraction comparison.

$1/5 < 2/4$
$2/4 > 1/5$
$2/4 < 3/3$
$3/3 > 2/4$
$2/4 = 1/2$
$3/3 = 1$

Showing the Knowing in the Picture Smart Group

Four students indicated some strength in picture smart (visual-spatial intelligence). They were given the task of making pictures of the fractions and creating a diagram. The students drew pictures on separate sticky notes and moved around these pictures as they compared the fractions. After a few revisions, they developed the chart in Figure 6–3.

The students displayed the fractions in a way that encouraged visual comparisons of the fractions.

Showing the Knowing in the Body Smart/Music Smart/People Smart Group

Three body smart (body-kinesthetic intelligence) students, two music smart (musical-rhythmic intelligence) students, and two people smart (interpersonal intelligence) students were grouped together and given the task of creating a game to describe and explain the order of the fractions.

With some guidance from the teacher, three of the students held fraction pictures and the other children in the group moved them into various orders. Each time they placed the students (holding fraction pictures) in order, they explained why the order was correct or incorrect. The group included sound effects (similar to those on game shows) be-

Figure 6–3

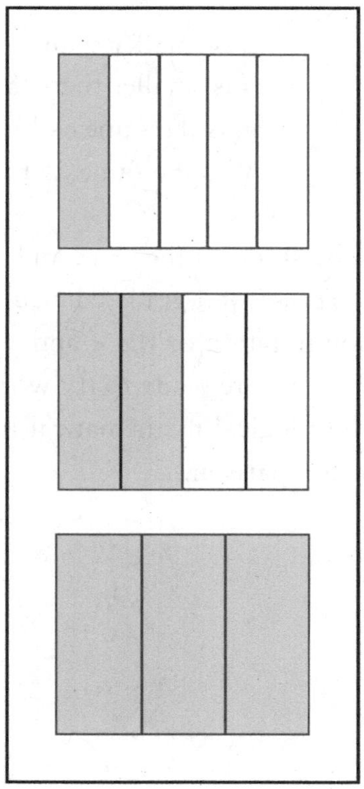

tween each question and answer period. The students incorporated music, large motor skills, and interpersonal skills to show what they know about fractions.

Showing the Knowing in the Nature Smart/Wondering Smart Group

The final group consisted of nature smart (natural-intelligence) and wondering smart (existential-intelligence) students. The students were asked to connect the fractions to something in nature. They were also asked to think of questions to *wonder* about. These students used circle fractions that they referred to as various phases of the moon. Each *moon* was given a fraction name and placed in order. The group explained the order and offered thoughts about the *moons* that would fit between the fractions in the given sequence.

In this second-grade example, the multiple intelligences were used as a means of *showing the knowing*. The students demonstrated understanding via their individual and combined personal strengths. The instruction was targeted to meet the learning needs of the students because the tasks and products were matched to specific intelligences.

Environmental Needs

The impact of our surroundings

Environmental needs include (but are not limited to) preferences regarding sound, light, temperature, and classroom design. The idea of attending to environmental needs is part of a learning style model developed by Dunn and Griggs (2000) for higher education. I find that these environmental preferences also exist among young children.

Some children prefer a quiet environment, while others learn better when there is sound around them. Sound can distract or focus children as they work in the classroom. What we need to do is find out how each child learns best. By analyzing performance and making interpretive connections to the environment, teachers can learn how sound influences learning for specific children. If a child hums to himself while working on a task he may either need sound to help him concentrate—or he might be superseding other sounds that he finds distracting. Teachers need to observe children. Teachers also need to talk to children to help them describe optimal learning situations regarding sound. The teacher may ask these and other questions: "Do you work best when it is quiet or when there is noise? Are there any sounds that distract you?

What does learning sound like to you?" When we find out which children prefer quiet and which children prefer noise, we can make adjustments in seating arrangements and locations of activities that will help students be successful.

The lighting of the classroom can influence how children learn. Concentration can be increased for some children with bright overhead lighting, but some children concentrate better with soft lighting. Some florescent lighting can actually increase hyperactivity in some children (Dunn, Dunn, and Price 1985). Given these and other findings associated with light and learning, it is important to consider lighting as we target mathematics instruction. We can adjust the setting to accommodate students' lighting preferences. Teachers can create workstations that are located by windows or lamps. The adjustments we make for students regarding lighting can have a positive impact on learning and performance.

As with lighting, temperature can affect learning. Some children like it warm when they are learning. Other children find it easier to concentrate when the temperature is cooler (Hart 1981). I have had the miserable experience of teaching in classrooms where it was so hot that I felt as if I couldn't breathe. The air conditioner was broken (or nonexistent, in some cases), yet the school day moved forward. Some children are just as uncomfortable as I was in extremely hot temperatures; other children seem unaffected. Likewise, some classrooms are too cold for learners. We need to find out which students prefer which temperatures. In some classrooms, the temperature is controlled by a central system rather than by the teacher in the classroom. In these cases, we need to encourage children to wear clothing that will help them adjust to the given temperatures.

How the classroom is designed can also affect how children learn. Some children are inspired by brightly colored decorations and classrooms filled with furniture and workstations. Other children find these environments to be overstimulating or congested. We need to observe students to learn if our classroom furniture, decorations, and other arrangements encourage learning or distract children. For example, in one first-grade classroom the teacher displayed children's work by hanging the work from the ceiling. One student spent much of his time blowing the paper that hung over his desk. In another classroom, the students were encouraged to use manipulatives to solve math problems, but the manipulatives were not accessible because they were kept in the closet under the paper supply. Children need easy access to supplies and they should see their work displayed; yet we need to keep in mind that some children could be distracted or frustrated by the location of supplies or displays.

The location and amount of furniture in the classroom can also serve to disrupt, distract, or bore students. Sometimes there is just too much furniture and at other times classrooms appear desolate. To create an optimal learning environment for students, teachers need to observe student performance and behaviors in relation to how the classroom is arranged and make adjustments accordingly.

Misconceptions About Environmental Needs

Misconception 1: All children need a quiet classroom to think. Not true. Many children actually need background noise to help them concentrate. Some children are distracted by sounds and others are not influenced by sound in the classroom.

Misconception 2: Bright lights will help all children focus. Unfortunately there is no magic formula for all children. Some children learn best when the lighting is bright, while this distracts others who prefer soft or natural lighting.

Misconception 3: The temperature in the classroom does not affect learning. This is not true. Hot temperatures and cold temperatures can influence concentration. Furthermore, students have different preferences regarding temperature.

Misconception 4: If the teacher moves things around in the classroom, the students will be upset or confused. This is not necessarily true. Students are often more flexible than we are when it comes to changes in the classroom environment. If something is distracting a child, we need to move it. If the mathematics manipulatives or other supplies are not easily accessible, we need to relocate them. If there is too much furniture, we need to find a way to remove it. The classroom arrangement influences learning and we want to set students up for success.

Misconception 5: Children must always work at desks/tables to keep the classroom organized. Not true. Some children may work best while seated on the floor. Other children prefer tables. We need to find out the students' specific preferences. This is not to say that some children will not have a desk. Each child needs a *home base* location, which is often a desk or specific seat at a table. During the course of the day, children work in their *home base* locations at times and other times children work in different locations.

Misconception 6: Children cannot distribute and organize materials. The teacher must do it. I definitely played the waitress role when I first started teaching. I brought supplies to children. I collected and distributed everything. I spent so much time being the waitress, that I had less time to be the teacher. Now I have turned many of these responsibilities over to my students. The students pass out supplies. The students go get the manipulatives that they need.

They put away the materials. They keep our math manipulatives organized. No, it is not perfect—and sometimes *we* have to reorganize things—but the time I can devote to teaching has increased! Moreover, the students often have excellent ideas for how to organize the materials and the environment. These ideas are often manifestations of environmental preferences.

Addressing these misconceptions and others will help us better implement environmental preferences as we target mathematics instruction for students. To better understand how to use environmental preferences, we will look at an example of how to target mathematics instruction.

Incorporating Environmental Needs

See:
Algebra, p. 63
Data, p. 85
Geometry, p. 88

In a kindergarten classroom the teacher strives to target mathematics instruction based on environmental preferences. The teacher has established various *neighborhoods* in the classroom, including the *quiet neighborhood*, the *soft-light neighborhood*, the *warm neighborhood*, and the *open-space neighborhood*. The *quiet neighborhood* is located in the back of the classroom where there is less movement and activity. The students understand that when they are working in this neighborhood, the goal is to work quietly. The *soft-light neighborhood* has a table, with a tablecloth and a lamp. The students know that when they work in this neighborhood, they are encouraged to use the lighting from the lamp to help them concentrate on the task at hand. The *warm neighborhood* is located by the heater. This is the warmest spot in the classroom. The children know that the temperature in this neighborhood is a bit higher than the temperature in other neighborhoods. (The *warm neighborhood* changes to the *cool neighborhood* when the weather gets warmer and the air conditioner is turned on!) The *open-space neighborhood* is located in the spacious front of the classroom. This area is also used for whole group time because it is a place where the whole class can be seated comfortably together.

Sometimes children choose to work in a specific neighborhood during independent work times. Other times the teacher directs children to try out a certain neighborhood when working. At the end of the day, the teacher guides a discussion about the specific environmental needs that can be met in various neighborhoods in the classroom. The children reflect upon their learning experiences related to the environmental characteristics of the neighborhoods.

Affective Needs

Effective attention to affective needs

The affective needs of learners include feelings, emotions, and self-esteem. These affective dimensions impact learning to a large extent. How children feel in the classroom can be connected to both their immediate and distant experiences. At any given time children may feel happy, sad, enthusiastic, anxious, receptive, grumpy, courageous, concerned, relaxed, sensitive, fascinated, sympathetic, tenacious, discouraged, surprised, desperate, impulsive, or indifferent. As teachers, we need to tend to the different feelings children have in ways that help their productivity. Often it is helpful to give students a venue for expressing feelings and emotions, because in this way students are encouraged to deal with them. Our job is not to hide the feelings students have; the students need to be given the opportunity to express and work through their feelings and emotions. We differentiate instruction as we give students avenues to express feelings and emotions.

As Caine and Caine note, "We do not simply learn. What we learn is influenced and organized by emotions and mind sets based on expectancy, personal biases and prejudices, degree of self-esteem, and the need for social interaction" (1991, 82). Therefore we need to give learners the opportunity to express feelings and emotions in ways that help them connect to learning situations.

Self-esteem is related to learning. When students feel good about themselves, they are more available for learning. They try new things, think about solutions in new ways, and accept the challenges that may go along with learning new things. Conversely, students who think poorly of themselves do not tackle new problems or try new ways of solving problems. They often shut down and become unavailable to learning. In our attempt to help students feel better about themselves, we often offer praise. While praise can be positive, it can also be empty and consequently unproductive. There are numerous posters and charts available that enumerate *100 Ways to Praise a Child*. The problem with many of these phrases is that they are too general to be meaningful. When we notice a student struggling with a concept, we may be inclined to encourage the child. If we say, "You are doing some good work," our intended praise may actually have a negative effect. The child may know his work is not the best because he is having difficulty. Our praise may actually send the message that poor work is good enough. Or worse yet, that our expectations for the child are very low. To reverse the potential negative effects in this situation, we would be better off to say, "I know this work is difficult. I like the way you are sticking with it and not giving up." These statements affirm the child's dedication and effort in ways that build the child's confidence and self-esteem. The comments are more specific to the behavior and intentions, and are therefore more likely to help the child's self-esteem. In essence, we need to differentiate the praise we give to students. The one-size-fits-all "Good job!" is not productive. We need to address specific behaviors, strategies, and decisions as we offer praise to children as a means for increasing self-esteem.

Differentiating mathematics instruction according to the affective needs of students is responsive teaching. "When students feel affirmation, affiliation, a sense of contribution, growing autonomy, accomplishment, and shared responsibility for the welfare of the group, the 'climate' for learning is good" (Tomlinson and McTighe 2006, 18). We want students to try new things, take a risk, and ultimately increase their knowledge and understanding. To do so, the students need to feel safe and they need to feel a strong, positive sense of classroom community. They need to know that their feelings will be accepted and respected. They need to feel good about their accomplishments and their attempts. As teachers, we need to be sensitive and aware as we target mathematics instruction based upon the affective needs of our students.

Misconceptions About Affective Needs

Misconception 1: Focusing on feelings and emotions is a waste of time. Absolutely not! While many of us are heavily burdened with curriculum pacing, we simply cannot leave out the emotional aspects. Students have emotions and feelings and we may end up spending more time trying to cover up repeatedly surfacing emotions than we will actually dealing with the emotions. Accepting students' feelings and emotions is the first step in differentiating instruction by students' affective needs.

Misconception 2: Feelings and emotions always impede learning. This is false. Feelings and emotions can actually enhance learning. Allowing children the opportunity to express their emotions and feelings encourages learning.

Misconception 3: Saying "Good job" to a student will increase the student's self-esteem. Not necessarily. Many teachers with good intentions try this mode of building self-esteem. Yet the general nature of the expression often leaves students feeling confused or artificially inflated. Our praise needs to be specific and sincere if our intentions are to increase students' self-esteem.

Misconception 4: We don't have time to build a strong, positive sense of classroom community. Honestly, we don't have time not to do so. The time invested in building an affirmative classroom community is well worth it. To enable students to share where they are in their learning journeys, we have to establish safe, inviting, and comfortable classroom environments.

Misconception 5: Responsive teaching is not proactive. Not true. Responding to students' affective needs involves making adjustments on the fly. While we can be proactive as we anticipate some potential needs, we are often in the thick of things when we realize we need to make adjustments. We need to accept that responding to the needs of all learners means that there are times when we should react to situations in ways that are helpful to learners.

Addressing these misconceptions and others will help us better implement affective needs as we target mathematics instruction for all students. To better understand how to incorporate affective needs, we will look at an example of how to use affective needs to target mathematics instruction.

Incorporating Affective Needs

See:
Algebra, p. 64
Data, p. 85
Geometry, p. 89
Measurement, p. 89

In a prekindergarten classroom, the students and the teacher use *I messages* to convey feelings and emotions. While many teachers implement *I messages* (a strategy developed by Gordon 1974) in their classrooms, not all teachers use *I messages* to target instruction in mathematics. The power behind *I messages* are that they are the opposite of *you messages* and therefore encourage the other person rather than making the person feel defensive. When Michael says to Eddie, "You messed up my number," Eddie may feel the need to defend his actions. However, if Michael says, "When you mess up my number I have to fix it and I feel frustrated," Eddie is invited to understand Michael's feelings and change his behavior. Notice that the *I message* includes three parts—a description of the behavior or situation, a description of the effect the behavior has on the speaker, and the attached personal feeling. Because *I messages* are nonjudgmental and straightforward, they serve as effective means of communicating feelings (Gordon 1974).

After many years of using *I messages*, I tweaked the order of the components in the *I message* to better meet the needs of young children. The feeling comes first, then the behavior, followed by the effect (i.e., I feel __________ when you __________ because I ___________). The teacher models the use of the *I message* prompt and encourages students to use the prompt to explain their feelings.

One way to target mathematics instruction by the affective needs of students is to use *I messages* to make adjustments in learning situations.

In a prekindergarten classroom, two children (Maria and Lynette) are using one-to-one correspondence to set the table for the class to have a snack. Maria has taken all of the plates and napkins and is setting the table without including Lynette. The teacher sees what is happening and encourages Lynette to use an *I message* to share her feelings with Maria. With the teacher's help, Lynette says, "I feel mad when you take it all because I have nothing." Maria looks at her armful of plates and napkins and says, "Sorry. Here, you can do the napkins." Lynette happily takes the napkins and follows Maria setting one napkin beside each plate.

In this way, the *I message* prompted a change in the learning situation based on the affective needs of Lynette and allowed the mathematics learning to take place, highlighting yet another way to target mathematics instruction in the prekindergarten through second-grade classroom.

Interests

The interesting things about interests

Children have varying interests. These interests motivate and inspire children to learn mathematics. Our goal is to engage children in mathematics learning. Using students' interests to target mathematics instruction is a powerful tool. Differentiating instruction by interest does not begin with who is *interested in math* and who is *not*. The interests we need to uncover are students' personal interests that we can use to *hook* students into learning situations.

Several years ago I was talking with a first-grade teacher who told me all about her space theme. She had a large display of the solar system in the classroom. The students spent several weeks connecting all of the disciplines (reading, writing, social studies, science, and mathematics) to the topic of space. They incorporated mathematics by finding patterns, measuring, using geometric properties, and applying number sense and computation to various authentic and contrived situations. When I visited the classroom, I was amazed with all of the connections to mathematics the class had made. I commented to one of the students, "Wow. Your class is really interested in space." The student responded, "Not really, but Ms. Kelley sure is." This response helped me realize that although connecting to interests can be powerful, we need to make sure it is the students' interests (not the teacher's) that are incorporated.

Some interests that children have are relatively constant while others are situational (Renninger and Hidi 1992). These interests tie to the relevance any given learning situation has for a particular child. If the learning situation is relevant, the child is more likely to be engaged in the mathematics.

Teachers need to get to know their students. We can't assume that students have particular interests. Using interest inventories to reveal enduring interests is an excellent place to start. The following is a list of prompts that can be used to uncover the interests students have:

Things I like to do with my friends . . .
Things I like to do with my family . . .
Things I like to do by myself . . .
Things I like to collect . . .
Places I like to go . . .
Games or sports that I like to watch or play . . .
Pictures that make me happy . . .
Music that I like to listen to . . .

Teachers can send these prompts home with students as homework assignments to be completed independently or with parents. Other times the prompts can be used in journal writing assignments or paired discussion times. The teacher can use the information gathered to create interest tasks to target instruction in mathematics (see Figure 6–4).

To uncover situational interests that students have, teachers need to observe behaviors and listen to conversations students have about the mathematics learning. Situational interests may be sparked due to a new math manipulative or a new authentic task that is deemed important by the students. Or there may be a circumstance that the class is faced with that evokes particular interest.

As teachers connect mathematics to students' enduring and situational interests, they are using the children's learning frameworks to differentiate instruction.

Misconceptions About Interests

Misconception 1: The teacher's interests are the same as the students' interests. Not necessarily true. Sometimes students have the same interests as their teacher. Most of the time the interests are not the same.

Misconception 2: Students' interests are collective. Rarely true. Typically, all the children in one classroom do not have the exact same interests. Although there are times that situational interests may be collective due to shared experiences, we cannot assume that all students are interested in the same thing.

Interest Inventory

Name ______________________________ Date ________________

Please answer the following questions.

1. What subject(s) do you like best in school?

   ____

2. Do you like to play sports? ________ What sports do you like to play?

   ____

3. What do you like to do with your free time? ______________________________

   ____

4. Do you like to play games (board games, dominoes, cards, etc.)? ______________

   What games do you like to play?

   ____

5. What do you do when you are at home?

   ____

6. Do you like to watch TV? What is your favorite TV show?

   ____

7. Do you like to listen to music? Do you like to sing?

   What are your favorite songs?

8. What do you like to eat?

   Where do you like to go out to eat?

Figure 6–4

9. What do you like to do with your friends after school?

____

10. What do you like to do on the weekend?

____

11. What do you like to do with your family?

____

12. If you had a million dollars, what would you do with it?

____

13. Do you like math? ________ Why or Why not?

____

14. What is your favorite number? ________ Why?

____

15. What is your favorite book? ________ Why?

____

16. Do you have any siblings? ________ If so, how old?

____

17. Do you collect anything? ________ If so, what?

____

18. Is there anything else you would like to share about yourself? Explain.

____

____

Figure 6–4 *Continued*

19. Draw a picture of something you like to do.

20. Draw a picture of something new you would like to try.

Figure 6–4 *Continued*

Misconception 3: Students' interests always remain constant. False. While enduring interests are more constant than situational interests, they can change. The child who was once mesmerized and engrossed with dinosaurs may eventually change his attention to some new topic of interest.

Misconception 4: Boys always have the same interests as other boys. Girls always have the same interests as other girls. Not true. Using stereotypical interests of genders is not a way to target instruction. It is false, for example, to assume that all boys like trucks and all girls like flowers.

Addressing these misconceptions and others will help us better implement interests as we target mathematics instruction for students. To better understand how to incorporate interests, we will look at an example concept and the associated ways of differentiating mathematics instruction.

Incorporating Interests

> Before the math lesson in a second-grade classroom, the teacher has each student write their favorite foods on pieces of paper. The teacher collects these papers and groups the students in twos and threes according to similar food interests.

See:
Algebra, p. 64
Data, p. 86
Geometry, p. 89
Measurement, p. 89

Because the math class is currently studying how to divide by partitioning sets, the teacher reads a book about sharing cookies called *The Doorbell Rang* (Hutchins 1986) to the whole class. The teacher incorporates the students' interests to target the mathematics instruction by having the students work in groups to write a similar story using their specific food interests.

One group writes about sharing pizza at a restaurant. Another group writes about sharing cake at a birthday party. Other groups write about candy, ice cream cones, hamburgers, chicken nuggets, and even macaroni and cheese. When the stories are shared, the other students in the class use dry-erase boards to represent the division in the stories.

Incorporating students' learning frameworks is a powerful mechanism for differentiating instruction in mathematics. Learning styles, multiple intelligences, environmental preferences, affective needs, and interests are ways to connect students with positive, prolific learning experiences. Students' motivation and commitment are increased as teachers incorporate learning frameworks.

CHAPTER 7

Personal Assessment

Using Graphic Organizers

Graph it!

Graphic organizers offer excellent ways to gather personal assessment information both for concepts and learning frameworks. Students indicate their level of comfort with or knowledge of a given topic by placing their names in specific locations on a graph. The teacher uses the information to target mathematics instruction. Exploring how specific graphic organizers can be used to target instruction does not imply that these are the *only* graphic organizers that can be used. We will take an in-depth look at a few examples, and hopefully spur your imagination to think of other graphic organizer possibilities.

T-Charts Show Personal Assessments of Number and Operations

See:
Algebra, p. 68
Data, p. 87
Geometry, p. 90
Measurement, p. 90

One of the most basic graphic organizers is a simple yes/no chart. Using the yes/no labels in the form of a T-chart, students are asked if they are comfortable with a specific math situation. For example, during a unit on fact families with first graders, the teacher may give the numbers 6, 4, 10 and ask the students if they know how to write the equations in the fact family.

Each student places a name card in the *yes* or *no* column. Sometimes instead of name cards the class can use clothespins with one student name on each. Each clothespin is clipped on the *yes* or *no* side of the chart by the students. The teacher can take a quick look and see which students believe they need to review the topic and which students believe they need an additional challenge (see Figure 7–1).

Yes/No charts can be used before, during, and after instruction. The teacher may begin the lesson by asking the students to share their levels of comfort with a math concept. Or the teacher may ask students to place their names on the yes/no chart during the lesson to find out how the students are currently feeling about the topic. Other times the teacher might ask students to place

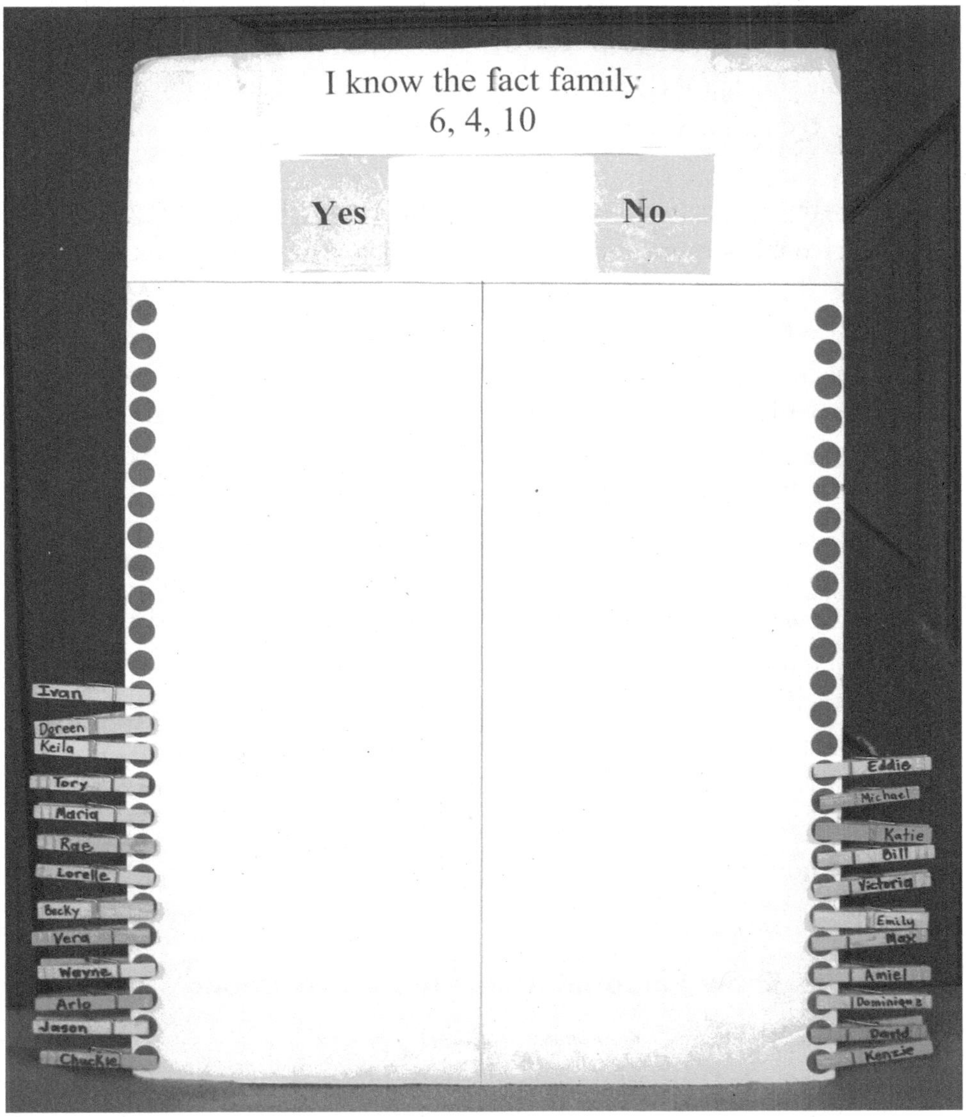

Figure 7–1 *A T-chart Used in a Class to Show Students' Knowledge*

names on the chart after the instruction. This information can be used to plan instruction for the next day.

> After working with her prekindergarteners on counting, the teacher asked the students to place their names on the yes/no chart. The question on the chart was *Can you count to 5?* The teacher read the chart to the students and asked them to place their name cards on the chart, as shown in Figure 7–2.
>
> Most of the children felt comfortable with counting to five. The teacher met with Aaron, Rozele, Calvin, and Amara in a small group setting. She first complimented the students on their courage and honesty. Then she targeted the instruction to meet their academic needs. By the end of the small group session, the four students felt comfortable enough to move their names to the *yes* side of the chart.

Using graphic organizers offers a twofold benefit. The teacher gathers important personal assessment data and students have more opportunities to engage in mathematics because the data can be used instructionally. Many times the teacher talks with the students about what the data show. Using math vocabulary as they analyze and interpret the information revealed in the graph offers children additional opportunities to experience real world mathematics.

For some students the act of displaying their current level of knowledge in public is a little intimidating. These students may be embarrassed if they do not know (or have a misconception about) something. To address these issues, teachers need to create classroom environments that allow students to be comfortable. We want to encourage students to be courageous and persistent. To do so, students need to know they will not be criticized by the teacher or their peers if they do not know something or give an incorrect answer. We need to teach students that the best way to learn something new is to identify what you already know about the topic and to reveal any misconceptions. The classroom environment must be a place both where people feel comfortable enough to admit not knowing something and where people can also make mistakes.

Bar Graphs Show Personal Assessment of Number and Operations

See:
Algebra, p. 71
Data, p. 89
Geometry, p. 93
Measurement, p. 93

Bar graphs are also powerful tools. For example, before beginning a lesson on ordinal numbers, the teacher may put up a bar graph shell titled *How much I know about ordinal numbers*. The labels include a large balloon (I know a lot), a medium-size balloon (I know some), and a small balloon (I know a lit-

Can you count to 5?

Yes	No
Remy	
Pierre	
Carly	
Austin	
Monty	
Peter	
Ricky	
Orrin	
Vito	
Brittni	Amara
Manda	Calvin
Yvette	Rozele
Greg	Aaron

Figure 7–2

tle bit). Students use sticky note cards to place their names in the category that represents how much they know, as can be seen in Figure 7–3.

The information is used to form groups and target instruction. After the lesson, students can change the placement of their name card if their comfort levels with the topic have changed; they may also write in their math journals about their change in level of understanding.

Comparison Circles Show Assessment of Number and Operations

See:
Algebra, p. 71
Data, p. 89
Geometry, p. 93
Measurement, p. 93

Comparison circles encourage math thinking and give excellent information. The teacher may use a single hoop or two (or more!) intersecting hoops. During a unit on addition, the teacher asked students to place their names inside or outside of the hoop to indicate their current knowledge. The title of the hoop was *I know all the addition facts up to sums of ten* (see Figure 7–4).

Using the data presented by the students, the teacher offered a two-tiered lesson. One group began working with addition beyond sums of ten. The other group began working on incorporating some new strategies for addition facts up to sums of ten. Everyone worked on addition and the instruction was suited to meet the academic needs of the students as perceived by the students.

The teacher used two intersecting hoops as the graphic organizer and asked the students to tell if they know how to represent the number 37 using base-

Figure 7–3

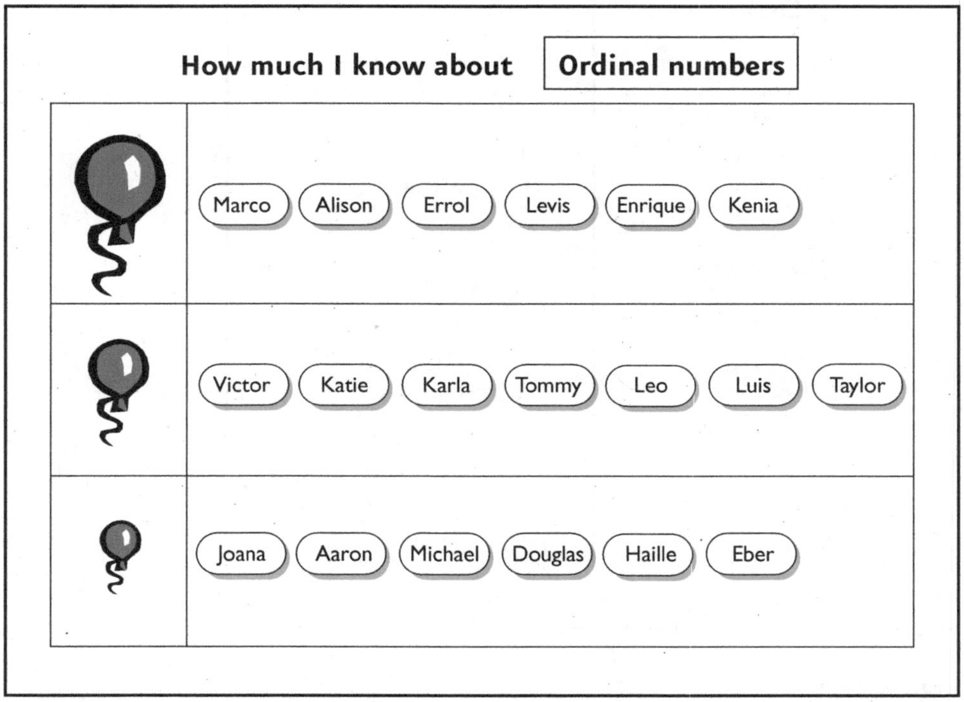

ten blocks and/or digi-blocks. The title of the comparison circle graphic was *I know how to show 37*. One hoop was labeled *Using base-ten blocks* and the other hoop was labeled *Using digi-blocks*, as shown in Figure 7–5.

The data indicate that many of the students are comfortable with representing the number 37 using both base-ten blocks and digi-blocks. Several students are comfortable representing 37 only with digi-blocks. Three students are comfortable using only base-ten blocks to represent 37. The teacher can offer targeted differentiated instruction to the students using the data presented in the comparison circles.

The teacher has many options for how to target the instruction. He can meet with each of the small groups and offer instruction using the manipulative they are not yet comfortable with. For example, the group that knows how to show numbers with digi-blocks could work on expanding their understanding of representing numbers by using base-ten blocks. With the group that already knows how to show 37 with both manipulatives, the teacher could focus on showing numbers that are more challenging.

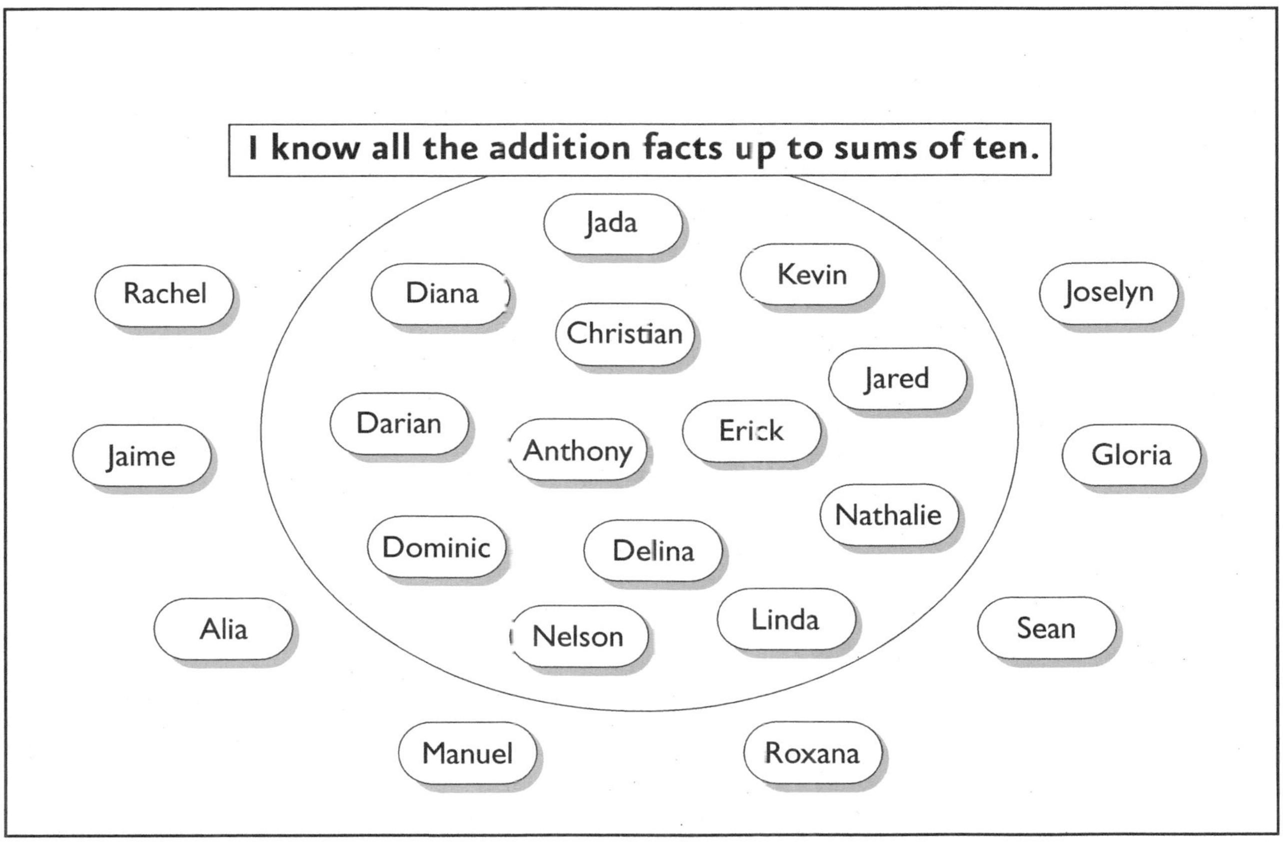

Figure 7–4

Another option for the teacher is to give students a task they can work on independently or with each other, while the teacher meets with small groups. If the students are working without the teacher, it may be most appropriate for the students to expand what they already know rather than move into something they are not yet comfortable with. For example, the students who know how to show numbers with both manipulatives could play a new game that involves showing and guessing numbers. In this way, the students engage in meaningful tasks without direct instruction from the teacher.

Pyramids Show Personal Assessments of Number and Operations

See:
Algebra, p. 74
Data, p. 91
Geometry, p. 96
Measurement, p. 96

Pyramid graphic organizers offer a way to show each student's current level of understanding in terms of high, middle, or foundational. Students place their name cards on the pyramid in the section that indicates level of understanding or comfort associated with a given topic.

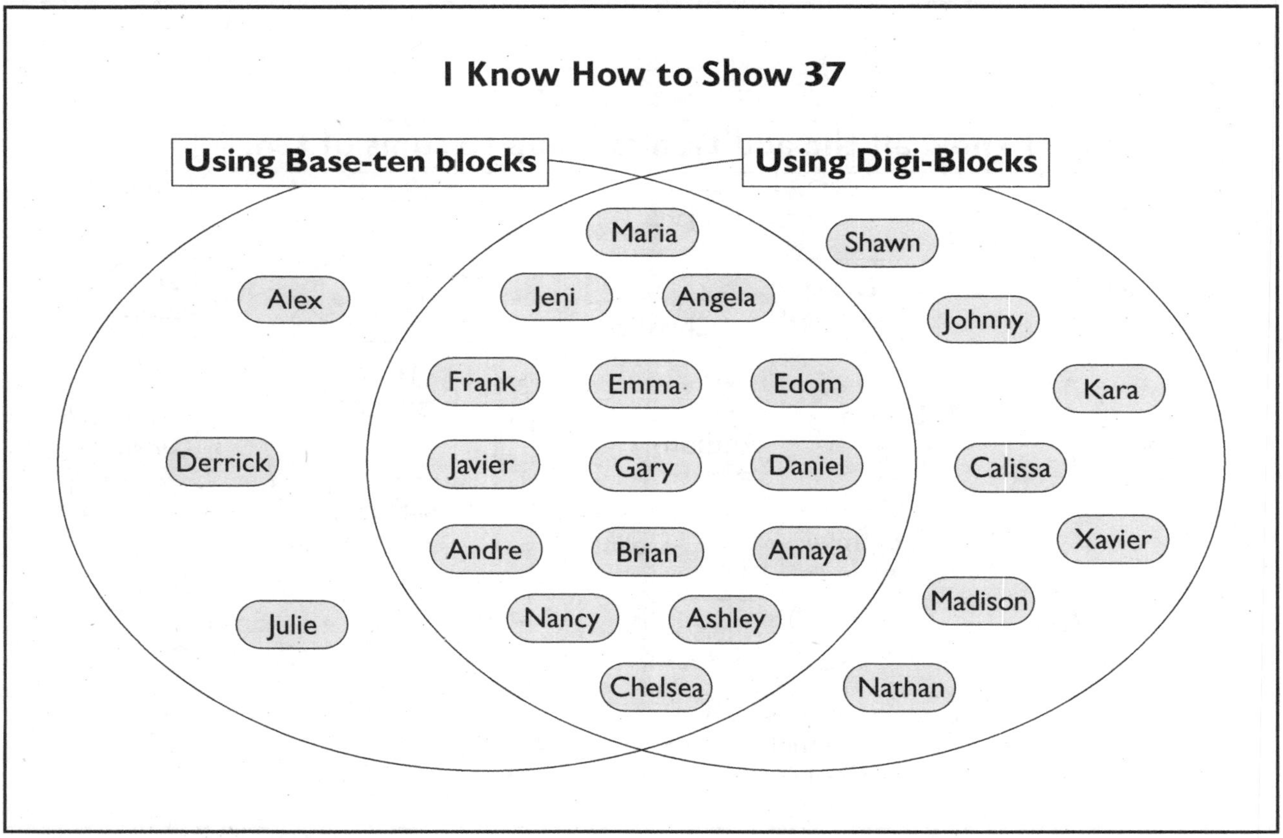

Figure 7–5

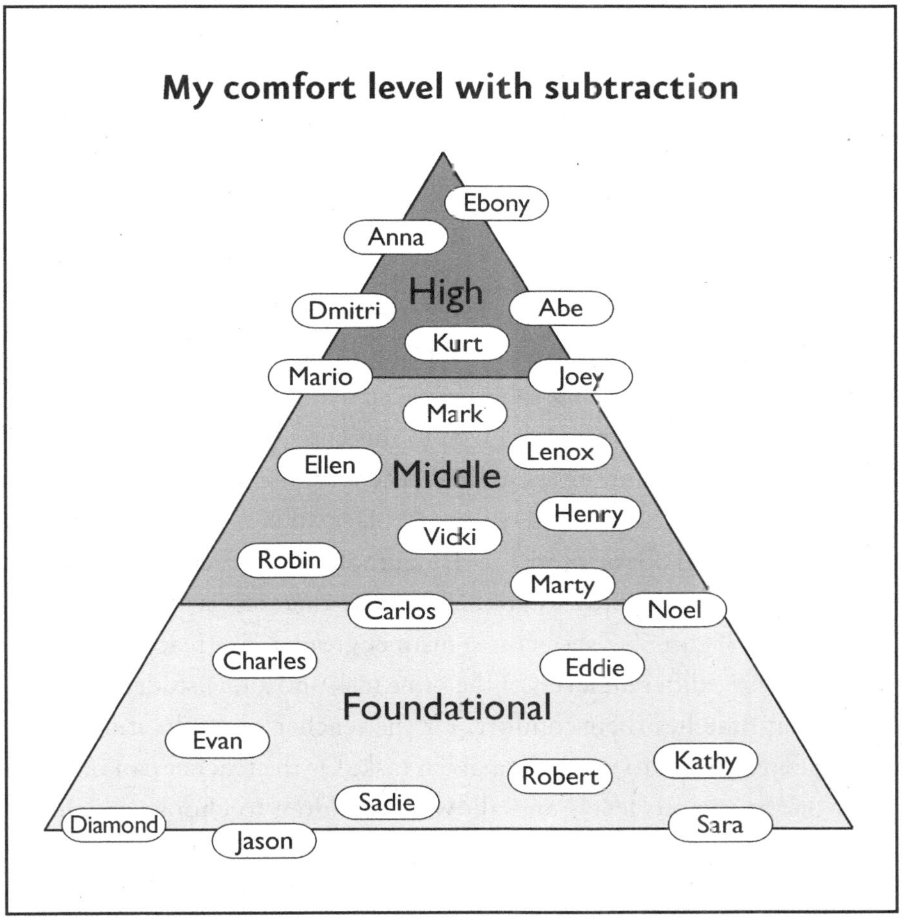

Figure 7–6

Using the pyramid as the graphic organizer, the teacher asked the students to place name cards in ways that show their levels of understanding. The title of the pyramid (see Figure 7–6) was *My comfort level with subtraction.*

The pyramid graphic allows students to show even more than one of three levels. They can actually place their names to designate levels within levels, such as high-middle or low-high. Some of the students shared their reasoning for their name card placement. Carlos said, "I am part middle and part low because sometimes I forget to minus." Joey said, "I am close to the high part because I am learning more and more."

Line Plots Show Personal Assessments of Number and Operations

See:
Algebra, p. 75
Data, p. 93
Geometry, p. 97
Measurement, p. 96

We do not need to wait until children reach intermediate grades to use line plots. There are a lot of high-quality math discourse and math thinking that can occur when using line plots. Essentially students indicate their level of knowledge or comfort with a number within a given range. The range can be small and simple, such as 1–3, 0–5, or 0–10. The range can also increase to 0–50 or 0–100, or decrease using fractions in a range from 0 to 1. The line plot range needs to be connected to the students' understandings of numbers and number lines.

Using a complex line plot that ranged from 0 to 1, the teacher asked the students to indicate their level of knowledge. The title of the line plot was *How much we know about estimation.* While the students had many experiences working with number lines and values between 0 and 1, this was one of the first personal assessment opportunities given to this class, so the teacher decided to make the pieces of data anonymous. The teacher hung the line plot behind an easel and allowed each student to privately place an X on the line. Sometimes students need several opportunities to use a graphic organizer in an anonymous fashion before they are ready to publicly display their levels of knowledge.

The data in Figure 7–7 show three distinct groups. The teacher can use the data to offer three different levels of the same task and allow students to choose the level that matches their comfort. Or the teacher can help students form heterogeneous groups to work on a given task. Or the teacher can offer small group work at various levels and allow the children to choose which group to attend. Or perhaps the teacher uses an informal assessment to target the instruction and the children use a different color X to privately indicate new level of knowledge following the instruction. Afterward, the class can analyze and interpret the data, highlighting growth trends.

Another similar way to show personal assessment data is to use individual number lines. Students simply make an X somewhere on the number line to in-

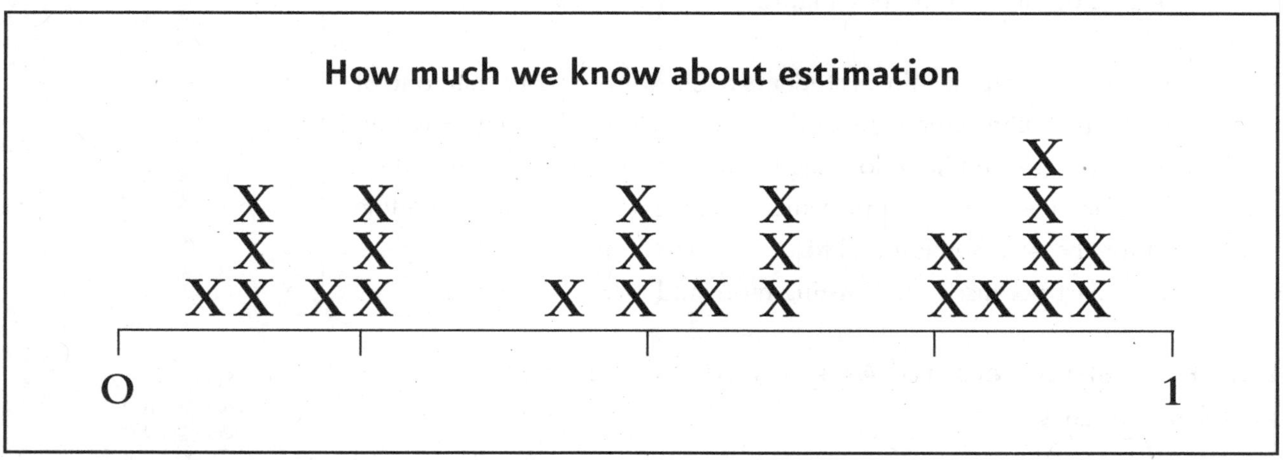

Figure 7–7

dicate a personal level of knowledge or comfort. Often using individual number lines is an initial step in helping students gain comfort with constructing line plots.

Fractions Grids Show Personal Assessment of Number and Operations

See:
Algebra, p. 76
Data, p. 95
Geometry, p. 98
Measurement, p. 98

The fractions grid is a great tool because it offers a way to show personal assessment data that can be analyzed using fractions. This example of the fractions grid has four sections. Each section represents a different level of knowledge—one whole (complete knowledge), ¾ (solid knowledge), ½ (some knowledge), and ¼ (little knowledge). The students place their name tags in the section that best represents their level of knowledge of the given concept.

While a class studied different types of word problems, the teacher posted this fractions grid and titled it *Portia has some candy. She gives 2 pieces of candy to her friend. Now she has 5 pieces of candy. How many pieces of candy did she start with?* Students who were completely confident with solving this (start unknown) word problem placed their name stars in the one whole section of the graphic. Students with solid knowledge (but not complete confidence) of how to solve it placed their name stars in the ¾ section. Students with some knowledge of how to solve it placed their name stars in the ½ section. Students with a little bit of knowledge of how to solve it placed their name stars in the ¼ section. If any students had zero knowledge of how to solve it, they could place their name stars outside of the graphic.

The teacher used the data seen in Figure 7–8 to plan for the next day's instruction. She offered a challenge for the students who indicated that they completely understood how to solve start unknown word problems. She offered targeted instruction to the ¾ group in a way that helped them move to complete understanding. She built more foundations with the ½ group and the ¼ group by targeting instruction. All of the students increased their levels of understanding.

Graphic Organizers for Learning Frameworks

Show how you learn!

Graphic organizers can also be used to show aspects of students' learning frameworks. Students can indicate learning styles, multiple intelligences, environmental needs, affective needs, interests, and a host of other learning

Portia has some candy.
She gives 2 pieces of candy to her friend.
Now she has 5 pieces of candy.
How many pieces of candy did she start with?

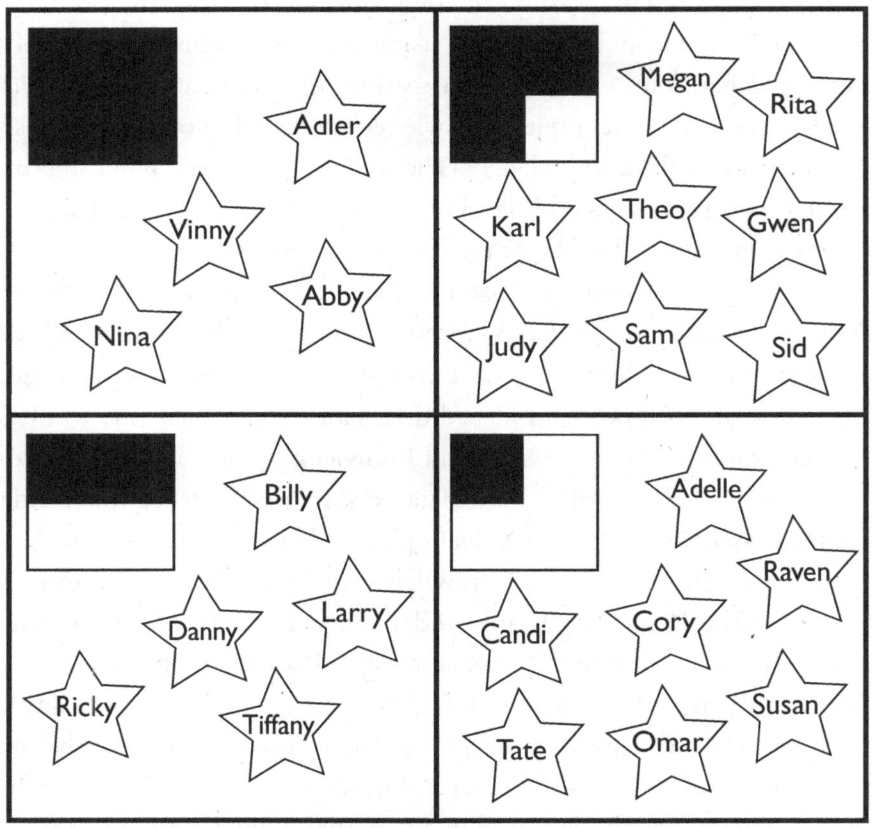

Figure 7–8

preferences. Just as students show levels of comfort or levels of knowledge, they can use name cards to indicate learning modalities, intelligences, and preferences.

T-Charts Show Learning Frameworks

Using a yes/no T-chart, a second-grade teacher asked her students to share which groupings they prefer. The label on the T-chart was *I want to work with a partner during center time today*. The children placed their name cards on the *yes* side or the *no* side of the chart shown in Figure 7–9.

I want to work with a partner during center time today

Yes	No
Caitlin	
Alvin	
Rene	Toni
Bruce	Jackie
Wayne	Max
Sherry	Liam
Carrie	Kenny
Craig	Ali
Gino	Koby
Brandy	Blake

Figure 7–9

The teacher used this information to form groups. All of the children on the *yes* side of the chart were assigned partners for center time. All of the children on the *no* side of the chart were given the opportunity to work alone during center time. Because the label included *today*, the children did not feel as though they were making a long-term decision. They could just decide the group structure they desired at the present time.

There are many others ways a T-chart can be used to collect students' learning framework data. The labels can be yes/no, agree/disagree, or true/false. The following list includes some options for T-chart titles:

Is moving around while you work helpful?
Does sunlight help you concentrate?
Do you like working at your desk?
Do you like to hum while you think?
I want to work in the quiet neighborhood today.
I like to work with puzzles.
I want to draw my answer.
I learned something new.

There are many other questions teachers can ask to help students identify aspects of their learning frameworks. It is important for the children to understand that these answers can change depending on situations, time, feelings, and circumstances.

Bar Graphs Show Learning Frameworks

Bar graphs offer a high-quality graphic organizer for students to indicate facets of their learning frameworks. The category labels can include learning styles, multiple intelligences, environmental needs, affective needs, or interests.

The teacher posted a bar graph template to gather information about learning styles. The title of the graph was *Ways we like to learn math*. The category labels included *Drawing or looking at pictures*, *Saying or hearing words*, *Building with objects*, and *Moving around*. Each label included a picture to help the children understand the categories. Each student placed a name card in one column to indicate preference (see Figure 7–10).

The teacher used the data to form groups of similar learning style. The visual learners indicated that they prefer to learn math by drawing or looking at pictures. The auditory group indicated that they like to learn math by saying or listening to words. The tactile group showed that they prefer to learn math by building with objects. The kinesthetic group preferred to learn math by moving around. The teacher modified the tasks to meet the learning style preferences of the students.

There are many other ways to use bar graphs to find out components of students' learning frameworks. The teacher could give several topics of interest and allow students to choose the topic that most interests them. The teacher could have category labels on the bar graph that include some or all of the multiple intelligences. Environmental and affective needs can also be displayed in the form of a bar graph. One first-grade class that I worked with constructed a bar graph related to noise in the classroom. The children indicated whether they could concentrate better with a lot of noise, some noise, a little bit of noise, or no noise. We made adjustments according to the students' preferences.

Ways We Like to Learn Math

8				
7	Adiel			
6	Jason		Emerson	
5	Asia		Marco	David
4	Jessie		Sylvia	Norman
3	Gilda		Alison	Deanna
2	Mary	Blanca	Zilma	Jared
1	Rusty	Molly	Vanessa	Douglas
0	Drawing or Looking at Pictures	Saying or Hearing Words	Building with Objects	Moving Around

Figure 7–10

Comparison Circles Show Learning Frameworks

To use comparison circles to gather student learning framework data, place name cards in the location that describes part of their learning frameworks. Sometimes students have dominant preferences, while at other times there are overlapping preferences. Comparison circles are a very appropriate graphic organizer to use because if students have more than one preference, they can place their names in the intersection. To find out which products the students want to use to express understanding or *show what they know*, the teacher used comparison circles. The title of the graphic organizer was *I prefer to show what I know with. . . .* The hoop labels included *Numbers, Pictures,* and *Words*. The students placed name cards on the graphic organizer in Figure 7–11 to share data about their learning frameworks.

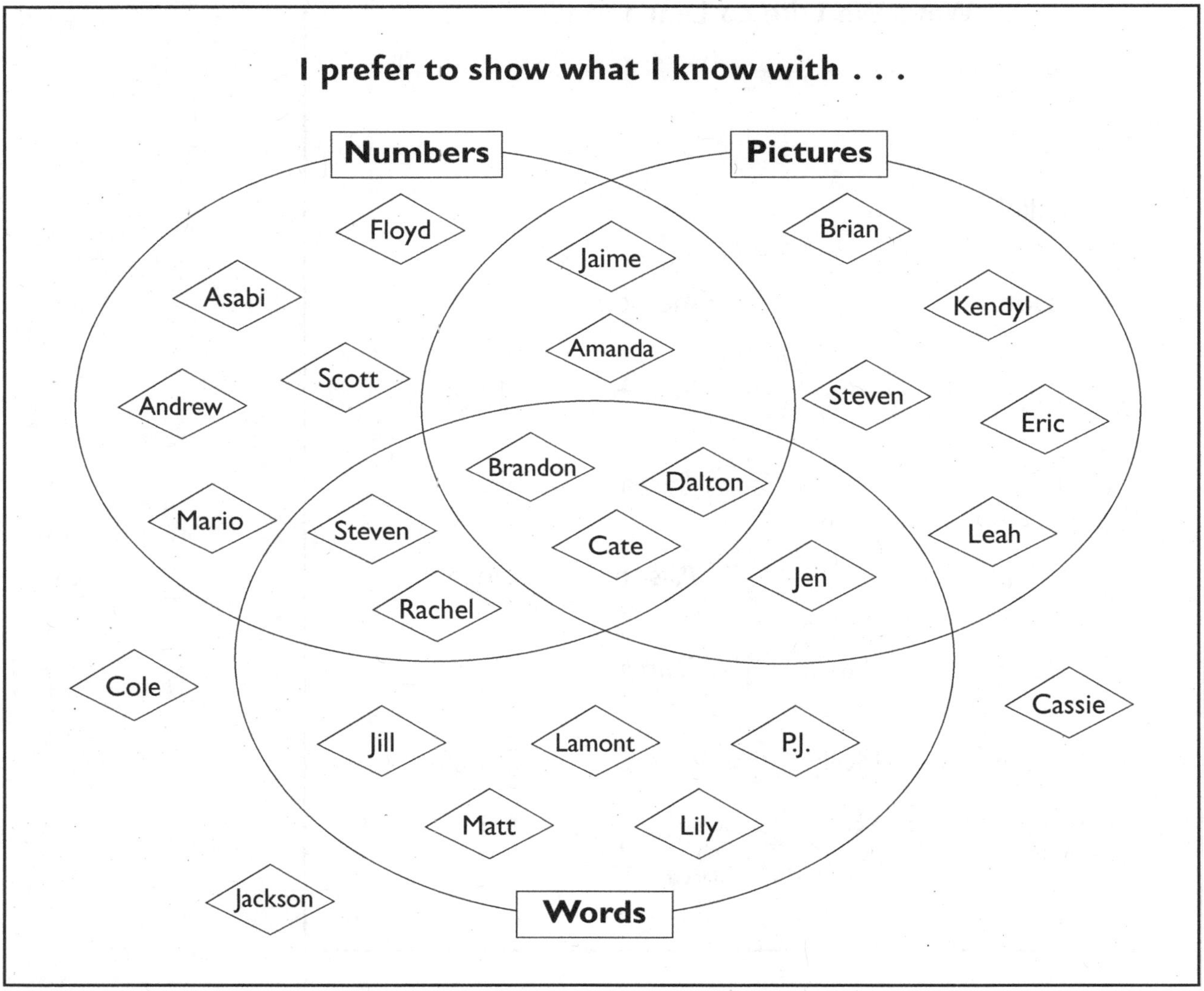

Figure 7–11

Some of the students prefer to *show what they know* using numbers, others with pictures, and others using words. Some prefer to use both numbers and pictures, numbers and words, or pictures and words. Three of the children prefer numbers, pictures, and words. It is important to note that when name cards are placed outside of the comparison circles, we still learn valuable information. Placement of a name card outside of the hoops indicates that the student prefers not to use numbers, pictures, or words. In this class, Cassie prefers music and Cole and Jackson prefer games.

Pyramids Show Learning Frameworks

When using the pyramid to show learning frameworks, the labels can represent levels, amounts, qualities, or other variations. For example, a second-grade teacher wanted to find the degree of body-kinesthetic intelligence held by her students as perceived by her students. She used a pyramid graphic organizer to gather the data. The pyramid was titled *I like working with my physical skills*. The pyramid was divided into three sections, including *Always*, *Sometimes*, and *Not often*. The students placed their name cards in specific locations (see Figure 7–12) to indicate the degree to which they prefer to work with their physical skills.

In this example, a few of the students indicated that they feel they have high preference for working with physical skills. This may indicate high body-kinesthetic intelligence for this group of students. The students who chose *Sometimes* may have some body smart intelligence or may be expressing some interest in this area. The students who placed their name cards in the *Not often* section are letting the teacher know that physical skills are not particular strengths or interests. The teacher can use these data to offer choices in activities for students.

Line Plots Show Learning Frameworks

To use a line plot for collecting data related to students' learning frameworks, an X or another symbol can represent the pieces of data on the line. Using name tags on a line plot, a teacher encouraged her students to share their affective needs prior to a lesson about odd and even numbers. She asked them to rate their feelings about the upcoming topic of study. She used a simple line plot (scaled 0–10) titled *How I feel about odd and even numbers*. The students placed name cards on the line plot, as is shown in Figure 7–13.

The faces really helped the young students understand how to rate their feelings on the line plot. When the class looked at the data, Hung and Marc shared that they were not very excited about studying odd and even numbers

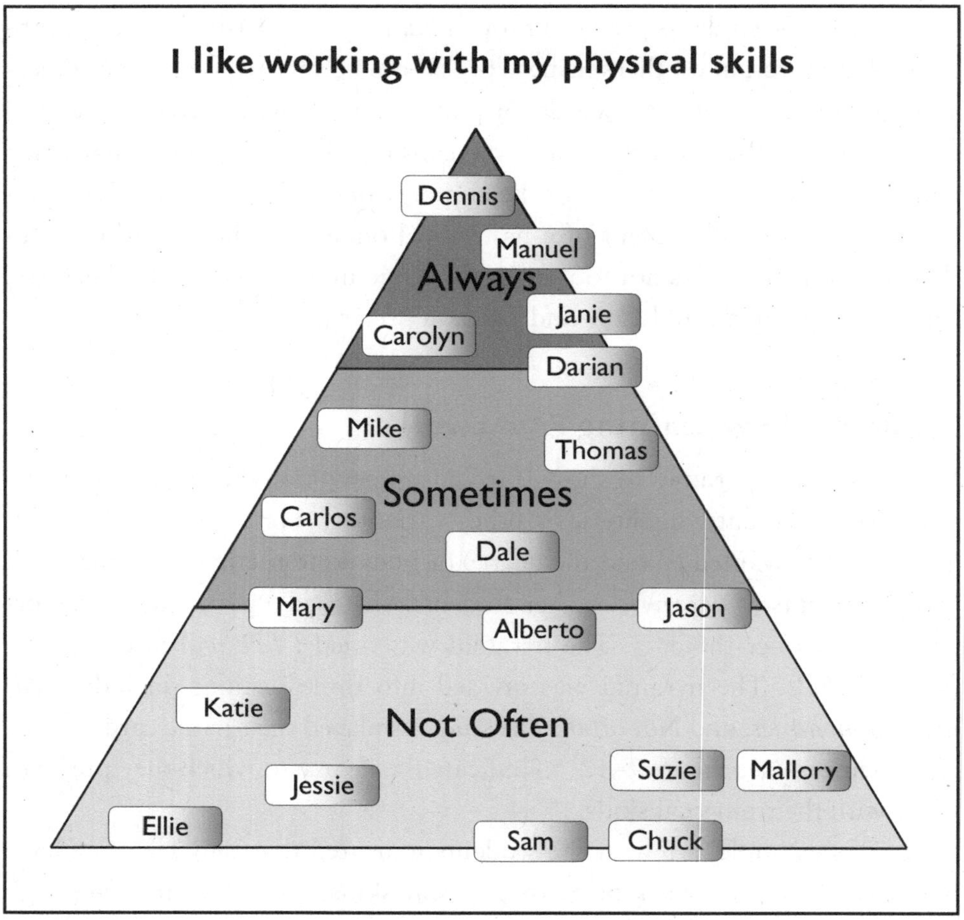

Figure 7–12

because they did not understand them. Lucy shared that she was not excited because she already knew about odd and even numbers. Amy shared that she was very excited about learning about odd and even numbers because her older brother told her about them. The class decided that it would be a good idea if the people who were excited about the new topic worked with the people who were not so excited to help them be more involved. In this way, the students offered heterogeneous grouping structures as a way to meet the affective and process needs of some of their classmates.

Fractions Grids Show Learning Frameworks

A first-grade teacher was working with her students on word problems. She planned to use a series of real-life scenarios that involved pets. She used a fraction grid to determine her students' degree of interest in cats. The four sections included complete interest (one whole square), somewhat solid interest (¾ of a square), some interest (½ of a square), and little interest (¼ of a square). The first graders placed their name cards in the location that best expressed their personal level of interest in cats (see Figure 7–14).

As it turned out, many of the students were interested in cats, but some were not. Therefore the teacher worked with small groups to target the instruction according to students' interests. She used the real-life word problem scenarios with the group that was interested in cats and she used different scenarios for the other students—they were more interested in other pets such as dogs, hamsters, and snakes (as indicated on different graphic organizers). The targeted, differentiated instruction according to interests was highly successful.

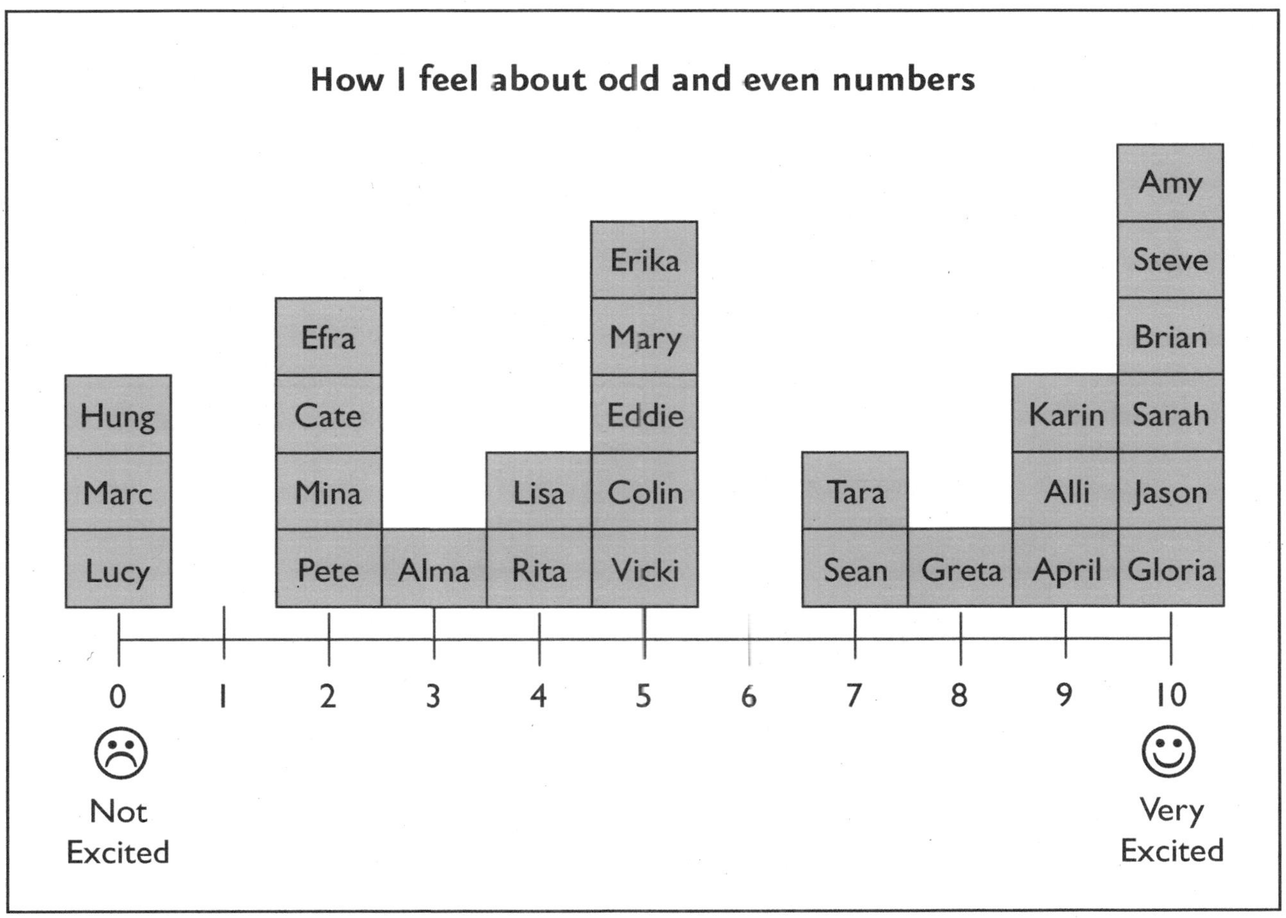

Figure 7–13

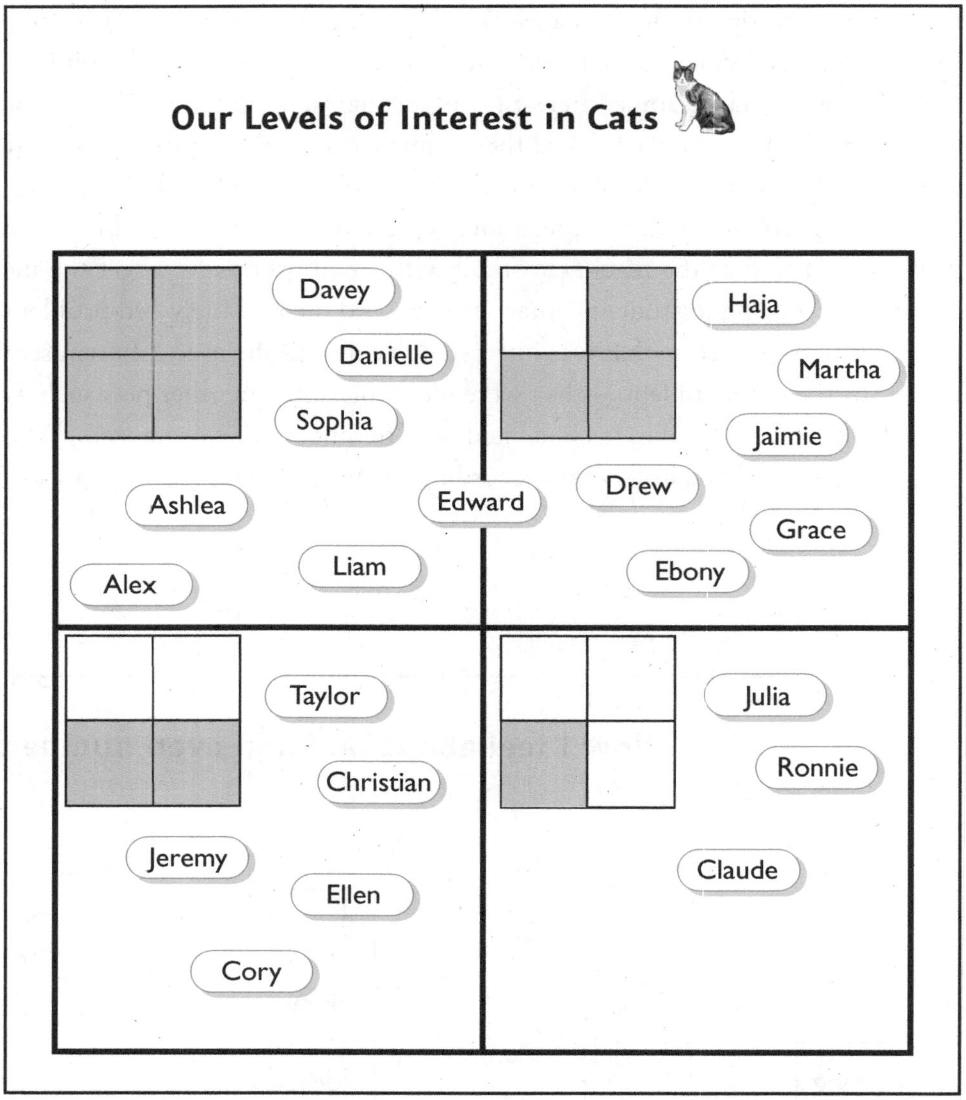

Figure 7–14

Using Graphic Organizers in Other Ways

Graphs give oodles of information

Personal preassessment is but one way to use graphic organizers. Teachers can also use graphic organizers to gather informal preassessment data. When presenting a problem or math situation for students to solve, the teacher can request that the answers be displayed in a graphic form. The teacher can give a problem and solution and ask students if they agree or disagree using a T-chart.

The teacher can present several ideas or solutions as labels on a bar graph, and students can indicate the answer they believe to be accurate by placing name cards in specific columns. Likewise, students can be presented with a math situation and then place their name cards in a specific location on the comparison circles to designate their answers. Using pyramids presented as always, sometimes, and never, the teacher could ask about operations or characteristics of numbers. Line plots can serve as a beneficial way for students to estimate answers. Fraction grids can offer ways for students to show the degree to which a representation accurately portrays a computation situation. The possibilities are seemingly endless.

These additional uses of graphic organizers are not personal assessment, but informal assessment because the students are not assessing themselves. The teacher determines the level of accuracy of each student. But like personal assessment, the students can adjust their responses after the differentiated mathematics instruction. As one first grader shared, "It is so funny that I used to think the answer was this, but now I know the right answer is that!" Nothing like trading this for that!

CHAPTER 8

Reflecting on Practice

Analyzing Learning Progress and Making Adjustments

Is it working?

Evaluating students' learning progress and making needed adjustments are core aspects of reflecting on classroom practices. Reflection is the vehicle for learning from our experiences. Reflecting means analyzing where we have been and determining where we will go next, interlaced with practice. We can't just think about it. We need to do something with the knowledge we gain through analysis and reflection. "Reflective practice is more than just thoughtful practice; it is the process of turning thoughtful practice into potential learning" (Jarvis 1992, 180). It is this transformation that gives us new meaning and provides direction.

As we reflect, we need to ask ourselves *is it working?* Monitoring student progress is vital. When some children are not learning, we need to make adjustments in our instruction. When some children already know the material, we need to modify our instruction. Frustrated students require change if we are to meet their needs. Bored students need academic challenges. The goal is optimal instruction for all students. True differentiation leads to more efficient and more accurate instruction to meet that goal.

A Differentiated Instruction in Mathematics Observation Rubric

The differentiated instruction in mathematics observation rubric is intended to help math educators implement best practices. Each component of the rubric presents degrees of implementation to allow educators to see where they are and where they can go. The rubric in Figure 8–1 can be used as a self-assessment tool for teachers or by supervisors as they observe a classroom.

Content Areas Are Connected to the Standards

Optimal mathematics instruction is directly connected to national (NCTM's Principles and Standards for School Mathematices [PSSM]), state, and local district standards. The power behind a standards-based curriculum stems from the comprehensive and coherent nature of the design. A standards-based curriculum promotes a focus on core mathematics and sense-making. While integration is common and encouraged and differentiation is the goal, an observer should be able to identify which content standards are being taught in any given differentiated mathematics lesson.

Preassessment Is Utilized

Using preassessment means more than *giving* preassessments. The teacher needs to incorporate the information gathered from the preassessments. While an observer may not directly see the preassessment during the observed part of the lesson, the degree to which preassessment is utilized can easily be discussed during preobservation and postobservation conferences. The teacher should be able to share how the preassessment data were used to drive the instruction. If personal preassessment is used, there may be a graphic organizer displayed in the classroom. If the teacher is self-evaluating the lesson, the degree to which preassessment is utilized is known.

Group Structure Is Purposeful, Flexible, and Fluid

Purposeful groups are strategic, not random. Whether heterogeneous or homogeneous grouping is used, the teacher should know why the students are grouped together. Flexible grouping means the same students are not always working together. An observer may notice ways to organize continuously changing groups (e.g., charts, movable name tags, lists). Fluid grouping means students flow in and out of groups. The groups are not rigid; instead there is smooth transition from one group to the next (e.g., small group to small group) or from one type of structure to the next (e.g., whole group to small group).

	4	3	2	1	Comments
Content areas are connected to the standards (national, state, local)	directly connected	connected	vaguely connected	unconnected	
Preassessment is utilized	clearly utilized	utilized	vaguely utilized	not utilized	
Group structure is purposeful, flexible, and fluid	clearly evident	evident	slightly evident	not evident	
Students engage in active participation	clearly evident	evident	vaguely evident	not evident	
Problem solving and real-world context are included	clearly included	included	vaguely included	not included	
Manipulatives are available	clearly available	available	randomly available	not available	
Students engage in rich math discourse	exceptional math talk	reasonable math talk	little math talk	no math talk	
Teacher-posed questions are of high quality	excellent questions	reasonable questions	mediocre questions	poor questions	
Ongoing assessment is evident	clearly evident	evident	slightly evident	not evident	
Levels of cognitive demand are adjusted	significantly adjusted	adjusted	slightly adjusted	not adjusted	
Instruction is targeted	clearly targeted	somewhat targeted	slightly targeted	not targeted	
Students' learning frameworks are implemented	extensively implemented	implemented	vaguely implemented	not implemented	
Student progress is monitored	often monitored	sometimes monitored	seldom monitored	never monitored	
Reflection is incorporated	extensively incorporated	incorporated	vaguely incorporated	not incorporated	

Developed by Jennifer Taylor-Cox

Figure 8–1 *Differentiated Instruction in Mathematics Observation Rubric*

If an observer only sees whole group instruction, the preobservation and postobservation conferences should reveal when the small group structure occurs and how purposeful, flexible, and fluid the groups are. Of course, if the teacher is self-evaluating the lesson, the evidence of purposeful, flexible, fluid group structure is obvious.

Students Engage in Active Participation

Optimal mathematics instruction includes students engaging in active participation. When students actively participate they construct personal, meaningful knowledge. Active participation encourages intrinsic motivation and serves as a key factor in learning mathematics. Active participation is evident in the actions, words, and gestures of the students. An observer or the teacher (in the process of self-evaluation) can find out how actively involved students are by watching students and asking them questions.

Problem Solving and Real-World Context Are Included

Problem solving and real-world context make mathematics more meaningful to the students and help them make sense of mathematics concepts. We want students to understand the power and significance of mathematics. Using problem solving and real-world contexts also allows us to teach for understanding. An observer or the teacher may notice students talking to one another, asking questions, relating the mathematics to their own lives, or making math connections with other content areas. When including problem solving and real-world contexts, the instruction and related tasks the teacher provides are not just procedural in nature.

Manipulatives Are Available

The degree to which math manipulatives are available reveals a great deal about how actively involved students are in the learning process. This is not to imply that every student needs to be using manipulatives at every moment. Instead it means that math manipulatives should always be available to students. An observer or the teacher should see that students have easy access to various mathematics manipulatives. The classroom climate needs to allow and encourage students to identify, locate, retrieve, and use manipulatives during the math lesson.

Students Engage in Rich Math Discourse

Student-to-student math discourse is paramount. There are two major characteristics of classroom math talk—quantity and quality. Exceptional math talk means plenty of high-quality student-to-student math discourse. The observer may hear students using math vocabulary (in context) and students asking each other questions about the math. The observer or teacher may notice that the quality and quantity of the student-to-student math talk are at the same level; however, sometimes they are not. If the quantity is high but the quality is low, for example, this can be noted in the comments section. It takes time and experience to reach rich levels of student-to-student math discourse.

Teacher-Posed Questions Are of High Quality

The quality of the mathematics questions posed by the teacher is vital. Excellent questions promote math thinking, while poor questions immobilize learning. Some examples of poor questions may include rhetorical questions and questions that fail to prompt discussion and decisions. It is important to realize that when differentiating instruction, the teacher may at times need to use lower-level questions. This does not mean the quality of the questions is weak. The questions may be valuable because they are aimed at meeting the academic needs of students. However, we do not want to fall into a trap of always providing low-level questions to the students who are struggling. We need to balance the questions we give to students in ways that empower thinking. To identify the quality of teacher-posed questions in a math lesson, the observer may need to watch the students' responses and the teacher's reactions. Sometimes the best questions are given after the initial question because they are based on the reactions and responses the students have. In cases of self-evaluation, the teacher may need to record the students' dialogue to help with the analysis.

Ongoing Assessment Is Evident

While preassessment is listed previously on the rubric, ongoing assessment actually includes preassessment along with assessment during instruction and postassessment. The assessments used may be formal, informal, or personal. While the observer may not see the preassessement or postassessment during the lesson, the observer should see evidence of assessment during instruction. The preobservation and postobservation conferences will also provide further clues on how evident ongoing assessment is in the classroom. In self-evaluation, the teacher needs to analyze the degree to which ongoing assessment is evident.

Levels of Cognitive Demand Are Adjusted

The level of cognitive demand (LCD) needs to be adjusted to meet the specific needs of students. Educators should understand that the LCD is the degree of thinking and ownership required to fully grasp the mathematics at hand. As educators gain comfort with LCD, they adjust levels as they differentiate instruction. The observer may notice the teacher adjusting LCD in problem solving, reasoning and proof, communications, connections, representations, and levels of thinking and questioning. During preconferences and postconferences the teacher can further clarify the degree to which the levels are adjusted through the tasks and assignments provided to the students. During self-evaluation, the teacher reviews and evaluates ways the LCD is adjusted.

Instruction Is Targeted

The degree to which the instruction is targeted to meet the needs of the students is essential. The targeted instruction may include back-mapping, forward-mapping, scaffolding, compacting, tiering, activating prior knowledge, or other strategies. The observer should see the teacher differentiating the instruction by content to groups of students. The preobservation and postobservation conferences should provide further information about how the targeted instruction is driven by the ongoing assessments. When the teacher self-evaluates, specific strategies and assignments should be considered.

Students' Learning Frameworks Are Implemented

Students' learning frameworks provide channels for students to learn mathematics. These may include learning styles, multiple intelligences, environmental needs, affective needs, and interests. The observer or the teacher may examine personal assessment graphics, modifications to assignments, and revisions to ways of engaging in mathematics processes and products. Applying students' learning frameworks serves as a powerful tool in planning, implementing, and assessing differentiated mathematics instruction.

Student Progress Is Monitored

Monitoring student progress is a key factor in differentiating mathematics instruction. While this may be revealed in the ongoing assessments implemented in the lesson, it may also be revealed in grouping changes, task modifications, targeted instruction, and incorporation of students' learning frameworks. The point is that the teacher knows where the students are and what they need next in their learning journeys.

Reflection Is Incorporated

The incorporation of reflection is twofold. The teacher encourages the students to reflect and the teacher reflects. Evidence of reflection may include students sharing what or how they learned or what they plan to learn next. The teacher's reflection may be present in any of the differentiated instruction components, if it is based on analysis and needed revisions. Much of the teacher's reflection may be revealed during the preobservation and postobservation conferences or with colleagues.

What's the Purpose of the Rubric?

The differentiated instruction in mathematics observation rubric is intended to be a guide for educators to evaluate differentiated instruction in mathematics. While no single rubric can capture everything that happens in the classroom, this rubric has been used and revised multiple times. The comments column provides a place to note qualitative information. The differentiated instruction in mathematics rubric is a tool that can be used for coaching, mentoring, and evaluating. Like all tools, it works best when used in the right way. The rubric is not a report card or a scorecard—or worse yet, a means for playing the "got-you" game. It is a tool to help mathematics educators cultivate the art of teaching. To inspire educators to continue to improve, we need to help them see what they do well and what they can focus on next.

Where Are You Now? What Is the Next Step?

Which aspects of differentiated instruction do I implement well? Which aspects do I need to improve? It is nearly impossible to move from a nondifferentiated classroom to a completely differentiated classroom overnight. Change takes time. We have to identify where we are and where we want to go next.

If you currently teach whole group lessons most of the time, your next step may be to work with small groups more often. If you currently meet with small groups but you teach the same thing to each group, your next steps may include adjusting the levels of cognitive demand and target instruction. If you only have heterogeneous groups, your next steps may include creating some homogeneous groups. If your groups do not change, your next step is to make your groups more flexible and fluid. If you use assessment only at the end of instruction, your next step is to try preassessments. If you give preassessments but only refer to these in terms of pre-evaluations versus postevaluations, your next step is to use the data in your instructional plans. The goals and focal points are different for different math teachers. It may sound humorous, but the truth is we actually need to differentiate our learning and implementation of differentiated instruction based on where we currently are and what we need to learn, implement, and revise next.

A Professional Development Model

Helping math educators differentiate instruction in mathematics

How do math educators become more comfortable with differentiating mathematics instruction? One way is to engage in professional development opportunities that include three key ideas: study, apply, and reflect (see Figure 8–2).

Study

Teachers need time to study the components of differentiated instruction in mathematics. We also need resources that help us identify what we do well and what we should work on next. We need to be allowed and encouraged to stretch our comfort zones by trying productive strategies that may be new or different.

Gaining comfort with the math is also essential. Using back-mapping and forward-mapping requires knowledge of the previous and subsequent mathematics concepts. We need time and resources so we can better understand the math we teach.

Apply

Applying what we study involves implementation with support. Strategic coaching and peer observation are very beneficial. A strategic coach observes, encourages, suggests, directs, and supports. Just as the teacher takes on many

Figure 8–2

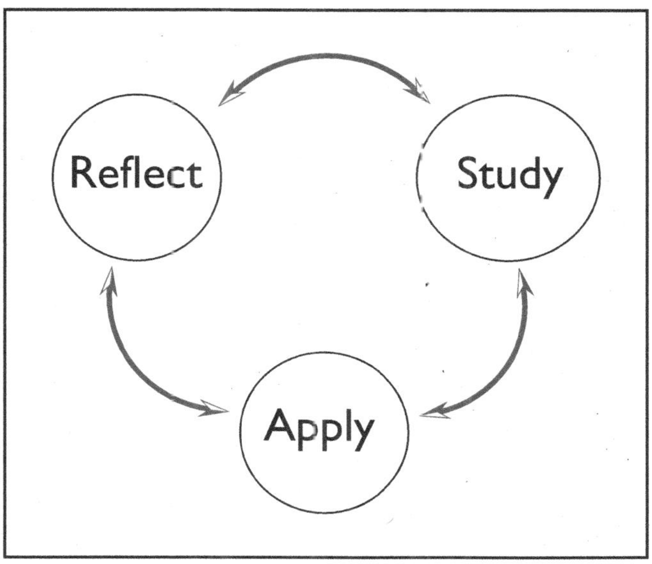

roles in the classroom, strategic coaches take on various roles as they provide constructive feedback that helps teachers move to the next level in their teaching.

Peer observation offers a valuable way for teachers to collaborate as they gain comfort with differentiating mathematics instruction. Peer observation gives teachers the opportunity and forum to share ideas and collaboration. The peer observations should not be evaluative, but informative—to the observer and the teacher.

Reflect

The reflection component is all too often slighted in professional development, yet reflecting is crucial because it is the way we transform. Educators need to engage in reflection through discourse and writing. Journal writing is a powerful way to reflect on classroom practices. Using reflective communication and candor, we can develop a community of learners who support and challenge each other. Teachers need time and resources to do so.

The study-apply-reflect professional development model is continuous. We learn something new, we try it out, we analyze it, we refine it; then we study more, apply more, and reflect more. As the process continues, our math classrooms become more differentiated and our students achieve at higher levels.

The Differentiated Instruction in Mathematics Cycle

The cycle continues

The differentiated instruction in mathematics cycle helps teachers understand the significant components of differentiated instruction and it serves as a map providing direction for teachers as they implement differentiated instruction in mathematics (see Figure 8–3).

Typically, the process begins with defining the concepts. The teacher should know and understand the specific math concepts that will be taught. The teacher needs to use back-mapping and forward-mapping to identify previous and subsequent concepts. This first step gives the teacher greater command of the content allowing the differentiated instruction to be implemented effectively and efficiently.

Using the concepts as the core, ongoing assessments (which may be formal, informal, or personal) are utilized to gather important data about the students' current knowledge or comfort levels. These data are used to form

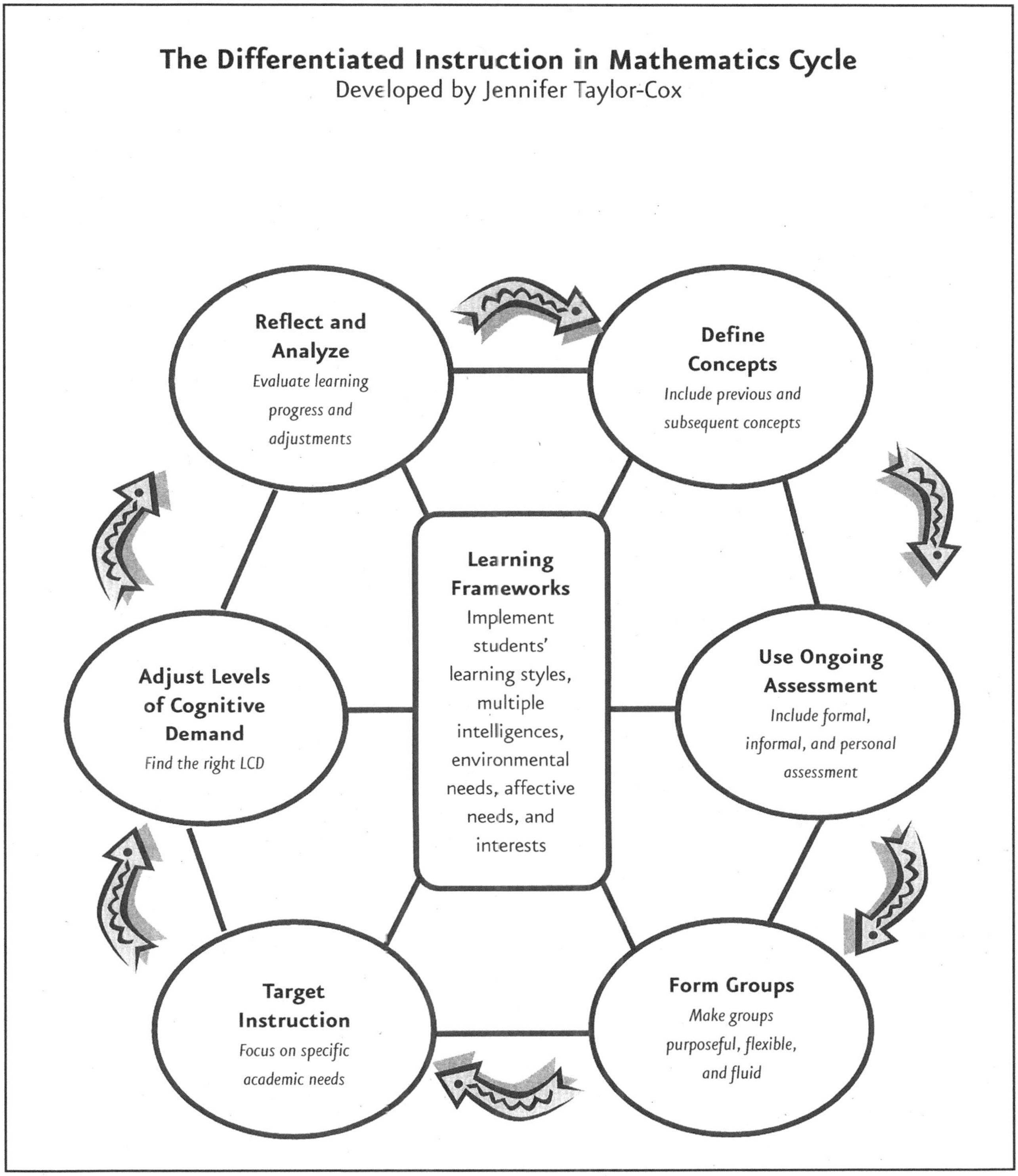
The Differentiated Instruction in Mathematics Cycle
Developed by Jennifer Taylor-Cox
Reflect and Analyze
Evaluate learning progress and adjustments
Define Concepts
Include previous and subsequent concepts
Learning Frameworks
Implement students' learning styles, multiple intelligences, environmental needs, affective needs, and interests
Adjust Levels of Cognitive Demand
Find the right LCD
Use Ongoing Assessment
Include formal, informal, and personal assessment
Target Instruction
Focus on specific academic needs
Form Groups
Make groups purposeful, flexible, and fluid

Figure 8–3

purposeful, flexible, and fluid groups of students and to steer the instruction. The instruction involves targeting instruction and adjusting the levels of cognitive demand. The teacher may implement other forms of ongoing assessment or move into the analysis and reflection phase. Students' learning frameworks are considered during all phases of the differentiated instruction in mathematics cycle. Incorporating the students' learning frameworks can and should occur in any cycle phases. In many ways incorporating students' learning frameworks serves as the heart of the differentiated instruction in mathematics cycle.

The cycle can also be interpreted as a hexagon—yes, the vertices are hidden, but there is a hexagon underneath. Each vertex is highlighted with a phase of the differentiated instruction in mathematics cycle. The hexagon's vertices also connect to the center where students' learning frameworks serve as the core of the cycle. All of these connections create triangles, parallelograms, and trapezoids that are minicycles within the larger differentiated instruction cycle. There are multiple paths within and including the hexagon that can serve to provide direction as we differentiate instruction in mathematics.

The Future of Mathematics Instruction

From the past to the future

Years ago nearly all mathematics classrooms were traditional. The teaching involved mostly lecture and some demonstration. Then hands-on learning made its way to the forefront. We learned that students need to construct their own knowledge through active learning. Most of us left behind passive math instruction and started teaching in ways that we believe to be more beneficial for students. Hands-on learning is a concept that all educators are familiar with—I believe that someday differentiated instruction in mathematics will be as preferred and as common as hands-on learning in mathematics. We will understand the power of differentiated instruction and we will help each other implement it.

The future of mathematics instruction *is* differentiated instruction. We can no longer pretend that a steady dose of whole group, aim-for-the-middle math lessons meets the needs of all students anymore than nondifferentiated reading lessons meet the needs of all students. Your strong command of the math content and implementing of these strategies will enable you to focus on ongoing assessment, grouping students, and targeting instruction to meet the needs of *all* students.

EPILOGUE

ENTER MY CLASSROOM

The teacher said, "Enter my classroom."
Some of the students said, "But we already know it."
The teacher again said, "Enter my classroom."
Some of the students said, "But we aren't ready to learn it."
The teacher continued, "Enter my classroom."
Some of the students said, "But we don't learn by watching."
The teacher persevered, "Enter my classroom."
Some of the students said, "But we don't learn by listening."
The teacher said again, "Enter my classroom."
Some of the students said, "But we are interested in something else."
The teacher persisted, "Enter my classroom."
Apprehensively, the students walked into the classroom.
The teacher declared, "You will each learn."
The students asked, "How will you meet all of needs in your classroom?"
The teacher explained, "Now that you are here, it is not my classroom.
It is our classroom."
The students persisted, "But how will you meet all of our needs?"
The teacher smiled and replied, "I believe in you.
I will give you the gift of differentiated instruction."
And everyone learned.

REFERENCES AND ADDITIONAL READING

Anderson, L., and D. Krathwohl, eds. 2001. *A Taxonomy for Learning, Teaching, and Assessing: A Revision of Bloom's Taxonomy of Educational Objectives.* New York: Longman.

Barnett-Clarke, C., and A. Ramirez. 2004. "Language Pitfalls and Pathways to Mathematics." In *Perspectives on the Teaching of Mathematics*, edited by R. Rubenstein. Reston, VA: National Council of Teachers of Mathematics.

Baroody, A. 1995. "The Role of the Number-After Rule in the Invention of Computational Shortcuts." *Cognition and Instruction* 13 (2): 189–219.

Behr, M., S. Erlwanger, and E. Nichols. 1980. "How Children View the Equal Sign." *Mathematics Teaching* 92: 13–15.

Bermejo, V. 1996. "Cardinality Development and Counting." *Developmental Psychology* 32 (2): 263–268.

Bloom, B., M. Englehart, E. Furst, W. Hill, and D. Krathwohl. 1956. *Taxonomy of Educational Objectives: The Classification of Educational Goals—Handbook I: Cognitive Domain.* New York: Longmans Green.

Brewer, D., D. Rees, and L. Argys. 1995. "Detracking America's Schools: The Reform Without Costs?" *Phi Delta Kappa* 77 (3): 210–215.

Caine, R., and G. Caine. 1991. *Making Connections: Teaching and the Human Brain.* Alexandria, VA: Association for Supervision and Curriculum Development.

Cantor, G. 1915. *Transfinite Numbers.* Chicago: Open Court Publishing.

Clements, D. 1999. "Subitizing: What Is It? Why Teach It?" *Teaching Children Mathematics* 5 (7): 400–405.

Clements, D., and J. Sarama, eds. 2004. *Engaging Young Children in Mathematics: Standards for Early Childhood Mathematics Education.* Mahwah, NJ: Lawrence Erlbaum Associates.

Copley, J. 2000. *The Young Child and Mathematics.* Washington, D.C.: National Association for the Education of Young Children.

Dienes, Z. 1960. *Building Up Mathematics.* London: Hutchinson Educational.

Dienes, Z., and E. Goldring. 1971. "Learning and Proficiency in Mathematics." *The Mathematics Teacher* 51 (8): 620–626.

Dunn, R., K. Dunn, and G. Price. 1985. *Learning Style Inventory.* Lawrence, KS: Price Systems.

Dunn, R., and S. A. Griggs, eds. 2000. *Practical Approaches to Using Learning Styles in Higher Education.* Westport, CT: Bergin & Garvey.

Falkner, K., L. Levi, and T. Carpenter. 1999. "Children's Understanding of Equality: A Foundation for Algebra." *Teaching Children Mathematics* 6 (4): 232–236.

Fennema, E., T. Carpenter, L. Levi, M. I. Franke, and S. Empson. 1999. *Children's Mathematics: Cognitively Guided Instruction—Professional Development Materials.* Portsmouth, NH: Heinemann.

Freeman, F. N. 1912. "Grouped Objects as a Concrete Basis for the Number Idea." *Elementary School Teacher* 8: 306–314.

Gallagher, J. 1993. "Ability Grouping: A Tool for Educational Success." *College Board Review* 168 (Summer): 21–27.

Gardner, H. 1983. *Frames of Mind.* New York: Basic Books.

Gardner, H. 1993. *Multiple Intelligences: The Theory in Practice.* New York: Basic Books.

Gardner, H. 1999. *Intelligence Reframed: Multiple Intelligences for the 21st Century.* New York: Basic Books.

Gentry, M., and S. Owen. 1999. "An Investigation of the Effects of Total School Flexible Cluster Grouping on Identification, Achievement, and Classroom Practices." *Gifted Child Quarterly* 43 (4): 224–242.

Goldring, E. 1990. "Assessing the Status of Information on Classroom Organizational Frameworks for Gifted Students." *Journal of Educational Research* 83 (6): 313–326.

Gordon, T. 1974. *T.E.T.: Teacher Effectiveness Training.* New York: Peter H. Wyden.

Hart, L. 1981. "Do Not Teach Them, Help Them Learn." *Learning* 9 (8): 39–40.

Howden, H. 1989. "Teaching Number Sense." *Arithmetic Teacher* 36 (6): 6–11.

Hutchins, P. 1986. *The Doorbell Rang.* New York: William & Morrow.

Jarvis, P. 1992. "Reflective Practice and Nursing." *Nurse Education Today* 12 (3): 174–181.

Jensen, E. 1998. *Teaching with the Brain in Mind.* Alexandria, VA: Association for Supervision and Curriculum Development.

Kagan, S. 1997. *Cooperative Learning.* San Clemente, CA: Resources for Teachers.

Kamii, C. 2000. *Young Children Reinvent Arithmetic*, 2nd ed. New York: College Teachers Press.

Kaufman, E. L., M.W. Lord, T. W. Reese, and J. Volkman. 1949. "The Discrimination of Visual Number." *American Journal of Psychology* 62: 498–525.

Kohlberg, E., and L. Dacey. 1999. *The Digi-block Program: Number Sense and Operations for Elementary Grades—Comprehensive Teacher's Guide.* Cambridge, MA: Digi-block.

Kramer, M. J. 2005. "The Key to Raising Achievement: Four Guiding Principles." *AASA New Superintendents E-Journal* (3). http://www.aasa.org/publications/content.cfm?ItemNumber=7039, April 25, 2008.

Kulik, J. A. 1992. *An Analysis of the Research on Ability Grouping: Historical and Contemporary Perspectives.* Storrs, CT: National Research Center on the Gifted and Talented.

Kulik, J. A., and C. C. Kulik. 1992. "Meta-Analytic Findings on Grouping Programs." *Gifted Child Quarterly* 36 (2): 73–77.

Lou, Y., P. C. Abrami, J. C. Spence, C. Poulsen, B. Chambers, and S. d'Apollonia. 1996. "Within-Class Grouping: A Meta-Analysis." *Review of Educational Research* 66 (4): 423–458.

Loveless, T. 1998. *The Tracking and Ability Grouping Debate.* Washington, D.C.: Thomas B. Fordham Foundation.

Loveless, T. 1999. "Will Tracking Reform Promote Social Equity?" *Educational Leadership* 56 (7): 28–32.

Ma, L. 1999. *Knowing and Teaching Elementary Mathematics: Teachers' Understanding of Fundamental Mathematics in China and the United States.* Mahwah, NJ: Lawrence Erlbaum Associates.

McIntosh, A. J., B. J. Reys, and R. E. Reys. 1993. "A Proposed Framework for Examining Number Sense." *For the Learning of Mathematics* 12 (3): 2–8.

Molina, M., and C. Ambrose. 2006. "Fostering Relational Thinking While Negotiating the Meaning of the Equals Sign." *Teaching Children Mathematics* 13 (2): 111–117.

National Association for the Education of Young Children and National Council of Teachers of Mathematics. 2002. *Early Childhood Mathematics: Promoting Good Beginnings, A Joint Position Statement.* Reston, VA: National Council of Teachers of Mathematics.

National Council of Teachers of Mathematics. 2000. *Principles and Standards for School Mathematics.* Reston, VA: National Council of Teachers of Mathematics.

Oakes, J. 1985. *Keeping Track: How Schools Structure Inequality.* New Haven, CT: Yale University Press.

Oakes, J. 1988. "Tracking in Mathematics and Science Education: A Structural Contribution to Unequal Schooling." In *Class, Race, and Gender in American Education*, edited by L. Weiss. Albany, NY: State University of New York Press.

Oakes, J. 1990. *Multiplying Inequalities: The Effects of Race, Social Class, and Tracking on Opportunities to Learn Mathematics and Sciences.* Santa Monica, CA: Rand Corporation.

Ogle, D. S. 1986. "K-W-L Group Instructional Strategy." In *Teaching Reading as Thinking*, edited by A. S. Palincsar, D. S. Ogle, B. F. Jones, and E. G. Carr. Alexandria, VA: Association for Supervision and Curriculum Development.

Olszewski-Kubilius, P. 2003. "Is Your School Using Best Practices of Instruction for Gifted Students?" *Talent Newsletter.* Evanston, IL: Center for Talent Development, Northwestern University. http://www.ctd.northwestern.edu/resources/talentdevelopment/bestinstruction.html, May 5, 2008.

Oxford English Dictionary, 2nd ed. online. April 11, 2007. New York: Oxford University Press.

Piaget, J. 1964. "Development and Learning." In *Piaget Rediscovered*, edited by R. Ripple and V. Rockcastle. Ithaca, NY: Cornell University Press.

Piaget, J. 1970. "Piaget's Theory." In *Carmichael's Manual of Child Psychology*, edited by P. H. Mussen. Vol. 1, 3rd ed. London: John Wiley and Sons.

Reis, S. M., D. E. Burns, and J. S. Renzulli. 1992. *Curriculum Compacting: The Complete Guide to Modifying the Regular Curriculum for High Ability Students.* Mansfield Center, CT: Creative Learning Press.

Renninger, K., and S. Hidi. 1992. *The Role of Interest in Learning and Development.* Mahwah, NJ: Lawrence Erlbaum Associates.

Renzulli, J. S., and L. H. Smith. 1978. *The Compactor.* Mansfield Center, CT: Creative Learning Press.

Renzulli, J. S., L. H. Smith, and S. M. Reis. 1982. "Curriculum Compacting: An Essential Strategy for Working with Gifted Students." *The Elementary School Journal* 82: 185–194.

Richardson, K. 2004. "Making Sense." In *Engaging Young Children in Mathematics: Standards for Early Childhood Mathematics Education*, edited by D. Clements and J. Sarama. Mahwah, NJ: Lawrence Erlbaum Associates.

Senz-Ludlow, A., and C. Walgamuth. 1998. "Third Graders' Interpretations of Equality and the Equal Symbol." *Educational Studies in Mathematics* 35: 153–187.

Slavin, R. E. 1987a. "Ability Grouping and Its Alternatives: Must We Track?" *American Educator* 11 (2): 32–36, 47–48.

Slavin, R. E. 1987b. "Ability Grouping and Student Achievement in Elementary Schools: A Best Evidence Synthesis." *Review of Educational Research* 57 (3): 293–336.

Slavin, R., H. Braddock, and H. Jomills. 1993. "Ability Grouping: On the Wrong Track." *College Board Review* 168: 11–18.

Smith-Maddox, R., and A. Wheelock. 1995. "Untracking and Students' Futures: Closing the Gap Between Aspirations and Expectations." *Phi Delta Kappa* 77 (3): 222–228.

Starkey, P., and R. G. J. Cooper. 1995. "The Development of Subitizing in Young Children." *British Journal of Developmental Psychology* 13: 399–420.

Taylor-Cox, J. 2001. "How Many Marbles in the Jar? Estimation in the Early Grades." *Teaching Children Mathematics* 8 (4): 208–214.

Tomlinson, C. 1995. *How to Differentiate Instruction in Mixed-Ability Classrooms.* Alexandria, VA: Association for Supervision and Curriculum Development.

Tomlinson, C. 1996. *How to Differentiate Instruction in Mixed-Ability Classrooms Professional Inquiry Kit.* Alexandria, VA: Association for Supervision and Curriculum Development.

Tomlinson, C. 1999. *The Differentiated Classroom: Responding to the Needs of All Learners.* Alexandria, VA: Association for Supervision and Curriculum Development.

Tomlinson, C. A., and J. McTighe. 2006. *Integrating Differentiated Instruction and Understanding by Design.* Alexandria, VA: Association for Supervision and Curriculum Development.

Vygotsky, L. 1962. *Thought and Language.* Cambridge, MA: MIT Press.

Wheelock, A. 1992. *Crossing the Tracks: How Untracking Can Save America's Schools.* New York: New Press.

Wiggins, G. 2003. "'Get Real!' Assessing for Quantitative Literacy." In *Quantitative Literacy: Why Numeracy Matters for Schools and Colleges*, edited by B. Madison and L. Arthur. Princeton, NJ: National Council on Education and the Disciplines.

Wiggins, G., and J. McTighe. 1998. *Understanding by Design.* Alexandria, VA: Association for Supervision and Curriculum Development.

Wirtz, R. 1980. *New Beginnings.* Monterey, CA: Curriculum Development Associates.

Wood, D., Bruner, J., and G. Ross. 1976. "The Role of Tutoring in Problem-Solving." *Journal of Child Psychology and Psychiatry* 17 (2): 89–100.

Wynn, K. 1992. "Addition and Subtraction by Human Infants." *Nature* 358: 749–750.

INDEX

4500939772-0607-2026
Printed in the U.S.A